D.H. LAWRENCE

Edited and Introduced by

PETER WIDDOWSON

LONGMAN
LONDON AND NEW YORK

Longman Group UK Limited,
Longman House, Burnt Mill,
Harlow, Essex CM20 2JE, England
and Associated Companies throughout the world.

Published in the United States of America
by Longman Publishing, New York

First published 1992

British Library Cataloguing-in-Publication Data

A catalogue record for this book is
available from the British Library

Library of Congress Cataloging-in-Publication Data
D.H. Lawrence / edited and introduced by Peter Widdowson.
    p. cm. – (Longman critical readers)
   Includes bibliographical references (p. 000) and index.
    ISBN 0-582-06156-3 (csd) : £19.99. – ISBN 0-582-06155-5 (ppr) : £9.99
    1. Lawrence, D.H. (David Herbert), 1885–1930--Criticism and
interpretation. I. Widdowson, Peter. II. Series.
PR6023.A93Z623374 1992
823'.912 – dc20   91-28958
                                                                                  CIP

Set in 9/11½ Palatino
Produced by Longman Singapore Publishers (Pte) Ltd.
Printed in Singapore

Contents

Contents

WEST GRID STAMP

NN		RR	7/00	WW	
NT		RT		WO	
NC		RC		WL	
NH		RJ		WM	
NL		RP		WT	
NV		RS		WA	
NM		RW		WR	
NB		RV		WS	
NE					
NP					

General Editors' Preface

The outlines of contemporary critical theory are now often taught as a standard feature of a degree in literary studies. The development of particular theories has seen a thorough transformation of literary criticism. For example, Marxist and Foucauldian theories have revolutionised Shakespeare studies, and 'deconstruction' has led to a complete reassessment of Romantic poetry. Feminist criticism has left scarcely any period of literature unaffected by its searching critiques. Teachers of literary studies can no longer fall back on a standardised, received, methodology.

Lectures and teachers are now urgently looking for guidance in a rapidly changing critical environment. They need help in understanding the latest revisions in literary theory, and especially in grasping the practical effects of the new theories in the form of theoretically sensitised new readings. A number of volumes in the series anthologise important essays on particular theories. However, in order to grasp the full implications and possible uses of particular theories it is essential to see them put to work. This series provides substantial volumes of new readings, presented in an accessible form and with a significant amount of editorial guidance.

Each volume includes a substantial introduction which explores the theoretical issues and conflicts embodied in the essays selected and locates areas of disagreement between positions. The pluralism of theories has to be put on the agenda of literary studies. We can no longer pretend that we all tacitly accept the same practices in literary studies. Neither is a *laissez-faire* attitude any longer tenable. Literature departments need to go beyond the mere toleration of theoretical differences: it is not enough merely to agree to differ; they need actually to 'stage' the differences openly. The volumes in this series all attempt to dramatise the differences, not necessarily with a view to resolving them but in order to foreground the choices presented by different theories or to argue for a particular route through the impasses the differences present.

The theory 'revolution' has had real effects. It has loosened the grip of traditional empiricist and romantic assumptions about language and literature. It is not always clear what is being proposed as the new agenda for literary studies, and indeed the very notion of 'literature' is questioned by the post-structuralist strain in theory. However, the uncertainties and obscurities of contemporary theories appear much less worrying when we see what the best critics have been able to do with them in practice. This series aims to disseminate the best of recent criticism, and to show that it is possible to re-read the canonical texts of literature in new and challenging ways.

RAMAN SELDEN AND STAN SMITH

The Publishers and fellow Series Editor regret to record that Raman Selden died after a short illness in May 1991 at the age of fifty-three. Ray Selden was a fine scholar and a lovely man. All those he has worked with will remember him with much affection and respect.

Acknowledgements

I would like to record my thanks to the library staff on the Enfield site of Middlesex Polytechnic for their invaluable and always good-humoured assistance. But the real debt of gratitude is to Jean Tonini, secretary of the Schools of English and Philosophy at the same institution, who has typed, xeroxed, and put up with my pernicketiness way beyond the call of duty. Without her, no book.

We are grateful to the following for permission to reproduce copyright material:
Associated University Presses for the article 'The Power of Nothing in *Women in Love*' by Daniel O'Hara in *Bucknell Review: A Scholarly Journal of Letters, Arts and Science*, Lewisburg, PA, Special Issue: ed. Harry R Garvin, *Rhetoric, Literature and Interpretation*, 1983, 28 (2), pp151–64, (Bucknell UP and Associated UPs, Lewisburg); Basil Blackwell Ltd for extracts from Chapter 5 'Psychoanalysis' in *Literary Theory, An Introduction* by Terry Eagleton (1983); Doubleday, a division of Bantam, Doubleday, Dell Publishing Group Inc and the Author's Agent for extracts from Chapter 5 'D. H. Lawrence' in *Sexual Politics* by Kate Millett. Copyright © 1969, 1970 by Kate Millett; Duke University Press for Chapter 12 'The Symbolic Father and the Ideal of Leadership' from *D H Lawrence and the Devouring Mother: The Search for a Patriarchal Ideal of Leadership* by Judith Ruderman. Copyright 1984 Duke University Press; Gill and Macmillan Limited for extracts from Chapter 6 'Transition' in *D H Lawrence, History, Ideology and Fiction* by Graham Holdernesss (1982); Harvester-Wheatsheaf/Barnes & Noble Books for extracts from Chapter 6 'Contexts of Reading: The Reception of D. H. Lawrence's *The Rainbow* and *Women in Love*' by Alistair Davies in *The Theory of Reading* ed. Frank Gloversmith (Harvester Press, 1984); Harvester-Wheatsheaf/University of Iowa Press for extracts from Chapter 2 'Northernness and Modernism: *The Trespasser, The Rainbow and Women in Love*' in *D. H. Lawrence* by Tony Pinkney (Harvester-Wheatsheaf, 1990)/Copyright © 1990 by University of Iowa Press; Open Books Publishing Ltd for extracts from Chapter 5 'Taking a nail for a walk: on reading *Women in Love*' by Gāmini Salgādo in *The Modern English Novel: the reader, the writer and the work* ed. Gabriel Josipovici (1976); Open University Press for Chapter 6 'D. H. Lawrence and Class' by Graham Martin in *The Uses of Fiction, Essays on the Modern Novel in Honour of Arnold Kettle* eds. Douglas Jefferson and Graham Martin (1982); Routledge for extracts from Chapter 3 'Lawrence, Feminism and the War' in *D. H. Lawrence and Feminism* by Hilary Simpson (Croom Helm, 1982); South Atlantic Modern Language Association for extracts from the article 'Alternatives to Logocentrism in D. H. Lawrence' by Daniel J. Schneider in *South Atlantic Review* May

For
(Lady) Jane
with love

WARNING!

These beautiful, innocent-looking books are packed with dynamite!

Richly grained bindings lavishly stamped in gold

HANDLE WITH CARE

A Heron Books Collection

" . . every man is a sacred and holy individual never to be violated. I think there is only one thing I hate to the verge of madness and that is bullying."

D. H. Lawrence 1885–1930

Unless you are willing to feel . . . to love . . . and to live to your full God-given capacity . . . *these books may be dangerous to read!*

Perhaps the censors were right when they banned D. H. Lawrence. Perhaps the police were right when they seized his books. Reading Lawrence can be dangerous . . . even today!

Not dangerous because of his use of basic Anglo-Saxon words! Not dangerous for his candid portrayal of relations between men and women. No, Lawrence is dangerous because of the *ideas* he can put in your *mind*. Reading Lawrence may give you inklings of unsuspected heights (or depths) which your feelings can reach . . . realizations that there can be far more to the husband-wife relationship than most couples settle for . . . suspicions that broad currents of human experience may be passing you by.

Mind-expanding, and Dangerous

Unless you know how to handle such revelations, they can be dangerous. But if you are mature and open-minded, reading Lawrence will be an illuminating experience.

But the first thing to expect from Lawrence is entertainment. He was a novelist and storyteller before all else. And though his tales are set some 40 to 80 years ago, they couldn't be more contemporary. For Lawrence was always ahead of his time. In 1912 he was writing in a style other writers adopted in the 1920's. By then he was pursuing the travel and action fashionable writers followed in the 30's and 40's. And his most famous novel *Lady Chatterley's Lover*, did not become a best-seller until 1960 – *32 years after it had been written!*

His Greatness Recognised

And now he is recognised (as F. R. Leavis notes): "a great novelist . . . incomparably the greatest creative writer in English in our time."

Poor Lawrence! In his lifetime he was pilloried by the press, persecuted by the police, banned by censors and ostracised by Establishment writers. He was penniless and ravaged by disease most of his life. And, he died in exile at 45!

His books however, live – honoured at last by critical acclaim. And now, honoured further by Heron Books' beautiful new Connoisseur Edition.

The Custom-bound Look

To all appearances, these are the custom-bound volumes you might find in a wealthy collector's house. The beautifully-grained deep green Skivertex covers have the look and soft feel of bookbinder's calf. They are richly gold stamped, the type is clear, the illustrations plentiful, and the detail immaculate right down to the silken bookmark.

They look expensive, but appearances can be deceptive. We offer them to subscribers for only 21/- each – scarcely more than you'd expect to pay for cheaply-bound commercial books.

AND YOUR FIRST VOLUME IS FREE! To receive the first two volumes in this exquisite collection, post the coupon below. Then after reading and examining them for ten days, decide: either to return them without payment or comment, or accept *Sons and Lovers* FREE, and keep *The Rainbow* for only 21/- as your first subscriber purchase. What's more, you may continue to receive further Lawrence books (about one a month) at the same low subscribers' price. You may cancel this subscription anytime if you wish – without buying another book.

While the supply lasts, you may also receive as a BONUS, the *Masterpieces of Maupassant* described here, and add their priceless beauty to your home. But act now, your chance to make such savings may expire soon. so post coupon today!

PLUS this extra bonus

accept FREE 'Sons and Lovers'

as your first volume of the D. H. Lawrence Collection

This famous Lawrence story is of a son (actually Lawrence himself) and his beautiful but terrible relationship with his mother who gives him the warmth and feeling she denies her 'inferior' husband . . . and his conflicts, as later he attempts emotional and sexual involvements with young women. Doubly enjoyable because it also prepares the reader for deeper appreciation of Lawrence's later books. *"A great landmark of autobiographical fiction"* —Magill

You also receive 'The Rainbow'

The first of many novels that caused Lawrence to be banned by the police, and ostracised by the literary set. It compares the marriages and matings of three successive generations – shows how sex sometimes helps, sometimes interferes with a true spiritual union. Many unforgettable characters including Anna Lensky who wanted to be pregnant again and again . . . and who spurned her husband every time she was.

You receive *'Sons and Lovers'* FREE when you accept *'The Rainbow'* – your first volume of the Collected Works of D. H. Lawrence, for the low subscribers' price of 21/-. **NO FURTHER PURCHASES ARE NECESSARY, unless you wish.**

THE MASTERPIECES OF MAUPASSANT

Brilliant translations of the famous novels and short stories of French writer Guy de Maupassant–world-famous master of the short story!

Maupassant was a master of style. He was a realist, who took hot and earthy passion, intimate relationships, even brutality, and presented it more vitally and vividly than life itself.

Maupassant's own vigorous pursuit of love and life coloured everything he wrote, adding a uniqueness and vitality to his characters that has rarely been equalled.

In stories like *Bel Ami, Une Vie, Pierre et Jean, Boule de Suif, La Maison Tellier, Miss Harriet, Mademoiselle Fifi, Claire de Lune* and the other 18 magnificent examples of Maupassant's genius as novelist and short story writer which we offer you in these 4 volumes, you have his finest works, all for just 15/–! Almost a gift!

4 volumes lavishly bound in rich, gold-embossed Skivertex, for only 15/-

also FREE 3 BEARDSLEY PRINTS

Aubrey Beardsley brought pen and ink drawing to heights never before or since equaled. His style was at once daring, morbid and sensual. Like Lawrence, he was a forerunner of a new wave. Sadly, this acknowledged genius died only 26. You may keep these 3 ready-to-frame 13" x 10½" prints even if you decide to return the books. This is our way of saying "thank you" for having confidence in us.

Heron Books, 18 St. Ann's Crescent, London S.W.18.

EXTRA GIFT FOR PROMPTNESS

Lawrence Memorial Medal Struck in enduring bronzed metal

☐ Tick here if you post coupon within 5 days and we will reward your prompt reply (it helps our long-range planning), by sending you ENTIRELY FREE this handsome medal. You may keep this collector's item, even if you decide to return your books.

FREE BOOK AND ART PRINTS COUPON

To: D. H. Lawrence Collection, Dept. 752/108
Heron Books, 18 St. Ann's Crescent, London S.W.18.

To introduce me to the joys of enriching my mind and beautifying my home with the world's most beautiful books, please send me for FREE examination *Sons and Lovers* and *The Rainbow* by D. H. Lawrence (2 volumes), plus the *Masterpieces of Maupassant* (4 volumes).

If I wish, I may return these books within 10 days and owe nothing. But if I would like to add these beautiful books to my library, I may keep the complete 4-volume set of *Masterpieces of Maupassant* for only 15/- (plus p. & p.) *Sons and Lovers* will be mine FREE, and for *The Rainbow*, I will pay only the special low subscribers' price of 21/- (plus a small p. & p. charge). Then each month you may send me another great D. H. Lawrence volume, exquisitely bound to match, at the same low subscribers' price, until I decide my collection is complete. It is understood I will also receive free the 3 Aubrey Beardsley prints, and my medal for promptness, all of which will be mine to keep whether or not I decide to return the books.

SIGNATURE
(Parent's signature if under 21)
NAME
ADDRESS

SEND NO MONEY NOW

C3

This offer applies only in the British Isles

Back cover of Family Circle *magazine, October 1968*

1 Introduction: Post-modernising D.H. Lawrence

Lawrence's coming of age

In October 1968, on the back cover of *Family Circle* magazine, appeared a glossy, full-colour advertisement whose main legend read: 'WARNING! These beautiful, innocent-looking books are packed with dynamite!' A hand holding a rubber-stamp and intruding from the margin has just impressed the bright-red message 'HANDLE WITH CARE' below it, and adjacent is a familiar portrait of . . . well, D.H. Lawrence. For this was a sales-pitch for the Heron Books' edition of Lawrence's novels. Bound in 'beautifully-grained deep green Skivertex covers [which] have the look and soft feel of book-binder's calf . . . [and] are richly gold stamped', they represent 'the custom-bound volumes you might find in a wealthy collector's house'. And all for 21s per volume (plus p. & p.). In case this wasn't enough, with your order you also received four 'lavishly bound' volumes of 'French writer' Guy de Maupassant's stories for 15s the lot; *Sons and Lovers* FREE when you accepted *The Rainbow* as your first purchase; 'three Beardsley Prints' FREE (yours to keep whatever – 'our way of saying "thank you" for having confidence in us'); and as an extra gift 'for promptness', a 'Lawrence Memorial Medal struck in enduring bronzed metal'. Where are they all now, one is tempted to ask: are there flaking 'bronzed metal' medallions of D.H. Lawrence gathering dust in countless older people's homes throughout the land (or perhaps increasingly in Oxfam shops), and Skivertex-wrapped, unread, volumes of *Aaron's Rod* and *The Lost Girl* still belying a 'wealthy collector', but really bought so that one favoured generation could have the opportunities their parents had missed – most particularly to become 'cultured'? The advertisement is in fact a flashy period amalgam of new American sales techniques, sixties' consumerism, and a serious, if over-hyped, notion of the popularisation of culture. There is a quotation from Lawrence himself appropriate to the sixties' *mentalité*: 'every man [sic] is a sacred and holy individual never to be violated'; there are tempting trailers for a (largely female?) *Family Circle* readership in the late sixties of

1

what *Sons and Lovers* holds in store: 'his beautiful but terrible relationship
with his mother who gives him the warmth and feeling she denies her
"inferior" husband . . .'; and raunchy tasters of 'the many unforgettable
characters [in *The Rainbow*] including Anna Lensky who wanted to be
pregnant again and again . . . and who spurned her husband every time
she was' (you never see literary criticism make that point!). There are
seductive suggestions that the censors and police were perhaps right to
ban Lawrence's work, so 'dangerous' is reading it 'even today!' But
equally, the advertisement neatly reverses the expected hard-sell of *Lady
Chatterley*/Lawrence, claiming that it is not the 'basic Anglo-Saxon words'
nor his 'candid portrayal of relations between men and women' which
make him important, but 'the *ideas* he can put in your *mind*' (their italics;
e.g. 'realisations that there can be far more to the husband–wife
relationship than most couples settle for . . .'). Finally, and most
whimsically, there is an attributed quotation from that severest defender
of a 'minority culture', F.R. Leavis: 'a great novelist . . . incomparably the
greatest creative writer in English in our time'. One wonders whether
Leavis himself became the proud owner of a complete Skivertex
Lawrence on the strength of this, or whether his fee (always supposing
he got one) turned out to be thirty pieces of silver.

In my context here, however, this advertisement is more than just a
curiosity of popular culture: it is, rather, a very pointed conjunctural
sign. Appearing in late 1968, it is effectively at the start of the period this
Critical Reader is to cover; only eight years after the *Lady Chatterley* trial,
it is nevertheless published on the back of a *gemütlich* family magazine –
but we are now, of course, at the other end of the sixties; it promotes
Lawrence in the libertarian-consumerist mode of the sixties, but it also
includes a seemingly unlikely reference to a serious literary critic who
had by then become the single most influential figure in constructing
Lawrence's reputation as *the* great English modern novelist. Mark Spilka,
an American critic introducing the 1963 collection of *Twentieth-Century
Views* on Lawrence (see also pp. 4–5, 6 below), notes that he 'is now
generally recognized as the foremost English novelist of his generation',
and puts that down to Leavis – 'the ablest of Lawrence critics and the
chief progenitor of his revival'.[1] As a number of essays in the present
volume also attest, it was Leavis's partial and strategic reading of
Lawrence which centrally shaped him as arch-proponent of 'Life' against
the mechanisation and dehumanisation endemic to the 'technologico-
Benthamite'[2] civilisation of modern industrial society. Compound this
with the dialectical connection between the *Lady Chatterley* trial and
sixties' sexual liberation (cf Philip Larkin's poem '*Annus Mirabilis*')[3] –
Lawrence as both 'Prophet of Life' and 'Priest of Love' – and we may
well say that in and around 1968 his reputation and popularity – well
beyond the academy – were at their highest point ever. 'Lawrence' had

become (and in some ways remains) the creature of cultural production – a cultural *figure*, rather than merely 'a writer'. He had, as Marion Shaw has remarked, 'led his people out of Victorian darkness by the historical necessity of elevating sex, making it holy. . . . [But] this apotheosis led to its own decay . . .'⁴ So we may also note that within a year or so (i.e. at the moment the present volume opens), Lawrence's work was being subjected to a searching negative critique. It is for this reason that the earliest (and indeed longest) piece included in the Reader is from Kate Millett's excoriation of Lawrence in *Sexual Politics* (1969). From *Family Circle* to *Sexual Politics*, from kitsch domestication to feminist anathema, 'Lawrence' changed dramatically, entering a period of what his critical acolytes hopefully call 'revisionism', and from which he has not – indeed, in my view, cannot – emerge. It is the business of the next part of this Introduction to map in something of the critical construction of Lawrence prior to the end of the sixties; and that of later sections, together with the body of the Reader, to indicate some of the forces which so traverse his work over the next twenty years as to radically reshape it.

F.R. Leavis and the 'moral formalism' of the sixties

Lawrence's critical reputation was in abeyance during the later thirties and forties. It is only in the late forties and early fifties that a Lawrence revival began, initiated mainly by Mark Schorer's 'Technique as Discovery' essay in *Hudson Review* (1948); by Leavis's *Scrutiny* essays (1950–52) on 'The Novel as Dramatic Poem'; by the publication of Harry T. Moore's biography, *The Intelligent Heart: the Story of D.H. Lawrence* (1954, later revised in 1962 as *The Priest of Love*); and of Leavis's *D.H. Lawrence/Novelist* (1955). By 1960, Penguin Books had already successfully printed up to 15,000 copies each of fifteen titles by Lawrence and were planning a further eight, including *Lady Chatterley's Lover⁵*; but the revival really took off, of course, in the decade after the famous trial in 1960. As James C. Cowan's *Annotated Bibliography* of Lawrence makes clear, leaving aside the large numbers of memoirs, bibliographies, psychoanalytic studies and miscellaneous other groupings also to do with 'the man' and 'the life', there has developed a huge corpus of criticism dealing with Lawrence's literary writing. (The second volume of the Bibliography, Cowan tells us, spanning 1960–75, is of similar length to the first, which covered the years 1909–60 and had itself contained 2,061 annotated entries. Equally, the variety of approaches and topics is making them 'hard to categorise'.)⁶ Much of this work – up to the early seventies – is celebratory, either receiving its charge from Leavis's view of Lawrence as the modern continuator of the English 'great tradition' passionately articulating life-values in a destructive industrial/ materialistic civilisation, or from a sixties' view of him as a radical mystic or visionary, rebelliously challenging and subverting, as a free individual spirit, the repressions and conventions of bourgeois society. Much is made, variously, of his romanticism, his empathy with nature, his 'dark gods' and 'demonic' power, his 'religion of the blood', his 'metaphysic', his aesthetic of 'felt life', his analysis of the 'relations between men and women', his symbolism, mythology, typology, psychology and so on. The Lawrence volumes in two series which are, in effect, the ur-texts for the present Critical Readers – *Twentieth-Century Views*, edited by Mark Spilka (1963), the first serious collection of critical essays to appear on Lawrence, and the Macmillan 'Casebook' on *The Rainbow* and *Women in Love*, edited by Colin Clark (1969) – represent as well as anything the celebratory tone and critical directions of the period. Spilka emphasises, in the American context particularly, the connection between New Criticism and the Lawrence Revival although it is Leavis, as Spilka is happy to pronounce, whose 'spirit haunts the whole anthology'[7] and who mediates the shift from the 'puristic formalism' (Spilka (ed.), *Introduction*, p. 6) of the older New Critics to the 'morally committed formalism' which Leavis himself propagates. It is the latter which has released younger British and American New Critics into a situation where 'intelligently sympathetic criticism' can concentrate on Lawrence's achievements 'without blinking at his faults, and which is formally imaginative and acute yet amenable to the prophetic possibilities of art' (Ibid. p. 13). It is this 'moral formalism' which Spilka's collection of essays represents, finding in Lawrence's work 'mature, serious, complex writing' which also evinces his 'fierce engagement with wasteland culture, his urgent sense of the modern death-drift, and his creative attempts to transcend it' (Ibid., p. 12). The potent mix of Leavis and a sixties' mindset is clearly apparent in Spilka's Introduction – the ideological implications of which I will return to in a moment; and the body of the collection bears it out in essays by, for example, Dorothy Van Ghent, Marvin Mudrick, Mark Schorer, Harry T. Moore, Julian Moynahan, Monroe Engel, Graham Hough, Vivien de Sola Pinto and early Raymond Williams. It is perhaps worth adding here, since it is also part of the post-sixties debate (see below pp. 13–14), that Spilka acutely and correctly ascribes to Leavis, not just the 'New Critical' practice of close scrutiny of long texts as though they were 'Dramatic Poems', but also – and partly by way of this technique – a further form of 'discrimination': 'establish[ing] something like a Lawrence canon'. He has, says Spilka, 'been instrumental, in fact, in another New Critical process: the creation of new hierarchies of accepted texts. Largely through Leavis's efforts, *Women in Love* and *The Rainbow* are now recognised as Lawrence's greatest novels; *Sons and Lovers* has slipped to third place, *Lady Chatterley* to fourth . . .' In contrast to twenty years later, when such ranking would constitute a fundamental animus for the critique of Leavis, Spilka approves the necessity and probity of his discriminatory exclusion of the 'weaker novels, and the inclusion of more integral achievements' (Spilka, (ed.), p. 4). One could ask for no clearer instance of the two major tactics of New and Leavisian criticism working together to naturalise each other, or of the factitious and contingent construction of a 'great writer' in the image of the criticism which forges it. Alternatively, Colin Clarke, in the Macmillan 'Casebook', reprints S.L. Goldberg, Wilson Knight, Moynahan again, H.M. Daleski, George H. Ford, Ronald Gray, Frank Kermode and himself, in order to correct (while still honouring) Leavis's unitary conception of Lawrence's celebration of positive life-forces by bringing out another, 'demonic', Lawrence, ambiguously fascinated by corruption, disintegration and dissolution. This emphasis is not a negatively critical one, however, but rather yet more complex evidence of Lawrence's ability to tap into the psycho-history of twentieth-century civilisation; and Clarke, too, accepts that Leavis 'has established the claims of *The Rainbow* and *Women in Love* to be great artefacts, and the peaks of Lawrence's achievement'.[8] Spilka's and Clarke's collections of essays have remained the two most dominant 'Readers' – at least as far as students of Lawrence are concerned – for the past twenty years.

Despite the connections with New Criticism, however, and the emphasis on 'moral *formalism'*, John B. Humma, reviewing some recent Lawrence biographical criticism in 1987, pointed to the 'standard' tendency to treat Lawrence's work 'thematically', so ignoring the 'artistic' elements of his writing. (It is soberingly indicative of critical drift to read, this late, that 'the critic who does not make his first allegiance "the words on the page" indeed is a potential castrator of literature'.)[9] Be this as it may, in addition to the 'thematic' issues and formally related features like imagery and symbolism, there has, in fact, also been considerable attention paid to Lawrence's 'new' psychological characterisation (rejecting 'the old stable ego of the character'); to his prose style and narrative structure; to his place within modernism; his relationship to European and American writers; his place in the English realist tradition; to his 'theories' of the novel and practice of it in relation to his 'metaphysic'; to what types of novel Lawrence wrote, and whether they are successful or not in terms of his own dictum: 'Never trust the novelist, trust the tale.' Clearly these interests and concerns did not cease in 1970, and it would seem to me that despite the disruptions and challenges which the present Reader seeks to represent, much of the orthodox discourse within Lawrence Studies continues to rehearse and recycle this characteristically 'Lawrentian' agenda.

What is common to it, I think, and despite its apparent diversity, is the sense of the Individual as Romantic Hero, the Artist as Man of Passion, not merely as a tribute to Lawrence but as a potent ideology in the post-war period. It may allude to Leavis's tradition of individual, humanist-artistic opposition to 'Society' (no doubt one of the reasons, too, for Lawrence's profound influence on British post-war 'working-class' novelists – Wain, Sillitoe, Waterhouse, Storey – with their own sharply individualistic, apolitical 'rebellion' against capitalist class society); it may allude to Cold War fears of totalitarianism; to philosophical existentialism; or to sixties' liberationism; but it focuses centrally on the notion of the free spirit, the quintessential individual – exemplified in 'the Artist' – still able to controvert the massing, if not massed, forces of authority, control, power and repression. A quotation from the Spilka essay considered above conveys something of the tone and substance of what Lawrence's 'moral vision of the age' meant for 'the crisis-ridden sixties':

> If, as [Eliseo] Vivas holds, that vision enables us to grasp 'the specific process of disintegration of which we are the victims', it may also help us, *individually if not collectively*, to reverse that process. The moral formalists, those who have rescued Lawrence from comparative oblivion, suggest that it will. More important, the works themselves suggest it through images of quickness, aloneness, wholeness, balance, tenderness, communion, resurrection and restoration – through images, that is, of promise.
>
> (Spilka (ed.), p. 12; my italics)

This touching and revealing sixties' litany depends on a potent and bewitching vision – one also which haunts all of Lawrence's writing, including his non-fictional 'political' prose. But it is potent and bewitching precisely because it is an ideological chimera, one which abjures and rejects collective political thought and action, and so in the end works only on behalf of those very forces it so bravely appears to challenge and threaten. It is for this reason, I believe, that Lawrence became the immensely popular figure he did in the sixties, and for this reason, too, that such an image of him was so rigorously demolished by Marxists and feminists (and just as fiercely defended) in the seventies and eighties. A great deal was at stake here politically: Lawrence, the representative icon of humanist individualism who must be defended at all costs, or Lawrence the ideological veil of patriarchy and bourgeois cultural hegemony which had to be ripped down if people were to see what lay behind it. The conflict goes on, but in the later eighties and the nineties the lines are less clearly drawn – both 'the sixties' and '1968' are now a long way off; and as the later part of the present volume suggests, while there is no consensual agreement about Lawrence, there is less partisan certainty about him either: he is the victim, like the rest of us perhaps, of post-modern depoliticisation. In the second half of this introductory essay I shall explore further the critical movements in and around Lawrence in the period since the sixties. But first, in good post-modern fashion and also so that they do not get buried in the backyard of the Introduction, I want to make some self-reflexive remarks about this Critical Reader itself.

Decoding this Critical Reader

Even a selective computer-search of books and articles on Lawrence's work over the past twenty to thirty years reveals a mountain of possible materials from which to choose the thirteen or so essays for a new 'Critical Reader' volume of the present kind. In part this bears out my point above that by 1970 Lawrence sustained a cultural significance and popularity of staggering proportions for a 'serious' writer; it also indicates that despite some senior Lawrence scholars' distaste for the term, there is indeed a 'Lawrence Industry' and that it is appropriately named in so far as it does continuously process and reprocess its 'product'. What that product looks like in the 1990s is a matter I shall return to later in this essay: but it is questionable whether such a process ever delivers a fuller sense of 'Lawrence' (*any* Lawrence) at all. On the contrary, is it not simply fuller proof of what was always true but not so evident before: that the 'product' is in fact the critical metadiscourse itself – which is all we ever really study – and never (because illusory) Lawrence's fiction as unmediated essence? For the moment, however, one thing is absolutely undeniable; the sheer proliferation of writing about Lawrence means a real problem for the editor of a volume such as this. Which essays to include and how to select them? Are they to be 'the Best of Lawrence Criticism', or are they to be 'representative', and if so of what? Which of those many Lawrences that criticism has constructed are to be brought into bold relief? If the dominant 'literary critical/history of ideas' representations of Lawrence must still receive space proportionate to their bulk, how will this new Critical Reader differ – except in chronology – from the earlier 'Twentieth-Century Views' and 'Casebook' volumes it is supposed to supersede? Should the selection be centred on 'approaches' to Lawrence, i.e. identifying for the reader the models and modes of address most commonly/dominantly deployed in Lawrence criticism, or seek to 'cover' as many of his works as possible? Are we, indeed, talking about *all* of Lawrence's *oeuvre* or just a part of it?

To start at the end with the easy one: this Reader is solely concerned with Lawrence's fiction – the short stories occasionally, but primarily with the novels. Arbitrary and distorting this may be, but then, as I shall suggest below, the apparently neutral and even-handed business of compiling 'Anthologies' or 'Selections' of anything is the most flagrantly manipulative activity in the whole 'disinterested' field of literary scholarship. Be that as it may, it is incontrovertibly obvious that to try and cover the critical writing about all of Lawrence's work – poetry, plays, paintings, non-fictional prose, as well as the fiction – in one volume, and make any sense of the directions in which these metadiscourses have moved over twenty years, is out of the question. So the fiction alone it has to be. Which leads me back, then, to my penultimate question above: 'approaches to', or 'coverage of', Lawrence's fictional *oeuvre*? First, pragmatically again, it becomes apparent that there are simply too many novels and shorter fictions for individual coverage to produce anything other than an unwieldy, or eclectic and disconnected, collection of discrete essays. My selection, then, fairly obviously and conventionally focuses principally on the novels which have received most attention – *Sons and Lovers, The Rainbow, Women in Love, Lady Chatterley's Lover* – and this despite my contention elsewhere (in relation to Thomas Hardy)[10] that the suppression of so-called 'minor' fiction is a central function in literary criticism's construction of a particular cultural/ideological version of a 'great writer' (cf. Mark Spilka's remarks above about Leavis's praiseworthy discrimination of Lawrence's work into hierarchies of value). Let me make it quite clear here, however, that this volume's orientation towards the 'major' novels is not the result of a residual inflexion of such literary evaluation on my part; it is simply because, on the whole, that is where the action is. In partial self-defence, too, I may also point out that most of Lawrence's novels are treated somewhere in the selection, and that wherever possible I have strategically included a piece on less-favoured texts – *The Lost Girl*, for example, or the so-called 'leadership novels' of the early twenties. The second, and more substantive, point to make on this 'approaches/ coverage' issue is that in the end I have simply assumed, in the context of the critical and theoretical debates of the past two decades, that we *have to be* primarily concerned with 'approaches'. No one now, I think, of whatever persuasion, believes that literary criticism is 'neutral', 'disinterested', 'innocent': it is generally accepted that all modes of address to literature are based on a model or theory which relates – somewhere down the line – to the social and cultural (ideological) *locus* of the critic. And Lawrence, for reasons which I have suggested above, is an especially serious 'site for contestation' (as we used to say) in the cultural and wider politics of our time: possession of Lawrence's signification represents an important ideological advantage.

This Reader, therefore, even if it chose not to, could not help but take sides. In fact, however, it *does* choose to: hence the inevitable emphasis on 'approaches'. Having acknowledged this, a number of answers to the other questions posed above flow from it. First, in the context of an approach-centred literary culture it is clearly impossible to conceive of a neutral 'Best of Lawrence Criticism' (which would imply, of course, an undifferentiated body of criticism ranked only by its proximity to revealing the 'true' Lawrence). Certainly some essays will be more interesting than others, but it is precisely wherein that 'interest' lies that short-circuits the issue and takes us back to the approach. The essays in this collection, then, have not been selected on the principle of somehow being 'The Best' – although to be fair to the individual pieces included, they seem to me to be as good, in their own terms, as anything else I have read; they have been chosen instead as most effectively representing a tendency or approach in recent Lawrence criticism. What the most significant approaches or tendencies are, of course, is much more contentious, and I will return to my selection of those in a moment. But the 'significant approaches' device, related to certain key contemporary debates, does allow me to resolve the question of how to represent the vast bulk of that earnest, worthy – if often idolatrous – literary criticism which has continued to explore every nook and cranny of 'Lorenzo's' life and work: family, friends, place of origin, travels, libido, imagery, symbolism, typology, philosophy, psychology, and so on and so forth. For the most part, I have left it out: it is almost impossible to 'represent', being at once so similar and so diverse. There are occasions when one questions whether there is any need at all for yet more critical monographs on 'Great Writers', for anyone reading through a shelf-full of such works quickly realises that despite an obsessive self-presentation of *difference*, they are all very much the same – inscribed as they are with the tic and mindset of their period. And in the end it is only that tic and mindset which is of interest. Later in this essay I will return to the question of whether, in the post-modern period, there is indeed anything left to say about Lawrence, or whether Lawrence has anything left to say to us.

Explaining the Reader's sections

But to return for a moment to the particular cast and construction of this Critical Reader and its evident emphasis on certain approaches: I am fortunate with Lawrence as my subject in one respect in particular. As I have indicated earlier, the point at which this book's remit begins, around 1970, is the point at which Lawrence had become a cultural icon on a grand scale and was indeed about to experience sharp iconoclasm. Initiated by the *Lady Chatterley* trials (in America, the novel sold six million copies in the months following the trial; in Britain, 1,986,121 between 10 November and 31 December 1960 and a further 1,240,435 over the next six months,)[11] and propelled throughout the sixties by an odd but heady compound of Leavisian and liberationist energies, Lawrence's reputation soared. But with the particular character of 1968 And All That, infused especially with militant feminism and New Left Marxism, it was bound to falter. If sex and sexuality had been a key issue in the sixties – both generally and in relation to Lawrence – it was rapidly reinflected thereafter as *gender*, and the Lawrence who had been perceived as a guru of sexual liberation became the phallocratic oppressor of gender politics. Equally, issues of social class and class relations had been central at once to the novel of *Lady Chatterley's Lover*, to the trial, and indeed to the meritocratic, consensual, consumerist, *'déclassé'* sixties. The cross-class coupling of the Lady and the Gamekeeper, and the notion of individual regeneration by way of a sexually-achieved 'separate peace', are discourses both of the novel and of the sixties. It is often said that the prosecution lost the trial at the moment when the Crown asked the jury whether this was a book 'you would want your wife or servants to read?' – not so much because of the sexism ('your wife'), but because the prosecutor was so *socially* out of touch as to assume the average juror would still have servants. And for Leavis (plus all those others at once liberated and frustrated by post-war realignments in the British class system), Lawrence was the working-class and provincial 'genius' who had blasted his way through the deadening snobbery and exclusiveness of metropolitan literary culture; who was, in his novels, an 'unsurpassed', 'incomparable', social historian of England; was profoundly perceptive about 'class' (see Chapters 2 and 3 of *D. H. Lawrence/Novelist*);[12] and who dynamically subverted the upper-class and bourgeois values on which rested the whole urban–industrial complex that crushed the lives of individual human beings. But as with the shift from sex to gender, so after 1968 liberal/socialistic interest in class relations was overtaken by the hard class-politics and theories of ideology of the New Left; and Lawrence, the proletarian writer-hero and prophet of Life, became the *déraciné* intellectual and proto-fascist mythologiser of cultural politics.

Two central axes of the present Reader, then, are the effects feminism and Marxism have had on the critical formation of Lawrence since the sixties. Without too much *parti pris*, I think it is safe to say that these have been, in general, among the most interesting theoretical developments in criticism over the past twenty years, and the perspectives they offer more specifically on Lawrence are equally so. Indeed, one of the fundamental effects of these movements has been to demystify and denaturalise any of the practices associated with literary criticism – from writing critical monographs to editing Critical Readers:

hence, I hope, the relentlessly self-reflexive tenor of this introductory essay. I may also note in passing here – to be picked up again later – that it was as much as anything this pervasive subversion by Marxism and feminism of bourgeois criticism which paved the way for their own rapid and paradoxical incorporation in the radically unstable, deconstructed terrain of post-modern indeterminacy. For we may now perceive that all that critical praxis ever is, is the continual reproduction of past writing within and on behalf of present cultural history; that literature exists only to be shaped and recuperated by and for its moment of consumption. Forget any notion of 'definitive' studies, editions, anthologies or Critical Readers (we would all have long been out of business if such were possible), and recognise that criticism's future rests precisely on the fact that every historical moment 'writes' the literature it wishes to read largely by way of the ceaseless flow of ephemeral monographs and collections of critical essays. Which is no more than to say that the present volume, while attempting to challenge and fracture earlier, now more conventional, representations of Lawrence by way of its emphasis on class and gender, in no sense purports to correct a misrecognition of the 'real' Lawrence which it then brings into view, but is itself constructing yet another partial version derived from different historical and ideological determinations. Indeed, this Reader's main theoretical thrust as a whole is at once to reveal how the metadiscourse of criticism itself largely constitutes the literature it then analyses so 'objectively', and to consciously implicate itself in the process by which 'D. H. Lawrence' is formed and reformed in the consumptional reproduction which any historical culture promotes in the course of realising its own world-view.

The sectionalising of the book in the light of the above is then, for the most part, fairly obvious: Marxism, feminism, post-structuralism. What this principally omits, however, in terms of giving proportionate coverage to widespread critical practices over the past twenty years, is the sophisticated formalistic work which increasingly dominated mainstream criticism in the seventies and beyond. Frank Kermode (see Further Reading) would be exemplary evidence of this general tendency, as would Gāmini Salgādo (represented in the present volume, perhaps unfairly, as a kind of unwitting proto-post-structuralist). But it is most clearly exemplified in the work of David Lodge, where the emphasis on form and language, often drawing opportunistically on linguistic and structuralist theory (one of his books is significantly entitled *Working With Structuralism*, 1981), gives a new impetus to traditional notions of practical criticism and close reading. But – and this has been the main reason for not representing it here – it is nevertheless clearly part of the tradition of New Criticism. It purports to be essentially descriptive, eschewing interpretation even, in its search for the neutral but complex exposition of how a literary text works. A good example of this is Lodge's analysis, by way of Roman Jakobson, of a passage from *Women in Love* in *The Modes of Modern Writing* (1977),[13] but even more to the point is a second essay on Lawrence in his most recent critical work, *After Bakhtin* (1990), which opens: 'The object of this essay is to bring Mikhail Bakhtin's theory and practice to bear on the fiction of D.H. Lawrence – primarily in the hope of enhancing our knowledge and understanding of the kind of literary discourse Lawrence produced; but also to test the usefulness of Bakhtin's concepts and analytical tools.'[14] This is, of course, explicit admission of the utilitarian and empiricist recuperation at the heart of a project of 'working with' radical theory: Bakhtin, effectively, will be used to *describe* Lawrence, and along the way his theory's 'usefulness' – solely as a descriptive 'tool' – will be 'tested' (in the process being defused of any subversive potential). Not surprisingly, then, Lodge's essay spends much of its time 'describing the dialogic quality of Lawrence's fiction' (Lodge, p. 65); refuses to offer an interpretation of *Women in Love* for fear of 'monologizing it' (Ibid., p. 63); and significantly ends by recognising that while the relationship between Lawrence and Bakhtin is 'more than merely formal' ('carnival behaviour' and 'instinctual life' are both suppressed by the 'same social forces' of bourgeois capitalism): 'to pursue that parallel further is beyond the scope of this essay' (Ibid., p. 74). For what is particularly noticeable – in contrast to the critical movements which this theoretically informed but neutral(ising) new empiricism is effectively attempting to contain and displace – is its resolutely apolitical stance. That is not to say, of course, that it is in any sense ideologically innocent, but that it assumes and purports neutrality (in fact, its presumption of being objective, almost 'scientific', aligns it with a liberalism which also holds itself to be non-partisan and disinterested). Equally, and as a further measure of how far and how fast criticism moved in this period, Salgādo's 1976 piece reprinted here for example – while itself almost proleptically deconstructive in its treatment of Lawrence's language in *Women in Love* – would nevertheless be inconceivable, in its residual positivism, once Deconstruction had properly been taken on board. It is instructive to compare this essay with the one, also reproduced here, by Daniel O'Hara, only seven years later: both say not dissimilar things about the language of the novel, but the cast and tone of the arguments are markedly different. (See below pp. 20–1 for further consideration of these two essays.)

The first two Parts of the Reader, then, are those which pick up and develop the class/history and gender strands outlined earlier. Both may be said to be driven by seminal essays, published in 1969 or 1970, which now appear to have 'turned' Lawrence studies over the next two decades: one, Kate Millett's, is represented here and is discussed rather more fully later (p. 14–15 and Headnote to Chapter 6); the other, Raymond Williams's chapter on Lawrence from *The English Novel From Dickens to Lawrence* (1970), sadly is not (a determinate absence). And so, as a way of introducing the general features of Part One, I offer a brief synoptic account of the latter's significance.

Materialist approaches

Raymond Williams's essay pre-dates his development into Marxist literary theory and evinces strong signs of his 'Left-Leavisism' at the time. But it nevertheless at once signals the Left's attempt to recuperate 'great tradition' writers from bourgeois culture – itself a hotly contested strategy (within Left criticism) in the seventies and eighties, and engages with the debate – announced by Leavis and the 'moral formalists', but also permeating much later criticism (especially of a materialist slant) – as to where Lawrence's 'true' achievement lies: in the earlier 'realist' work (up to and perhaps including *The Rainbow*), or in the 'modernist' phase, of which the masterwork is of course *Women in Love*. Williams's obvious inclination towards the 'miracle of language' and 'knowable community' of the earlier fiction, and his presentation of *Women in Love* as a 'radical *simplification* of the novel', as 'abstract', 'isolated' and 'a masterpiece of loss' ('the loss of . . . the experience of community'),[15] dislodges the Leavisian orthodoxy and opens the way for the extensions and reorientations of the debate represented in Part One by the work of Eagleton, Martin and Holderness.

The short piece on Lawrence from Terry Eagleton's influential book, *Criticism and Ideology* (1976) – the harbinger in Britain in the seventies of the impact of European (especially French: Althusserian, Machereyan) theory on literary criticism – indicates how a new Marxist critic 're-reads' a canonic author. In fact, the whole chapter from which this extract comes recasts much of the 'Culture and Society' tradition, and often appears to be shadowing precisely Williams's *The Novel from Dickens to Lawrence* mentioned above. In this, Eagleton at once remains paradoxically bound to the 'great tradition' (a point Alistair Davies makes in a later essay in this collection), but also offers a materialist critique of it, and especially its complicity in the workings of bourgeois ideology. Graham Holderness and Graham Martin, both working from a materialist base, reconsider class and history in Lawrence's work. As with a number of other essays in this Reader, Martin's confirms Leavis's central place in the 'making' of Lawrence (see Alistair Davies, again, for an interesting account of the ideological imperative for this), and notes how seldom, therefore, Lawrence's treatment of 'class' has been rigorously analysed in the secondary literature up to that point (1982). Martin goes on to show, in partial disagreement with Williams and with Holderness, that Lawrence exhibits a progressively more complex representation of class in his fiction, implying that the shift from realism to 'abstraction' may not necessarily mean a loss of depth and grasp in this context. Holderness also challenges Leavis – and especially Leavis's promotion of *The Rainbow* as an 'incomparable' social history of England (see above p. 10) – in his argument that the novel effectively substitutes 'myth' for 'history' in its comparative treatment of the various social communities depicted. As a formal enactment of this, he sees Lawrence's increasing rejection of realism not as 'progressive', but as a way of legitimising the process by which 'real historical forces are abstracted into separable myths'. In this, and in his opposition to Eagleton, Holderness continues the debate about the relative status of *The Rainbow* and *Women in Love* compared to the earlier works, and hence, of course, further challenges the modernist orthodoxy of the post-Leavisian moral formalists of the sixties. Both essays display, in my view, the way in which fiction may be made to 'speak' something entirely different to what it has hitherto appeared to say when a different set of questions are put to it. Both are careful, empirical analyses – no more wildly speculative than most other literary-critical readings – and yet they cast Lawrence in an altogether different mould. Finally, Eagleton's second short piece on *Sons and Lovers* (from his later *Literary Theory: An Introduction*, 1983) is an attempt to exemplify the way a psychoanalytic (or neo-Freudian) analysis of literature can also be coupled to a social and material understanding of it. In miniature, then, Eagleton is attempting here to close one of the major fissures in modern criticism: the divide between 'apolitical' psychological/Freudian, and 'depersonalised' historicist/Marxist, approaches.

Feminism

In Part Two on 'Gender', Kate Millett's early essay focuses the feminist critique of Lawrence's sexual politics, which, as one major bibliographer has put it, 'seemed at the time to have been launched almost single-handedly' by her intervention; and he adds that the questions it 'brought to the forefront of critical debate . . . have reverberated in Lawrence criticism from then on.'[16] It is also worth saying, given the hammering Millett has received over the years from sensitive (usually male) literary critics, that her essay is still one of the wittiest and most savagely ironic pieces of literary demolition one could hope to find (and in Lawrence circles solemnity is often sadly *de rigueur*). Angry, engaged, assertive, 'distorting' it may be, but few would disagree that somewhere along the line she rings a bell that is still tolling for the pretensions of Phallic Man. I have not, however, included further examples of Millet-influenced, anti-Lawrence feminist criticism (a number of which, together with others less negative, appear in Anne Smith (ed.), *Lawrence and Women*, 1978). Nor have I attempted to redress the balance with any of the several defences of Lawrence which followed Millet (the earliest, and certainly the wackiest, being Norman Mailer's assault on her in *The Prisoner of Sex*, 1971); Lydia Blanchard, for example, (represented here by a later, more sophisticated essay) wrote a measured piece (1975)[17] attempting to rescue Lawrence from the 'sexual politics' furore and reconsider his treatment of women as more complex and perceptive than feminist attacks had allowed. As might be expected, there have been a number of male players in the Lawrence-and-Feminist-Criticism League, with the most paranoid recent one being Peter Balbert, whose *D. H. Lawrence and the Phallic Imagination: Essays on Sexual Identity and Feminist Misreading* (1989) is, the cover blurb tells us, 'one of the first full-length works to respond to revisionist attacks against Lawrence', and one which, significantly, attempts to recycle Norman Mailer as part of the process. What precisely is implied by 'revisionist' here? The inference I draw is that such attacks are doctrinally unsound and so betray the 'true Lawrence' who, by definition, is permanently present in his works, waiting only for the revisionist heresy to be exposed and destroyed so that he may again be seen for what he really is. Certainly Balbert is embattled, as his Introduction makes clear: 'the record of the last decade in Lawrence criticism may show that it was left to me – by the virtual default of the academy – to supply a missing voice in response to feminist charges'. And in its references to 'misreadings' and 'unequivocal distortion', to the 'evocation and explanation of his bedrock ethic' and 'the more nurturant impulses of Lawrence's framing vision',[18] it does seem to imply an essentialist Lawrence lurking there behind the revisionist caricature. It is interesting to see that even in 1989 there is still some life in the old sexual-politics dog yet: as I noted earlier, a lot more is at stake in who possesses Lawrence's 'meaning' than might be implied by wrangles over whether or not Connie and Mellors have anal intercourse in *Lady Chatterley's Lover* or Paul treats Clara badly at the end of *Sons and Lovers*.

But rather than fill the section with the heat and dust of now somewhat *passé* gender skirmishing, I include, first, a piece by Hilary Simpson from her widely respected book, *D.H. Lawrence and Feminism* (1982), which unpolemically attempts to explain, mainly in terms of historical determinations, the reasons for, and direction of, Lawrence's changing attitudes to women and women's movements, especially during the First World War; second, an example, by Judith Ruderman, of again unpolemical albeit gendered writing about Lawrence which represents the psycho-sexual spin-off from feminism, particularly in the United States, and exhibits the critical deployment of modern psychological theory; and third, an essay by Lydia Blanchard which, in its orientation to Foucault, could as well be in the following, post-structuralist, section as in this one. But I retain it here as an example of the way in which feminism has so entered our consciousness that, without polemicism or militancy, a mature essay of this kind is unmistakably informed by it. It needs no saying, really, that in this case – as indeed in that of the anti-feminist Peter Balbert – Lawrence has been indelibly feminised and must 'speak' differently than he did two decades ago. Anti-revisionist essentialism fails to see that the critical reconstruction of the past twenty years is now an integral part of the 'true' Lawrence.

Post-structuralism

The final section is more eclectic than the rest – and properly so. For although I might want to claim that Marxist and feminist studies have produced significant new criticism of Lawrence, I must recognise too that they have also spawned (either by their success or by their failure) the post-structuralist, deconstructionist and post-modernist tendencies of the eighties (and beyond?) – most evident in the tentativeness, uncertainty and self-consciousness of the work produced. Perhaps I should explain the apparent paradox of my claim here that Marxism and feminism have produced the most compelling recent readings of Lawrence, despite demonstrating both in the Introduction and the body of Reader that the celebration of indeterminacy (in critic and in text) seems now to be the order of the day. What Marxism and feminism did from the late sixties through the seventies in the area of cultural politics at least, was to offer such a devastating critique of existing attitudes, assumptions and approaches, and such an agoraphobic agenda of future possibilities, that only a relatively small amount of work – and that of a diverse kind – actually got done at the empirical level. There had been, then, only a fragmentary tangible achievement before the epistemological and methodological uncertainties endemic to the situation were themselves overdetermined by the political destabilisation incident on the rise of the New Right in the eighties and the apparent replay for the Left of 'The God that Failed'. Firm, clear, political statement, even in the cultural context, became deeply problematical on the Left, and it was compounded by the ascendancy in the eighties of 'post-modern' cultural forms and tendencies – the end of history, the recycling of images, re-production, the death of meaning, Style, self-reflexivity, egocentrism, etc. What we have yet to see is whether post-modernism is indeed our 'condition', or whether it was effectively only the cultural image of New Right supremacy in the eighties. Be that as it may, it seems to me perfectly acceptable to argue (and this explains my paradox) that certain approaches, fragmentary achievements and potentialities remain the most hopefully and progressively potent, even if the conditions for their realisation no longer effectively obtain. This is not to fix Marxist and feminist post-'68 initiatives in nostalgic aspic (the end of history indeed); it is merely to suggest that while indeterminacy, inconclusiveness and uncertainty may be our present condition – one which makes the ascription of meaning, the sense of a future and political belief difficult – it remains possible to insist that better 'conditions' may exist, that choices can be made, that meaning – if only temporarily – can be asserted. Perhaps, in the end, the most important bequest in the incomplete legacy of post-'68 Marxism and feminism will be the recognition that meaning exists only within history, is not permanently fixed, is contingent and determinate, is not owned by any one interest; that, conversely, it can be contested, taken, reinflected and reasserted; and that indeterminacy, as a 'condition', is probably more susceptible to the contestation of meaning than ideology in hegemonic form.

Meanwhile, let me glance briefly at the examples of this indeterminate 'condition' in Lawrence criticism, as represented by Part Three of the Reader, before returning to the phenomenon rather more fully in the final part of this Introduction. There are two main manifestations in the essays selected: one (Salgādo, Schneider, O'Hara – and we may reinclude Blanchard here), is the emphasis on Lawrence's language and its unstable self-deconstructing dynamic; the other (Davies most obviously), is the destabilisation of the critical 'figure' of Lawrence which occurs when he is removed from behind the dominant image manufactured by Leavis (in this instance, by Davies's relocating of Lawrence in the context of his early reception). The collection closes with a recent piece by Tony Pinkney from a book which is a bravura re-reading of Lawrence in its own right, but which, for my purposes here, is also an example – in its sequence of deconstructive turns, controlled intertextuality, re-engagement of close reading with cultural history, gendered and politicised discourse, and stylish post-modern *brio* – of the way theoretical developments now thoroughly inform critical practice and can re-present Lawrence in a guise quite unlike that which he bore some twenty years earlier. Indeed, one might say in Pinkney's case, and in the light of my comments above about the potentialities of indeterminacy, that the reader's gaze is shifted, in proper post-modern fashion, from what *Lawrence may be* to what the critical discourse *makes of him*. The focus, in other words, is now on the metadiscourse which reproduces, rather than on the 'original' discourse so reproduced. But then that, I

17

would argue, is what criticism has always actually been – indeed what 'understanding literature' can only ever be when the chips are down.

'Radical indeterminacy':[19] a post-modern Lawrence

Where does this leave Lawrence – or, to repeat my earlier questions: does Lawrence have anything left to say to us, and is there anything left to say about Lawrence? The whole drift of my argument, together with the substantive content of this Reader, give the answers: yes and yes. But in order to establish the logic of this conclusion, I must clarify and illustrate some of its premises.

The selection of essays, here, reveals that a number of very different Lawrences exist and often co-exist – the most extreme cases being, perhaps, those within the sexual-politics arena. Can there really be, simultaneously, the phallocrat/misogynist *and* the liberating writer of the phallic imagination? Surely one or other of these positions is simply *wrong* – Lawrence having been unacceptably distorted? But the Reader, and certainly its Introduction, suggests that the different constructions of Lawrence are by no means a matter – solely, if at all – of reading and misreading the text, but are productions of cultural politics, of positions formed and held, challenged and subverted, in which the possession of Lawrence's signification has much wider ramifications than disagreements as to what he might or might not have meant. Raymond Williams, in the Foreword to a volume of essays celebrating the centenary of Lawrence's birth in 1985, outlines three prevalent 'versions' of Lawrence: last exemplar of the great tradition in English fiction; first major producer of the English working-class novel; pioneer of a new kind of understanding and presentation of sexuality. On these he reflects:

> Can we say, consensually, that there is truth in each of these presentations? Not, usually, to those who are offering them. For quite apart from the deep-rooted attachments to the general positions which underlie the alternative presentations, there is the special problem that Lawrence is taken, again and again, not simply as an exemplary but as a campaigning figure. Indeed, he is often taken as in effect the private possession of this or that tendency. He is at once their justification, their promotional instance and, where necessary – which can produce the most curious results – the stick to beat the others with . . .

> Can we then say, consensually, that as against these selective interpretations Lawrence has to be seen as a whole? Perhaps, but it is

doubtful if that plausible formulation will serve. The real question may be *whether there is any whole, in that sense, to see.*[20]

Williams then notes how the appearance, first, of the Cambridge edition of Lawrence's work (including a large, newly published, part of the unfinished novel *Mr Noon*, with its subversively 'comic' and/or paranoid narrative voice), combined, second, with the progressive decoupling of early twentieth-century modernism from contemporary consciousness (particularly by way of feminism), are together affecting our understanding of the complex cluster of 'selectivities' which Lawrence already is (Williams, Ibid., pp. ix–xi). But he also finally adds (*à propos*, perhaps, of the remark quoted above that there may not be 'any whole . . . to see') that, in the nature of Lawrence's entire project, 'finish, settlement were never either the ends or the means' (Ibid., p. xi) – a point I shall return to shortly.

In another essay not included in the present volume, 'Lawrence's Cultural Impact' (1987), Kingsley Widmer charts the way 'Lawrence has called forth ranging and intense responses . . . which go beyond usual literary legacies' in three areas: 'the feminist–misogynist disputes; the obscenity–censorship conflicts; and the problematic role as a prophet of enlarged eroticism'.[21] In each case, Widmer offers an interesting account of the often entirely contradictory responses, interpretations and deductions different readers and sectional interests make of, or take from, Lawrence's work – to such an extent, indeed, that the essay itself can finally make no real sense of what Lawrence's 'cultural impact' may amount to. In one instance in particular (the misogynist–feminist disputes), Widmer concludes by, in effect, answering my question above as to how two totally opposed views of Lawrence can exist simultaneously without one of them being wrong. He posits that the disputes seem 'based on the simple-minded proposition that one cannot be both sensitively sympathetic to women and an extreme male chauvinist. Lawrence was obviously both . . . one who provocatively – unto perversity – contributed to a different, a *more conflicted*, awareness of man–woman relations' (Widmer, p. 163; my italics). And the whole essay ends on a note of almost paralysed ambivalence. Suggesting that Lawrence's imperative of a 'passional consciousness' may be his most important cultural legacy, Widmer quotes Lawrence's own dictum, 'Anything that *triumphs*, perishes', and reflects: 'If his prophecy has not completely perished, it is because his vivid consciousness of life has not triumphed' (Widmer, p. 174).

What emerges from both Williams and Widmer is that, on the one hand, 'Lawrence' is constructed, as I have kept repeating, differentially in relation to the cultural–political *loci* of different critics/readers, but on the other, that this is *also* a reflex of the radically unstable discourse that

Lawrence's work seems to be. Williams's notions of Lawrence's refusal of 'settlement' and the absence of 'any whole . . . to see', and Widmer's of his 'conflicted awareness', are both expressions of this.

That Lawrence's text is dynamically contradictory is by no means a new perception – but it is one, I will want to argue in a moment, that is given a wholly new dimension in the context of post-modernity. Critics have long pointed to the tensions, inconclusiveness and changes of view in Lawrence's *oeuvre*, both over time and within individual works. In *Women in Love*, in particular, it has often been noticed that Birkin, so obviously at times the 'Lawrence figure', is subjected to irony and ridicule, makes contradictory remarks at different points in the novel, is sometimes the dominant consciousness of the book, and sometimes gives way to Ursula – to the point where the reader does not know whether to 'trust the tale' or not. The case for the novel's 'radical indeterminacy' is well made by Gāmini Salgādo (the phrase is his) in his essay of 1976 included, in part, in this Reader. In the opening paragraph here, he notes that *Women in Love* 'is not merely a novel that accommodates contradictory readings, it positively invites and even compels them'. He then goes on to show how this is borne out generally by the structure of the novel and, in the part included here, specifically by its competing languages. Salgādo reflects that the reader

. . . will be more than usually at a loss to say what he has got [out of the novel], not because of the meagreness of the experience but because of its abundance. Working through the novel leaves one reader at least with the sense that its 'message' or 'messages' are snares and delusions: the final effect is the typically 'modern' one of having the experience and missing the meaning.

And he concludes:

Lawrence's novel does not merely deploy a series of paradoxes and contradictions in the service of a larger unity. It is centrally paradoxical because it is shot through with the continuous and continuously felt tension between the necessity of articulating a vision and its impossibility, and sometimes its undesirability.

However, in 1976, still immune to the logical negativity of nascent Deconstruction, Salgādo continues to hanker after some unifying principle, some notion of completion, rather than accepting that the text's 'radical indeterminacy' is a function of its own 'impossible' desire: to achieve, as Lawrence himself put it in the American Foreword of 1920, 'the passionate struggle into conscious being', the 'struggle for verbal consciousness [which] should not be left out in art'.[22] Daniel O'Hara's later, deconstruction-informed essay, 'The Power of Nothing in *Women in Love*' (1983), is however able to accept the 'repetitive self-cancellation that defines the structure of the novel' as an inflexion of Lawrence as 'apocalyptic ironist who says, in effect, a plague on all your houses' – including both Birkin and Ursula in this – and who leaves the reader with: 'not de Man's linguistic machine, or Foucault's discursive network, but simply "nothing" at all'. Daniel Schneider, too, in a more general context, and while not wishing to present Lawrence as a proto-deconstructionist, nevertheless sees him, in his attacks on idealism and logocentrism, as allied to deconstruction's 'frontal assault on traditional views of knowledge and logic'. Lawrence believed above all, Schneider says, that 'one must understand that language may bear no connection with a speaker's original intention and that the structures of convention which masquerade as sincere or authentic truth are mere structures, dead, static, final. No words, no ideas, can convey the breath of life. On the contrary, all knowledge is, strictly speaking, the death of life, the death of being.' But ironically, of course, as O'Hara points out, Foucault has criticised Lawrence's own stated desire – to 'realize sex. Today the full conscious realization of sex is even more important than the act itself'[23] – as also a controlling and hence a repressing of sexuality, which thus renders Lawrence's 'full conscious realization' merely one of those 'languages' or 'knowledges' that mark the 'death of being'. Lydia Blanchard, however, argues that Foucault underestimates the complexity and flexibility of Lawrence's grasp of 'the relation between language, sexuality, power and knowledge'. And in the case of *Lady Chatterley*, she suggests that Lawrence 'not only created a language of love, a lover's discourse, but has also shown the limits of such a discourse, even at its most eloquent and persuasive'. In this, I think we may perceive a further instance of that post-structuralist, post-modern Lawrence in whom ambivalence, contradiction and self-cancellation preclude 'knowledge' and 'truth' and allow only a temporary, glimpsed, ordering of the play of discourse. For Blanchard finally sees the novel as representing the tension between 'the need to rescue sexuality from secrecy, to bring it into discourse, and the simultaneous recognition that the re-creation of sexuality in language must always, at the same time, resist language.'

To add one further twist to this sense of a Lawrence who leaves us 'nothing at all', as his texts self-deconstruct both from the weight, ironically, of the critical elucidation they sustain and from their own sense of the impossibility of their task ('the struggle for verbal consciousness' – that is, the simultaneous deployment of, and resistance to, language) – let me proffer one observation of my own. I am not the first by a long chalk to puzzle over the 'radical indeterminacy' of the closing lines of *Women in Love*:

'Did you need Gerald?' she asked one evening.

'Yes,' he said.

'Aren't I enough for you?' she asked.

'No,' he said. 'You are enough for me, as far as a woman is concerned. You are all women to me. But I wanted a man friend, as eternal as you and I are eternal.'

'Why aren't I enough?' she said. 'You are enough for me. I don't want anybody else but you. Why isn't it the same with you?'

'Having you, I can live all my life without anybody else, any other sheer intimacy. But to make it complete, really happy, I wanted eternal union with a man too: another kind of love,' he said.

'I don't believe it,' she said. 'It's an obstinacy, a theory, a perversity.'

'Well – ' he said.

'You can't have two kinds of love. Why should you!'

'It seems as if I can't,' he said. 'Yet I wanted it.'

'You can't have it, because it's false, impossible,' she said.

'I don't believe that,' he answered.[24]

After all they have undergone, after all the intense *rites de passage* of Birkin and Ursula's relationship, what on earth does Birkin mean? Isn't Ursula quite right to reject his wishful-thinking as 'an obstinacy, a theory, a perversity'? Surely for once the novel stands firmly behind Ursula and judges Birkin? But somehow it doesn't quite read like that: after all Birkin gets the last word – 'I don't believe that' – and why should Lawrence (yes, I still find myself able to invoke that dead figure, 'the author') choose to end the novel in this way? It has, in the opening phrase, 'she asked one evening', a deliberate, coda-like tone which refuses to allow that Lawrence may not have intended the novel to end on quite this note. (Certainly, the 'fair-copy' manuscript-draft of the last chapter contains no break in the remarkably clean handwriting of the final page – with just the word 'wrong', instead of the printed 'false', appearing in the penultimate line.)[25] He may not, however, have intended its *effect*: for what Birkin is rejecting is the whole logic of the novel's apparent thesis up to this point. On a fairly simple reading, Gerald Crich has represented the 'consciousness' of a Western civilisation which is spiralling down to its own destruction (the First World War) because it has split into extremes of being ('Northern' intellect v 'primitive' sensuality). Gerald represents the Northern Mind/ Will of 'Society', and is symbolically frozen to self-determined death in the snow. Birkin has been unable to bond with him – hence Gerald's 'death' and Birkin's 'perverse' desire in the passage quoted above. But Ursula is right – it is 'false, impossible' – because the novel *has to* destroy Society (Gerald) precisely in order to 'free' Birkin/Ursula. Lawrence, at the extremity of the (il)logic of bourgeois individualism, has posited that the enemy of human individuals is Society, and that in order to save themselves they must, in Ernest Hemingway's phrase,[26] make a 'separate peace' before Society destroys them, along with itself, by its own inevitable deathly logic. The novel finally enacts this 'liberation' with Birkin and Ursula poised for withdrawal ('*Exeunt*') into the autonomy of their relationship. But just at the moment of the novel's closure, Birkin, it would seem, 'recognises' the flaw in the ideology of liberal individualism: that it is both impossible and futile to live *without* – in both senses of the word – social being. What the novel points up, by thus running so close to the extremity of its own ideology, is the latter's ultimate inadequacy. When Birkin desires a relationship with Gerald at the end (in its wistful pastoral form – 'to make it complete, really happy'), he is reopening a closure which represents the trajectory of the novel's logic, and is hence an 'impossibility' in its attempt to countermand it. He *cannot* have a relationship with 'Society' *and* be a free individual, and in any event Society is doomed by the terms of its own definition in the novel – its inherent deathliness. Ursula, of course, is right: it is 'a theory, a perversity, false, impossible' in respect of the 'world' the novel has proposed; but the novel at that moment recognises its own awesome negative logic, and flinches. When Birkin says 'I don't believe that', he (Lawrence? the novel?) is rejecting the entire fiction that has preceded the statement. The novel is effectively deconstructing itself at the last moment – in a recognition which it cannot of course sustain – that the ideology which informs it is fatally flawed. What I am suggesting, in short, is that *Women in Love* finally articulates the 'impossible': at once the propagation and the negation of its philosophy of life. And when an ideology recognises its own falseness, there are no hiding places left: only, on the one hand, political action; on the other, despair – and the re-erection of the ideological screen. Perhaps this accounts, then, for the presence of Major Eastwood (significantly named) in *The Virgin and the Gypsy* (written 1925–6, published 1930) – that 'great snow-bird of a major' with 'the abstract morality of the north blowing him, like a strange wind, into isolation' – but one who now recognises 'that desire is the most wonderful thing in life. Anybody who can really feel it, is a king, and I envy nobody else!' Pointedly, he almost immediately also tells Yvette:

> 'I'm a resurrected man myself, as far as that goes . . . I was buried for twenty hours under snow,' he said. 'And not much the worse for it, when they dug me out.'
> There was a frozen pause in the conversation.
> 'Life's awful!' said Yvette.
> 'They dug me out by accident,' he said.

'Oh!' – Yvette trailed slowly. 'It might be destiny, you know.'
To which he did not answer.[27]

In the 'happy' pastoral of this later fiction, Lawrence had to 'resurrect' Gerald in order to make the 'impossible theory' a realised possibility. We may accept this as a fiction; but, like Birkin, we 'don't believe' it either.

In the nineties, then, and as we approach the new millennium, we have a D. H. Lawrence who is composed of a multiplicity of cultural reproductions, both critical and extra-critical. The trial of *Lady Chatterley* still evokes public interest: on New Year's Eve 1989 *The Sunday Times* ran an interview, thirty years on, with Bernardine Wall (as was), the twenty-one-year-old Catholic girl who appeared as a prime witness for the defence all those years ago; in the accompanying visuals, a copy of the original Penguin edition of the novel was prominently displayed.[28] The image of Lawrence as passionate being and sexual pundit is still recycled by the now numerous films and videos based (more or less) on his life and work: *L'Amant de Lady Chatterley* (1959); *Sons and Lovers* (1960 – a very successful TV adaptation was also made by Trevor Griffiths in 1981); *The Fox* (1968); Ken Russell's *Women in Love* (1969); *The Virgin and the Gypsy* (1970); *Lady Chatterley's Lover* (1981, starring Sylvia Kristel, but wrongly titled – it is, in fact, based on *The First Lady Chatterley*); Christopher Miles's *The Priest of Love* (with Ian McKellan as Lawrence, 1981); a TV adaptation of *The Rainbow*, directed by Stuart Burge, in 1988; a 1986 Australian film version of *Kangaroo*, first shown on British television in January 1991; and a soft-porn film, *The Young Lady Chatterley*, widely available on video in Britain and the United States.

The year 1985 was the much-celebrated centenary of Lawrence's birth; there are tourist-guides to Eastwood and 'the Lawrence Country'; his work is always widely in print, and is on every secondary and tertiary education syllabus in the English-Literature-studying world; and there are thousands of books, articles, theses and other critical productions focusing on his life and work. I have just indicated, by way of reflecting on the orientation and trajectory of this Reader, that 'Lawrence' becomes more complex, more unstable, more 'unfinished', as the range and sophistication of the attention paid to him increases. In other words, and in typically post-modern fashion, the vast, and vastly differentiated, cultural reproduction of Lawrence's work means that we can make less and less sense of it in any absolute way – as its contradictory, heteroglossic, polyvocal discourse deconstructs beneath, and because of, our transfixed critical gaze. All we can do is reconstruct it, temporarily and partially, in our own image and for our own ends.

Let me finally, and with that in mind, return us once more to 1970, to Raymond Williams – with our two decades of Marxism, feminism, post-structuralism, deconstruction and post-modernism still ahead – to an essay I have suggested helped foster some of these developments . . . and re-run it. What was it that Williams perceived as the 'most redeeming sign' of that 'masterpiece of loss', *Women in Love*? Well, 'the inconclusiveness . . . of the final paragraph . . . [that] the ending . . . is inconclusive'. Lawrence had reached 'a condition to face, to live through, but never, never at all, to ratify'; and for Williams he therefore remained a human resource, because 'it is not after all an end with Lawrence. It is where in our time we have had to begin.'[29] A radical inconclusiveness may also be the place for us to begin again to construct meanings which ensure that history has not ended. And reproducing Lawrence as a post-modern figure who speaks to our condition may indeed be a part of this process. Which does not mean – and I add this at the end to disarm the many critics out there who will see all this metacritical hoo-ha as at once arrant presumption and arid nonsense on my part – that very large numbers of people, students and general readers alike, will not go on reading Lawrence with the intense pleasure and puzzlement his work so often induces, tapping into the strange sources of power his fiction seems to draw on, and so, at a stroke, sweeping all such sophisticated 'revisionism' aside in the immediacy of their exposure to the positive essences of the 'text itself'. But then, perhaps, they will turn to the present volume in the fond expectation that it will help them focus and clarify what they have read . . .

Notes

1. MARK SPILKA, Introduction, Spilka (ed.), *D.H. Lawrence: A Collection of Critical Essays* ('Twentieth-Century Views': Englewood Cliffs, N. J.: Prentice-Hall, 1963), pp. 1, 5.

2. The phrase is Leavis's. It may be found, for example, in the title of Chapter 4 ('Why *Four Quartets* matter in a Technologico-Benthamite age') of *English Literature in our Time and the University. The Clark Lectures, 1967* (London: Chatto and Windus, 1969).

3. The poem, first published in Larkin's collection, *High Windows* (1974), begins: 'Sexual intercourse began/In nineteen sixty-three/(Which was rather late for me) – /Between the end of the *Chatterley* ban/And the Beatles' first LP.'

4. MARION SHAW, 'Lawrence and Feminism', *Critical Quarterly*, **25**, 3 (Autumn 1983): 23.

5. Information derived from GERALD J. POLLINGER, '*Lady Chatterley's Lover*: A View from Lawrence's Literary Executor', in *D.H. Lawrence's 'Lady': A New Look at Lady Chatterley's Lover*, ed. Michael Squires and Dennis Jackson (Athens, Georgia: University of Georgia Press, 1985), pp. 236–7.

6. JAMES C. COWAN, 'Introduction', *D.H. Lawrence: An Annotated Bibliography of*

Writings About Him, Vol. II (De Kalb, Illinois: Northern Illinois University Press, 1985), pp. xxi, xxv.

7. SPILKA, *op. cit.*, p. 14.

8. COLIN CLARKE, 'Introduction', Clarke (ed.), *D.H. Lawrence: The Rainbow and Women in Love: A Casebook* (London: Macmillan, 1969), p. 17.

9. JOHN B. HUMMA, 'More Matter, Less Art: The Continuing Course of Lawrence Criticism', *Studies in the Novel*, **19**, 1 (Spring 1987): 88.

10. PETER WIDDOWSON, *Hardy in History: A Study in Literary Sociology* (London: Routledge, 1989). See especially the Introduction and 'A note on the case of the "minor novels"' in Part I, Chapter 1.

11. Information derived from KINGSLEY WIDMER, 'Lawrence's Cultural Impact', in *The Legacy of D.H. Lawrence: New Essays*, ed. Jeffrey Meyers (London: Macmillan, 1987), p. 167; and Pollinger, *op. cit.*, p. 238.

12. F.R. LEAVIS, *D. H. Lawrence/Novelist* (1955); Harmondsworth: Penguin Books, 1964). See Chapter 2, 'Lawrence and Class' (mainly about the short story 'Daughters of the Vicar'); and p. 151 especially, for the claims made for *The Rainbow*.

13. DAVID LODGE, *The Modes of Modern Writing: Metaphor, Metonymy, and the Typology of Modern Literature* (London: Edward Arnold, 1977). See Chapter 4, 'D.H. Lawrence', especially pp. 161–3. Much of the rest of the chapter is devoted to a reading of the short story 'England, My England'.

14. DAVID LODGE, *After Bakhtin: Essays on fiction and criticism* (London: Routledge, 1990), p. 57.

15. RAYMOND WILLIAMS, *The English Novel from Dickens to Lawrence* (1970); St Albans: Paladin, 1974), Chapter 8, 'D.H. Lawrence', *passim*, pp. 128–9, 143, 145, 147.

16. COWAN, *op. cit.*, p. xxx.

17. LYDIA BLANCHARD, 'Love and Power': a reconsideration of sexual politics in D.H. Lawrence', *Modern Fiction Studies*, **21**, 3 (1975): 431–43.

18. PETER BALBERT, *D.H. Lawrence and the Phallic Imagination: Essays on Sexual Identity and Feminist Misreading* (London: Macmillan, 1989), *passim*, pp. 12, 2, 6, 3, 11.

19. The phrase is Gāmini Salgādo's, from the essay included in the present volume. See below, p. 138.

20. RAYMOND WILLIAMS, Foreword (1985) to *The Spirit of D. H. Lawrence: Centenary Studies*, ed. Gāmini Salgādo and G.K. Das (London: Macmillan, 1988), pp. vii–viii (my italics).

21. KINGSLEY WIDMER, 'Lawrence's Cultural Impact', in *The Legacy of D.H. Lawrence: New Essays*, ed. Jeffrey Meyers (London: Macmillan, 1987), p. 156.

22. D.H. LAWRENCE, Foreword to *Women in Love* (American edition, 1920). The Foreword is reproduced in COLIN CLARKE's *D.H. Lawrence: The Rainbow and Women in Love*, op. cit., pp. 63–4, and as Appendix 1 of the Cambridge edition of *Women in Love* (Cambridge: CUP, 1987), p. 483.

23. The sentence (from Lawrence's *Psychoanalysis and the Unconscious*) is quoted by

Foucault at the end of his *The History of Sexuality*. See O'Hara's essay later in this volume for further references – especially p. 149–51 and his notes 8 and 9. Lydia Blanchard takes Foucault to task over the same point in her essay also included here (see especially pp. 120–1).

24. D.H. LAWRENCE, *Women in Love* (1921; Harmondsworth: Penguin Books, 1963), p. 541.

25. I have been fortunate to see a xerox copy of the original manuscript, which is housed in the Humanities Research Centre, The University of Austin, Texas.

26. See, for example, the italicised passage immediately preceding 'A Very Short Story' in Ernest Hemingway, *The Snows of Kilimanjaro and Other Stories* (Harmondsworth: Penguin Books, 1963), p. 81, where the wounded Nick Adams says to Rinaldi: 'You and me we've made a separate peace.'

27. D.H. LAWRENCE, *The Virgin and the Gypsy* (1930; Harmondsworth: Penguin Books, 1967), pp. 223, 229.

28. 'My Life and Lady C by the Convent Girl': the Valerie Grove Interview, *The Sunday Times*, 31 December 1989, p. A7.

29. WILLIAMS, *The English Novel*, op. cit., pp. 147, 148, 149.

Part One

Class, History, Ideology

2 D.H. Lawrence*

TERRY EAGLETON

Terry Eagleton, Warton Professor of English Literature at Oxford University, is the most influential, prolific and varied of the generation of British Marxist critics who emerged in the 1960s and 70s. *Criticism and Ideology* was particularly significant in importing Althusserian theory into the parochial world of British literary criticism (see Introduction, p. 13). This passage is the penultimate section of a long chapter entitled 'Ideology and Literary Form', which shows British nineteenth- and early twentieth-century literary culture enacting, in its increasingly apparent self-destruction of organic form, the mounting contradictions and tensions within liberal-bourgeois ideology. It is an early example of how the new Marxist criticism, by way of the concept of Ideology, can make a materialist *formal* analysis of texts, rather than merely situating them in their historical contexts.

Eagleton's many books and articles of Marxist literary theory and criticism include, more recently: *Walter Benjamin, or Towards a Revolutionary Criticism* (Verso, 1981); *The Rape of Clarissa* (Blackwell, 1982); *Literary Theory: An Introduction* (Blackwell, 1983); *The Function of Criticism* (Verso, 1984); *William Shakespeare* (Blackwell, 1986); *The Ideology of the Aesthetic* (Blackwell, 1990); *Ideology: An Introduction* (Verso, 1991); a novel (*Saints and Scholars*, Verso, 1987) and a play (*Saint Oscar*, Faber, 1990). He is currently working on Irish history and culture.

Of all the writers discussed in this essay, D.H. Lawrence, the only one of proletarian origin, is also the most full-bloodedly 'organicist' in both his social and aesthetic assumptions. As a direct twentieth-century inheritor

* Reprinted from Terry Eagleton, *Criticism and Ideology: a Study in Marxist Literary Theory* (New Left Books, 1976; London: Verso Editions, 1978), pp. 157–61; footnotes renumbered from the original.)

of the 'Culture and Society' Romantic humanist tradition, Lawrence's fiction represents one of the century's most powerful literary critiques of industrial capitalism, launched from a deep-seated commitment to an organic order variously located in Italy, New Mexico, pre-industrial England and, metaphorically, in the novel-form itself. The novel for Lawrence is a delicate, labile organism whose elements are vitally interrelated; it spurns dogma and metaphysical absolutes, tracing instead the sensuous flux of its unified life-forms.[1] Yet Lawrence is also a dogmatic, metaphysically absolutist, radically dualistic thinker, fascinated by mechanism and disintegration; and it is in this contradiction that much of his historical significance lies.

What Lawrence's work dramatises, in fact, is a contradiction within the Romantic humanist tradition itself, between its corporate and individualist components. An extreme form of individualism is structural to Romantic humanist ideology – an application, indeed, of organicism to the individual self, which becomes thereby wholly autotelic, spontaneously evolving into 'wholeness' by its own uniquely determining laws. This ideological component – at once an idealised version of commonplace bourgeois individualism and a 'revolutionary' protest against the 'reified' society it produces – is strongly marked in Lawrence's writing, and enters into conflict with the opposing imperatives of impersonality and organic order. His social organicism decisively rejects the atomistic, mechanistic ideologies of industrial capitalism, yet at the same time subsumes the values of the bourgeois liberal tradition: sympathy, intimacy, compassion, the centrality of the 'personal'. These contradictions come to a crisis in Lawrence with the First World War, the most traumatic event of his life. The war signifies the definitive collapse of the liberal humanist heritage, with its benevolistic idealism and 'personal' values, clearing the way for the 'dark gods' of discipline, action, hierarchy, individual separateness, mystical impersonality – in short, for a social order which rejects the 'female' principle of compassion and sexual intimacy for the 'male' principle of power. 'The reign of love is passing, and the reign of power is coming again.'[2]

In this sense Lawrence was a major precursor of fascism, which is not to say that he himself unqualifiedly accepted fascist ideology. He unequivocally condemned Mussolini, and correctly identified fascism as a spuriously 'radical' response to the crisis of capitalism.[3] Lawrence was unable to embrace fascism because, while it signified a form of Romantic organistic reaction to bourgeois liberalism, it also negated the individualism which was for him a crucial part of the same Romantic heritage. This is the contradiction from which he was unable to escape, in his perpetual oscillation between a proud celebration of individual autonomy and a hunger for social integration; he wants men to be drilled soldiers but *individual* soldiers, desires to 'rule' over them but not 'bully' them.[4] To 'resolve' this contradiction, Lawrence had recourse to a metaphysic which dichotomised reality into 'male' and 'female' principles and attempted to hold them in dialectical tension. The male principle is that of power, consciousness, spirit, activism, individuation; the female principle that of flesh, sensuality, permanence, passivity.[5] The male principle draws sustenance from the female, but must avoid collapsing inertly into it. Yet Lawrence's dualist metaphysic is ridden with internal contradictions, for a significant biographical reason: his mother, symbol of primordial sensual unity, was in fact petty-bourgeois, and so also represented individuation, aspiring consciousness and active idealism in contrast to the mute, sensuous passivity of his working-class father. This partial inversion of his parents' sexual roles, as defined by Lawrence, contorts and intensifies the contradictions which his metaphysic tries to resolve.[6] The mother, as symbol of the nurturing yet cloying flesh, is subconsciously resented for inhibiting true masculinity (as is the father's passivity), yet valued as an image of love, tenderness and personal intimacy. Conversely, her active, aspiring consciousness disrupts the mindless unity of sensual life symbolised by the father, but is preferred to his brutal impersonality. *Sons and Lovers* takes these conflicts as its subject-matter, on the whole rejecting the father and defending the mother; yet as Lawrence's fiction progresses, moving through and beyond the First World War, that priority is partly reversed. *Women in Love* struggles to complement a potentially claustrophobic sexual intimacy with the 'liberating' effect of a purely 'male' relationship; and the hysterical male chauvinism of the post-war novels (*Aaron's Rod, Kangaroo, The Plumed Serpent*) represents a strident rejection of sexual love for the male cult of power and impersonality. Lawrence's deepening hatred of women is a reaction both against bourgeois liberal values and the snare of a sensuality which violates individual autonomy; yet his commitment to sensual being as the source of social renewal contradictorily persists. In *Lady Chatterley's Lover*, the image of the father is finally rehabilitated in the figure of Mellors; yet Mellors combines impersonal male power with 'female' tenderness, working-class roughness with petty bourgeois awareness, achieving a mythical resolution of the contradictions which beset Lawrence's work.

Lawrence's particular mode of relation to the dominant ideology, then, was in the first place a contradictory combination of proletarian and petty-bourgeois elements – a combination marked by a severe conflict between alternative ideological discourses which becomes encoded in his metaphysic. Yet this fact is of more than merely 'biographical' interest: for the ideological contradictions which the young Lawrence lives out – between power and love, community and autonomy, sensuality and consciousness, order and individualism – are a specific overdetermination of a deep-seated ideological crisis within the dominant formation as a whole. Lawrence's relation to that crisis is then doubly overdetermined by his expatriatism, which combines an assertive, deracinated individualism with a hunger for the historically mislaid 'totality'. The forms of Lawrence's fiction produce this ideological conjuncture in a variety of ways. The 'symptomatic' repressions and absences of the realist *Sons and Lovers* may be recuperated in the ultra-realist forms of *The Rainbow* – a text which 'explodes' realism in its letter, even as it preserves it in the 'totalising' organicism of its evolving generational structure. After the war, Lawrence's near-total ideological collapse, articulated with the crisis of aesthetic signification, presents itself in a radical rupturing and diffusion of literary form: novels like *Aaron's Rod* and *Kangaroo* are signally incapable of evolving a narrative, ripped between fragmentary plot, spiritual autobiography and febrile didacticism. But between these texts and *The Rainbow* occurs the unique moment of *Women in Love*. That work's break to synchronic form, away from the diachronic rhythms of *The Rainbow*, produces an 'ideology of the text' marked by statis and disillusionment; yet it is precisely in its fissuring of organic form, in its 'montage' techniques of symbolic juxtaposition, that the novel enforces a 'progressive' discontinuity with a realist lineage already put into profound question by *Jude the Obscure*.

Notes

1. See 'The Novel', *Phoenix II* (London: Heinemann, 1968).

2. 'Blessed are the Powerful', *Phoenix II*.

3. See his comment in *St Mawr*: 'Try fascism. Fascism would keep the surface of life intact, and carry on the undermining business all the better.' Lawrence was not a fascist rather perhaps in the sense that he was not a homosexual. He thought both fascism and homosexuality immoral, but was subconsciously fascinated by both.

4. *Fantasia of the Unconscious* (London: Heinemann, 1961), p. 84.

5. This duality is imaged in Lawrence's work in a whole gamut of antinomies: love/law, light/dark, lion/unicorn, sun/moon, Son/Father, spirit/soul, sky/earth, and so on.

6. A contortion evident in the *reversibility* of some of Lawrence's symbolic antinomies: the Father, symbol of sensual phallic consciousness, is identifiable with the *female*; the lion may signify both active power and sensuality; the sun is sometimes male intellect and sometimes sensuous female warmth, while the moon may suggest female passivity or the cold abstract consciousness of the male.

3 D.H. Lawrence and Class*

GRAHAM MARTIN

Graham Martin, Professor of Literature at the Open University, is a materialist critic more in the tradition of British Marxist humanism than of that initiated by the incursion of European Marxist-structuralist theory in the seventies. The essay included here is interesting at once for its innovative, because serious, recognition that 'class' is a fundamental issue in Lawrence's work; for its contribution to the ongoing (realist/modernist) debate pioneered by Leavis and Raymond Williams (see Introduction, pp. 4–5, 13–14) about the relative status of *Women in Love* in Lawrence's overall achievement; and for its subtle textual analysis of how narrative structures reveal the pressure of class in Lawrence's informing consciousness. A second piece by Martin, '"History" and "Myth" in D.H. Lawrence's Chatterley Novels' (in Jeremy Hawthorne (ed.), *The British Working-Class Novel in the Twentieth Century* (London: Arnold, 1984)), should be read in conjunction with the present essay and with the following one by Graham Holderness.

Martin's other works include: (ed.) *Eliot in Perspective: a symposium* (Macmillan, 1970); (ed. with Bernard Waites and Tony Bennett) *Popular Culture: Past and Present: a Reader* (Croom Helm with the Open University Press, 1982); (ed., with W.R. Owens) *Arnold Kettle 1916–86. Literature and Liberation: Selected Essays* (Manchester University Press, 1988); and many study guides and course books for Open University literature and cultural studies units – most particularly on 'The Nineteenth-Century Novel and its Legacy', on 'Twentieth-Century Poetry', and on 'Popular Culture'.

In the extensive secondary literature that now clusters round Lawrence's fiction, the topic of 'class' scarcely receives a mention, and from one

---

* Reprinted from Douglas Jefferson and Graham Martin (eds), *The Uses of Fiction: Essays on the Modern Novel in Honour of Arnold Kettle* (Milton Keynes: The Open University Press, 1982), pp. 83–97.

point of view this is welcome. Early commentators who noticed Lawrence's awareness of class-distinction in English life either judged it unhealthy, even tinged with snobbishness (some memoirists, T.S. Eliot); or believed that it showed Lawrence settling for the petit-bourgeois proto-fascist route of escape from his working-class origins (Caudwell). Evidence for the first view was at best sparse and ambiguous, but for the second drew mainly on Lawrence's non-fictional writings, *Movements in European History* (1921), *Reflections on the Death of a Porcupine* (1925), some essays posthumously assembled in *Assorted Articles* (1931) and in *Phoenix* (1936), though also upon simplified readings of the 'political' novels, *Kangaroo* (1923) and *The Plumed Serpent* (1926).

But what of the fiction as a whole? As is well-known, it was by pressing this question that F.R. Leavis intervened so decisively in the history of Lawrence's reputation. The *Scrutiny* essays (1950–53) and *D.H. Lawrence: Novelist* (1955) shifted attention from Lawrence's express polemicizing, from what he himself would have called his preachy *Salvator Mundi* side, towards a proper consideration of his fictional art. Yet in so doing, Leavis may also be said to have removed 'class' from the agenda of relevant discussion of Lawrence's work. There was a general reason for this. The anti- or a-political nature of Leavis's conception of culture in itself entailed a refusal to explore the relevance of 'class' to literary-critical practice, except in the narrow sense of strictures on aspects of Bloomsbury and 'the metropolitan centre'. More immediately in Lawrence's case, Leavis's canonization of *The Rainbow*, *Women in Love*, certain *nouvelles* and short stories, as constituting the novelist's major achievement, had the implicit result of setting aside such novels as *Sons and Lovers* and *Lady Chatterley's Lover* in which 'class' is evidently an issue. And where Leavis led, Lawrence critics have, by and large, followed.[1]

But explicitly too, Leavis's own treatment of the issue had this effect as in 'Lawrence and Class', the chapter in *D.H. Lawrence: Novelist* (pp. 73–95), whose title I have adopted for this essay. There Leavis dismisses the charge of snobbery by means of an analysis of a previously unregarded *nouvelle* in *The Prussian Officer* (1914) collection of Lawrence's earliest short fiction, 'Daughters of the Vicar', which turns on a conflict of class values. Lawrence's handling of the issue (argues Leavis) shows not just that he was a close observer of a lamentable fact about English society, but that he perceived it from the vantage ground of 'classless truth', avoiding both sentimental idealisation of the working-class and animus against the middle-class. The sterile and repressed Lindley family, obsessed by 'proud class-superiority', push one daughter into a marriage whose sole recommendations are money and position. But the other daughter rebels by choosing 'life', her relationship with a young collier of the district, overcoming both the cold hostility of her family and the subtler barriers within her own and her lover's class-influenced feelings. For Leavis, this outcome contains the essence of Lawrence's view of 'class'. Class-division, class-feeling exist as poisonous facts about English society, and Lawrence hates them. But they can be overcome by 'life', that is to say, by individual men and women sufficiently courageous, tender, and fiery, to establish human relationships beyond 'class'.

The general application of this account to other of Lawrence's writings will, of course, be clear. Yet formulated in this way, it omits the crucial fact that the 'classless truth' affirmed by these lovers is not permitted to find an English home. Unable to prevent their daughter's scandalous *mésalliance*, the Lindleys insist that the young couple leave the district. They offer no resistance and plan to emigrate to Canada, where their offence will no longer retain the force of a direct challenge to the Lindleys' social position. Leavis is surely correct in identifying Lawrence's *authorial* view of this as a victory over 'class' at the personal level. But what we need to add is that the tale speaks more complexly, more interestingly, than the artist. The conclusion which so emphatically robs the Lindley ethos of its last vestiges of moral authority is equally emphatic in confirming its social *power*. Such a triumph of 'life' over 'class', however un-idealised at the personal level, bears an uncomfortable resemblance to defeat – certain individuals escape but the objective determinations of 'class' persist, scarcely recognised as such.[2] In this essay, I want to claim paradigmatic status for such narrative structures within Lawrence's work as a whole, and to propose that his perception of 'class', realized in these ways, gives us a measure of his achievement, both of its strength and its limitations.

A paradigm takes concrete form only in its variants, so some of these must now be considered. Amongst the early fiction, 'Daughters of the Vicar' broaches the 'class' issue with a clarity hardly to be repeated before *Lady Chatterley's Lover*. The question is more characteristically present as a contradiction, or counter-current, subverting the narrative authority of the main story. In *Sons and Lovers*, we meet this:

'You know,' [Paul] said to his mother, 'I don't want to belong to the well-to-do middle class. I like my common people best. I belong to the common people.'

'But if anybody else said so, my son, wouldn't you be in a tear. *You* know you consider yourself equal to any gentleman.'

'In myself,' he answered, 'not in my class or my education or my manners. But in myself I am.'

'Very well, then. Then why talk about the common people?'

'Because – the difference between people isn't in their class, but in themselves. Only from the middle classes one gets ideas, and from the common people – life itself, warmth. You feel their hates and loves.'

'It's all very well, my boy. But, then, why don't you go and talk to your father's pals?'

'But they're rather different.'

'Not at all. They're the common people. After all, whom do you mix with now – among the common people? Those that exchange ideas, like the middle class. The rest don't interest you.'

Sons and Lovers, pp. 314–15.[3]

H.M. Daleski uses this exchange (amongst other evidence) to argue for Paul's unconscious identification with his father, more generally, for a conflict between his overt and his suppressed feelings about each parent, and few critics would wish to deny some such sub-text in the novel's articulation of Paul's attitudes.[4] Yet the argument, characteristically psychological in emphasis, needs its complement. Lawrence has constructed Paul's thinking about 'class', by means of a binary opposition (middle-class = ideas / working-class = warmth) that persists throughout his work. Moreover, if we turn to the presentation of Morel's positive qualities, we can see that 'warmth, life itself' is further defined. The rare occasions when Morel is at one with his family occur 'when he worked and was happy at work . . . Then he always wanted several attendants, and the children enjoyed it. They united with him in the work, in the actual doing of something, when he was his real self again': mending boots, patching his pit-trousers as too dirty for his wife to mend, or making fuses with wheat-straws and gunpowder, a detail followed by one of the few direct glimpses of Morel's life in the mine, when he tells stories about the pit-pony and the mouse up his sleeve (pp. 102–4).

Indeed, critical foregrounding of the relationships *within* the Morel family lead one to forget how thoroughly Part I of the novel is imbued with the working rhythm of the colliers' lives, the trooping back and forth to the pit, the early returning when work is slack, the many references to Morel in his 'pit-dirt', in effect the uniform of his job, which holds the attention of the children in exactly the degree to which it repels them. Or again, when Paul and his mother first walk to the Leivers' farm they see Minton pit in the distance. Paul stops to sketch the pit-hill and the line of waiting trucks, saying 'I like the feel of *men* on things while they're alive. There's a feel of men about trucks, because they've been handled with men's hands, all of them' (p. 167). Paul's contradictory feelings about his father have, that is, their social dimension; and though the 'class' issue remains unformulated in narrative terms, the over-all rejection of Miriam, not of course middle-class but central to Paul's response to 'ideas', takes on an unexpected implication in the light of the conversation quoted above. Unlike his brother William, whose career involves becoming 'a gentleman' (p. 132), Paul remains in his own class, amongst 'the common people' whom he likes best.

Women in Love, however, is the first full-length novel in which class opposition is discernible, though occluded in form. Countering Leavis's emphasis on the contrast between the fates of Ursula and Birkin and Gudrun and Gerald, Raymond Williams has called the novel 'the tragedy of a single action' where all four protagonists combine, to register a root-and-branch negation, not just of the available social formation of pre-1914 England, but 'of humanity itself'.[5] Yet the question needs to be asked: does the novel present a *single* action? Modern criticism is so deeply (silently) committed to the notion that the significance of a text derives from its unity, that perhaps one shouldn't be surprised at the practice of discounting the novel's internal contradictions. Yet surely these are emphatic. Birkin himself is as much the site of unresolved debates as the semi-official spokesman he is usually taken to be. The residual obscurity of his final relationship with Ursula (does it or does it not realize the conception of marriage he has argued for? Is the desired further friendship with Gerald necessary to the permanent realisation of true marriage, and if so, why didn't we hear about it much sooner?) which *has* been debated, is only one aspect of this.

Birkin's attitude towards English society is equally unresolved. For Williams, the overriding note is the radical misanthropy of Birkin's final meditation over the death of Gerald. Here, he supposes that the human species may be an evolutionary mistake, which the ultimate 'creative mystery' will replace, as the horse replaced the mastodon. This ultimate negation constitutes the 'single action' of the novel. Yet this expression of it is interestingly qualified with 'it was very consoling to Birkin to think this' (p. 580) – consoling, that is, to Birkin's grief at the death of his friend. And just as emphatic is Birkin's inner conflict of love and hate for his native country, his admission of which prompts the more profoundly cynical Gudrun to gibe at him as 'a patriot' (p. 488). Nor does Birkin refuse this term. A similar ambivalence has already appeared when Birkin and Ursula decide to cut all their connections with society and together 'just wander about on the face of the earth', words which Birkin immediately counters when he confesses to 'a hankering after a further sort of fellowship . . . I always imagine our being really happy with some few other people – a little freedom with people' (pp. 451–2). This 'further fellowship' directly relates to Birkin's desired friendship with Gerald. It is usual to notice the personal, quasi-homosexual element in this, yet as with Paul's attitude towards his father, its social dimension is also clear. Gerald is the man of action, of effective social and political power, and Birkin's defeated hope that their friendship might have rescued Gerald from his self-destructive love for Gudrun, gestures towards a more creative future than the death in the Alps. The conflict in Birkin's mind can be summed up in this way. Do he and Ursula belong, with everybody else, in 'the river of corruption' which Loerke, the supreme nihilist, is exploring ahead of them all (p. 523)? Or have he and Ursula opened up a different possibility? The sense of an ineluctable process of history drawing pre-1914 English society towards a final destruction is one of the memorable features of *Women in Love*, and Birkin, a kind of latter-day Jeremiah, is its explicit voice. But whether he is part of the process, or opposed to it, is never finally settled.

Where does 'class' enter into this uncertainty? The important point to make is that *Women in Love* recognises the objective existence of class determination as no earlier work of Lawrence had done. In Chapter 17, we learn of the critical change in the relationship between the paternal late-Victorian capitalist Sir Thomas Crich, and his miners, brought about by a major strike. This event reveals to Sir Thomas that his Christian ethic is 'an illusion . . . and this really broke his heart. He must have the illusion and now the illusion was destroyed. The men were not against *him*, but they were against the masters' (p. 298). In this struggle, says Lawrence, the miners were driven by two hopelessly entangled emotions, democratic aspiration and 'cupidity'. But the first was only a mask for 'the desire for chaos', that is to say, the destruction of all hierarchic relationships, and therefore of relationship itself. Gerald then resolves the conflict by embroiling master, management and men in over-riding loyalty to 'the great productive machine' (p. 301). He initiates a thorough-going mechanisation of every aspect of the mining process. At first bitterly resentful of the change, eventually 'the men were satisfied to belong to the great and wonderful machine, even whilst it destroyed them. *It was what they wanted*' (p. 304, my italics). Now as David Craig has pointed out, we need to recognise the tendentiousness in Lawrence's account of this phase of English history, how little justice it does to the complex development of industrial trade-unionism and spreading the Socialist struggle of the years 1880–1914.[6] Yet it is also true that the underlying fact of 'class' opposition is clearly registered, together with a Lawrentian version of the process some historians have described as the bourgeoisification of the working-class during the later Victorian period. Moreover, not only is the process of historical change seen as a product of a contest over the means of material production, the novelist's attitude is detached, analytic. Gerald, the new-style capitalist, is in his personal life as much a victim of mechanisation as the miners, as his relationship with Gudrun reveals. Except in his purely mechanical role as the creator of the Machine, he becomes irrelevant to the productive process. The personal condition for his success as a mine-owner is the human emptiness which leads finally to his death.

On balance, certainly, Lawrence's concern is with the individual careers of his four protagonists. The particular social formation with which they finally break is, for Lawrence, irredeemably tainted, the history set in motion by Gerald and his like irreversible. Yet we have to add that its working-class members are nevertheless a significant presence, possessing an ambiguous attraction. In the scene where Ursula and Birkin give the antique chair to the young working-class couple, the man is seen as both repulsive and beautiful 'somewhere indomitable and separate, like a quick vital rat' (p. 450). Birkin calls them 'the children of men, they like market-places and street corners best', and says they will inherit the earth. The notion of a powerful subterranean life, both 'glamorous' and horrifying is more extensively conveyed in Gudrun's feelings about Beldover, following upon the episode in which the Brangwen girls watch Gerald master his horse.

> There were always miners about. They moved with their strange, distorted dignity, a certain beauty, and unnatural stillness in their bearing, a look of abstraction and half-resignation in their pale, often gaunt faces. They belonged to another world, they had a strange glamour, their voices were full of an intolerable deep resonance, like a machine's burring, a music more maddening than the sirens' long ago.
>
> *Women in Love*, p. 175

These are the same people later said to be completely in the grip of the great Machine established by Gerald. Gudrun feels their attraction as physical and sexual, threatening her precariously achieved individual identity. They are 'the common people', yet she cannot resist joining them on market-nights 'like any other common girl of the district' (p. 176). When, later, she is tutoring Winifred Crich, she and Gerald walk out one evening and pass under a railway bridge where 'she knew that . . . the young colliers stood in the darkness with their sweethearts, in rainy weather. And so she wanted to stand under the bridge with *her* sweetheart, and be kissed under the bridge in the invisible darkness' (p. 414). And so it turns out.

Gudrun's temporary sense of identification with the people of Beldover is in contrast with Paul's mere statement that he 'likes the common people best'. In Gudrun we are presented with her conflict of feelings, and for people clearly identified as a class formation in a world dominated by industrial capitalist production. That the mining village is seen 'as through a glass darkly' may be conceded. But the fact remains that its inhabitants *are* seen. We are reminded of that suppressed passion and energy when in the final discussion about England in which Gudrun calls Birkin a patriot, he says 'when the English really begin to go off *en masse*, it'll be time to shut your ears and run' (p. 385).

Finally, we should notice the more elaborate use of the binary opposition used by Paul Morel to distinguish the common people from the middle-class: 'life'/'ideas'. The Beldover miners and the young working-class man embody a distorted and subterranean vitality, while Ursula's peculiar attraction for Birkin derives from her special quality of 'life' (p. 270). 'Ideas', on the other hand, are associated with Birkin's world, a bohemian demi-monde of artists and intellectuals, with an upper-class dimension. 'Ideas', too, are no longer straightforwardly admirable. Sometimes, they amount to a falsifying 'idealism' which masks a ruthless will-to-power (Hermione, Sir Thomas Crich, Gerald). Their bohemian manifestation in Halliday and his set, is presented as vapid or (obscurely) corrupt. Birkin, a principal source of 'ideas' and with a foot in each camp, is characteristically a site of contradictions. Ursula discerns in his theorising about marriage a mere attempt to bully her. Part of Birkin's self-disgust arises from the suspicion that he *has* been dangerously complicit with Hermione's style of 'idealism'. Yet Birkin's own 'ideas' are also accorded respect, as he struggles to find the right formulation for his relationships with Ursula and Gerald. Gudrun's conscious rejection of the class position which marriage to Gerald would bring has a certain parallel in Birkin's rejection of 'ideas' in their false manifestations, whether located in the upper-class settings of Breadalby and Shortlands, or in the intellectual bohemia of Halliday's set. With this in mind, we can read the Birkin-narrative as a transition from 'ideas' (false form) to 'life', leaving the reader with a significantly unanswered question. What is the connection between the 'life' of the Beldover miners which attracts Gudrun and which Birkin recognises, and the 'life' in Ursula which Birkin consciously desires? Lawrence's novels are, of course, famous for avoiding resolution, and at the personal level (not altogether 'personal' in Ursula's and Birkin's unresolved debate about Gerald) *Women in Love* is a signal case. But the radical contradiction lies at a less conscious level, articulated through the opposition between 'ideas' and 'life' and their shadowy adumbration in terms of opposed classes. Here is the clearest index of a counter-movement opposing the dominant narrative authority which Williams proposes in his conception of the novel's 'single action'.

We have seen that in 'Daughters of the Vicar' the escape from 'class' into 'life', unproblematic from the narrator's point of view, is differently signalled in the narrative. In *Women in Love*, though again it is the narrative that articulates the deepest sense of unresolved contradiction, a dim consciousness of inner turmoil may be said to affect the narrator's sense of the issues at stake. The simplest illustration of this development lies in the conclusions of each narrative. In 'Daughters of the Vicar', the narrator confidently adopts what might be called the 'colonial solution': the fugitives from 'class' will emigrate to Canada. No such solution is available to Birkin and Ursula. They exultantly choose a life of wandering (Chapter 26), but they end back in England, in a sort of limbo, with nowhere to go. We shall see that in *Lady Chatterley's Lover*, the narrator's consciousness of the issues wholly accords with that of the narrative. But first, it will be useful to glance at two post-war *nouvelles* characterised by a movement of 'internal' exile, in contrast with the literal and explicit exile present in the earlier narratives.

'The Ladybird' and 'The Captain's Doll' are distinct tales, but they share a number of traits. Located respectively in an aristocratic and upper-middle class milieu, each turns upon a marital deadlock finally broken by a representative of that familiar Lawrentian type, the mysteriously potent 'dark' male figure. Both marriages are characterised, in Lawrence's analysis, by the imposition of 'ideas' upon the reality of passional 'life', a romanticization of sexual difference, which by trying to obliterate 'otherness' leads to mutual destruction (Gerald and Gudrun represent the fullest analysis of this condition). Both stories also register the impact upon English and European society of the 1914–18 war. The 'dark' hero is defined in opposition to the old social order, effectively cancelled by the war. The narrative structure in both cases involves the 'dark' hero's successful wooing of a woman initially a member of the old order. The heroes are, or become, exiles in the sense that their criticism of the pre-war social order is almost as radical as Birkin's in *Women in Love*. But the exile is 'internal'. The hero's success in persuading the woman to join him establishes a relationship of unresolved mystery, his 'darkness' being a coded allusion to this state of affairs. The wealth of biographical and psychological commentary on this symbolism has had the effect of obscuring its social dimension. Yet the tales' insistent location of the deadlocked marriages within specific class *milieux* makes this dimension inescapable. Moreover, the sense of unresolved contradiction within each class *milieu* arises primarily from the balanced pairing of the characters. In 'The Ladybird', the aristocratic English Major Apsley, the romantic day-time husband, is doubled against the aristocratic European Count Psanek (the name, we are told, means *outlaw*), victim of near-fatal war wounds, who becomes the night-time husband (and lord) of Lady Diana of English aristocratic lineage. The story ends with these two relationships in counter-poise, so that Lady Diana is in effect doubled into conflicting day-time and night-time identities. Apsley represents the mere survival of the old, but superannuated, aristocratic class; Psanek voices some of Lawrence's proto-fascist social theorising, a prominent feature of the later 'leadership' novels. But the tale ends in the mystery of Psanek's symbolic underworld, where he is lord of a reconstituted hierarchical order, a 'dark' mirror image of the dead day-time aristocratic world in which Lady Diana grew up.

This doubling is more intricate in 'The Captain's Doll'. Captain Hepburn is both the husband of Mrs Hepburn, married on 'romantic' terms of adoring worship, and Countess Hannelle's lover, the 'dark' Hepburn, with whom she nevertheless wants a 'romantic' marriage. Like Lady Diana, the Countess moves from one marriage-idea to another. Whereas she is of European aristocratic family displaced by the war, Hepburn is English upper-middle class, but neither is exactly a 'class' fugitive. Hepburn, moreover, evolves from his initially divided condition into a new 'dark' identity, and the conclusion even hints at a version of the 'colonial' solution: they might go and farm in Kenya. Yet this counts for less than the symbolic statement of Hepburn's new identity, which culminates in the tale's concluding sentence: 'He pulled back quickly into the darkness' (p. 251). We are left with an unresolved contradiction between this mysterious promise and the daytime world of postwar Europe represented in the socially formless and pleasure-seeking life of the Alps and Austrian sequences.

From the angle of 'class', we can read these tales as re-workings of the ambivalent ending of *Women in Love*. The impact of the war on the authority of the old upper-class is registered, yet the shadowy alternatives glimpsed in the novel are absent, the social relationship of the 'dark' hero and his bride to the altered class structure left unresolved. Sources of the new 'life', neither wanderers nor bohemian fugitives, they remain as socially-undeclared challengers of the post-war European order.

Of Lawrence's subsequent fiction, *Kangaroo* and *The Plumed Serpent* are too substantial to be discussed here, though their relevance to the argument may be briefly indicated. In *Kangaroo* the 'dark' hero's rejection of both proto-fascist and socialist responses to the aftermath of the war is justified in terms of 'life' as against falsifying political 'idealism'. But it is 'life' without social content, evoked only in the mysterious landscapes of Australia. *The Plumed Serpent* then represents Lawrence's struggle to clothe this 'life' with political and social form, sketching a kind of fascism without material 'base'. Only in *Lady Chatterley's Lover* do we find a substantial extrapolation of the 'life'/'ideas' opposition in terms of social class. The task of analysis is complicated by the existence of the three versions, the 'class' issue emerging in interestingly different ways from one to the next. Here, it will be necessary to concentrate on the third with only glancing reference to the earlier texts. A general point, though, may be made about all three. That disjunction between narratorial and narrative emphasis, between teller and tale, noticeable in Lawrence's earlier fiction has disappeared. The narrator is now entirely explicit that 'class' is a central issue in the novel, and unambiguously locates 'ideas' and 'life' within opposing class formations.

Clifford and his friends are the site of 'ideas' (Platonism, aestheticism), of an absence of warmth and tenderness characteristic of Clifford's 'class and race' (p. 74), and also of an underlying will-to-power transforming

Clifford from dilettante writer into the post-war industrial capitalist who successfully revives the profitability of the Chatterley mines. The opposing cluster of values signified by 'life' is to be located, though not without severe qualification, within the mining populations of the district. On the positive side, we can cite Mrs Bolton's surviving passion for her dead collier-husband, source of her secret antagonism towards the Chatterley family as of her decision to side with Connie when, having guessed that Mellors is her lover, she provides a protective alibi by starting the rumour that Connie might yet have Clifford's child (pp. 153–4). Mellors's origins place him in the same camp, though here the situation is more complicated. His opposition to the industrial machine is, of course, unambiguous; the spirit of 'life' which he sustains in his work and in himself is Clifford's determined enemy. The Connie-narrative recounts her journey from the site of 'ideas' (her own youthful enthusiasms, as well as initial complicity with Clifford's position) to that of 'life', and underscores the emphatic break with his class when she tells Clifford that if, lacking a divorce, she can't marry Mellors, she would rather their child were illegitimate than remain the Chatterley heir (Chapter 19). What of the people of the mining villages (Tevershall, Stacks Gate)? The duality of attitude mutely present in *Women in Love* is now fully articulate, though the emphasis falls more on the negative side. In the often-cited Chapter 11, describing Connie's drive through the district surrounding Wragsby, its people are seen as ugly, culturally impoverished, radically infected with a grasping materialism expressed in shallow leisure activities and an obsession with the money needed to pursue them. The miners seem to Connie subterranean 'animals of coal and iron and clay' (p. 166). Yet also, as victims of the 'leaders of men' (p. 159) who have brought this about, they are possessed of a 'weird inhuman beauty', product of the conditions imposed upon them. Considered in their human aspect, they are 'patient and good men', and Connie both laments the impotence of their virtue and fears its opposite: 'supposing the dead in them ever rose up! but no, it was too terrible to think of. Connie was absolutely afraid of the industrial masses.' (p. 166) The 'life' in the mining populations is thus suppressed, underground, and only Mellors, a child of these people, succeeds in affirming it in a new manifestation. In his final letter to Connie, he reiterates the criticisms voiced by the narrator in Chapter 11, and concludes: 'There's a bad time coming, boys, there's a bad time coming! If things go on as they are, there's nothing lies in the future but death and destruction for these industrial masses. I feel my inside turn to water sometimes, and there you are, going to have a child by me' (pp. 315–16). Connie and Mellors, then, are fugitives from their respective classes, hoping (somewhat desperately) to bring to birth the 'life' which in different ways each class denies, with the final responsibility for its denial being laid at the door of the upper-class represented in Clifford. Mellors' alienation from his class is conscious from the start, a frozen withdrawal from which he is revived by Connie, while the process of *her* alienation from her class is the story of the novel.

So, as with 'Daughters of the Vicar' though now with full narratorial consciousness, the question the novel leaves us with is: where will this 'classless' life find a *home*? We can see from the earlier versions that Lawrence struggled with this question. In *The First Lady Chatterley*, Parkin rules out both Canada and farming (Chapter 18), determines to stick to his job at the Sheffield steelworks partly because he had become branch secretary of the Communist League, leaving us with the possibility that he and Connie might marry and live near his work (Chapter 22). 'Class', moreover, is an issue which enters into their relationship. Connie is much more '*Lady* Chatterley' and he is bristlingly sensitive to possible patronage. 'Life' in this version of the novel prompts Lawrence to conscious, if inconclusive, exploration of its probable social and political manifestations in the English Midlands in the 1920s.[7] There is also a cautious *rapprochement* between 'life' and 'ideas', signalled in the character of Connie's intellectual friend Duncan Forbes, entirely on the lovers' side, and not unsympathetic to radical political change (Chapter 23). In *John Thomas and Lady Jane*, however, where again Parkin is distinctly a working-man whose social and economic vulnerability are unmistakable, the political dimension has gone and the conclusion is indeterminate. Connie vetoes the Canada solution voiced by Parkin (Chapter 13), though only for the vague alternatives of Italy, or farming – no place specified (Chapter 25). 'Class', moreover, is held to be an anachronism (Chapter 13) to be set aside by a few select individuals courageous enough to seek a full human relationship, while the sexual relationship is now more heavily stressed.

This second version shows Lawrence withdrawing from the complex formulations tentatively proposed in the first, a movement completed in the third where Parkin has become Mellors, working-class in origin, yet as has often been noticed, sufficiently de-classed by his war-years to feel entirely on terms with Connie's father. This enables Lawrence to dispense with the working-class *milieu* of the earlier versions (Sheffield, the Tewson family) entailed by the characterisation of Parkin as unambiguously working-class. 'Class' is no longer an issue which Connie and Mellors have to face in personal terms. It remains as a structure of the world which they are about to leave. 'Life' in their terms is only conceivable *outside* the social and economic conditions which the novel has presented. The evolution of the novel towards this final version strikingly demonstrates the structuring power of the 'life'/'ideas' opposition in Lawrence's thinking. Starting from the more complex first version, which implicitly challenges the terms of that opposition,

Lawrence simplifies and abstracts, reworking the material till it is more consonant with the basic formula. Yet at the same time, the full narratorial consciousness that 'class' is a central issue has its effect. As Mellors' letter indicates, there is as much despair as hope in the conception of 'life' which he and Connie represent. The power of the structures they are determined to escape has been too strongly stated to be easily forgotten.

In summary, we can identify three stages in Lawrence's work, seen from the angle of 'class'. The first notices 'class' as a state of affairs from which certain individuals can disengage, culminating with *Women in Love* in which disengagement leads nowhere and the notion that 'class' constitutes a set of determining social structures begins to press for narratorial recognition. The second stage, from about 1918 and evidently in response to the war, shows a clear narratorial consciousness about 'class', but of a limited kind. The social and economic structures glimpsed in the first phase are no longer present. There is an attempt to dissolve 'class' into imaginary political structures based on a resurrected, but also dematerialised aristocratic principle. This phase culminates in *The Plumed Serpent*. The third phase, probably initiated by Lawrence's visit to Eastwood in September 1926, a key event in the production of the *Lady Chatterley* novels,[8] combines a full consciousness about 'class' with an explicit grasp of its social and economic conditions, yet also renews the concern with disengagement, differing in this respect from the first phase in a greater sense of its difficulty. Dominating all three phases are the assumptions that 'life' can only be sought outside these determining structures, and that 'ideas' are often evidence of a sterile pretence to have escaped them. These assumptions have such a hold on Lawrence that they block the development of his more complex thinking about 'class'.

This aspect of Lawrence's work should surely figure prominently in our estimate of his achievement. For most novelists, 'class' is a matter of the social minutiae which signal sub-divisions within that amorphous and shifting category of 'the middle-class', a condition which it is supposed that narrator and reader can jointly view from a non-aligned position of 'classlessness'. Of some of Lawrence's work, and especially some of the tales and short stories, this can also be said. But as I have tried to outline here, several major texts register a deeper and more complex sense of 'class', and considered as a succession, show a pressing into consciousness, which is also a response to a changing history, that no other novelist of his time can equal. Lawrence's struggle both to articulate this new consciousness, and at the same time to resist it, opens up a perspective on his work that deserves wider and more detailed recognition.[9]

Notes

1. ARNOLD KETTLE's discussion of *The Rainbow* is a notable exception. He defines its theme as 'what bourgeois society does to personal relationship' (*Introduction to the English Novel*, Volume II, 1953, p. 129; London: Unwin Hyman, 1967). 'Class' as such, however, is a good deal less prominent in *The Rainbow*, than in the texts I discuss here. Ursula and Skrebensky talk about 'class', but it is hardly registered as a structure of the world Ursula inhabits. For some discussion of 'class' see John Goode's chapter on Lawrence in *The Twentieth Century* (London: Sphere Books, 1970, ed. Bernard Bergonzi, *Sphere History of Literature*, Vol. 7); and Graham Holderness *D.H. Lawrence: History, Ideology and Fiction* (Dublin: Gill and Macmillan, 1956).

2. As GRAHAM HOUGH points out in *The Dark Sun* (London: Duckworth, 1982), p. 43, the handling of 'class' in 'Daughters of the Vicar' is not unlike traditional nineteenth-century treatment of the theme.

3. Page references are to the Penguin version of this and subsequent Lawrence novels.

4. In *The Forked Flame* (1965; Wisconsin: University of Wisconsin Press, 1987), p. 113.

5. RAYMOND WILLIAMS, *Modern Tragedy* (London: Chatto and Windus, 1966), p. 135.

6. DAVID CRAIG, *The Real Foundations* (London: Chatto and Windus, 1973), pp. 143–67.

7. GEOFFREY STRICKLAND proposes that for this and other reasons, the first version is very much better than its successors. See A.H. Gomme (ed.), *D. H. Lawrence: a Critical Study of the Major Novels and Other Writings* (Hassocks: Harvester Press, 1978), pp. 159–71.

8. See 'Return to Bestwood' in *D. H. Lawrence: a Selection from Phoenix*, ed. A.A.H. Inglis (Harmondsworth: Penguin, 1971), recounting Lawrence's impressions of the General Strike in the Erewash Valley, especially pp. 152–7.

9. For a characteristically psychological reduction of Lawrence's sense of class difference, see his 'Autobiographical Sketch' (1929, in *A Selection from Phoenix* (ed. Inglis), p. 17.

4 Transition (*The Rainbow*)*

GRAHAM HOLDERNESS

Graham Holderness, Director of Studies for Humanities and Education at Hatfield Polytechnic, is one of the younger generation of Marxist critics who were stimulated and redirected by the impact of the new critical theory in the seventies. His work – implicitly in the book from which present essay derives: more explicitly in his later essays on Shakespeare – seeks to recuperate for the Left 'major writers' of the bourgeois canon by way, in part, of exposing their ideological construction as 'mythic' cultural figures. The following piece comprises sections 3 and 4 of a chapter entitled 'Transition', which also deals with the *Study of Thomas Hardy* and *The Fox*, and takes as its theme Lawrence's theory of social tragedy. Like other essays in this volume (see Introduction, pp. 13–14), it enters the debate about the relative merits of the 'realist' and the 'modernist' Lawrence, but in particular argues that, far from being, as Leavis claimed (see Introduction, p. 10), an 'incomparable' fictional history, *The Rainbow* substitutes myth for history in a remarkable feat of realist legerdemain.

Holderness specialises in Renaissance and Modern Literature and Theatre, and his numerous other publications include: *Shakespeare's History* (Gill and Macmillan, 1985); (ed.) *The Shakespeare Myth* (Manchester University Press, 1988); *D.H. Lawrence: Life, Works and Criticism* (York Press, 1989); (ed.) *The Politics of Theatre and Drama* (Macmillan, 1991); and a number of study guides to Shakespeare's and Lawrence's works.

The most interesting argument advanced in Terry Eagleton's brilliant but brief sketch of literary ideologies from Matthew Arnold to D.H. Lawrence

* Reprinted from Graham Holderness, *D.H. Lawrence: History, Ideology and Fiction* (Dublin: Gill and Macmillan, 1982), pp. 174–89; references renumbered from the original.

is his view that 'the fissuring of organic form is a progressive act', and one of the most interesting hints thrown out in his provocative but undeveloped passage on Lawrence is his suggestion that the development from *Sons and Lovers* to *Women in Love* is a progressive development:

> The 'sympomatic' repressions and absences of the realist *Sons and Lovers* may be recuperated in the ultra-realist forms of *The Rainbow* – a text which 'explodes' realism in its letter, even as it preserves it in the 'totalising' organicism of its evolving generational structure.[1]

Women in Love continues to 'enforce this "progressive" discontinuity with a realist lineage already called into profound question by *Jude the Obscure'*. Eagleton points out that such a position conflicts with 'a Marxist aesthetic tradition heavily dominated by the work of Georg Lukács'; he seems to remain unconscious, however, of the extent to which *his* evaluations align suspiciously with those of bourgeois critical orthodoxy. I would like to examine *The Rainbow* in the light of these comments and argue that the novel neither preserves nor explodes realism, but substitutes for it, in the form of metaphysics and mythology, a textual ideology of a peculiarly pure and non-contradictory kind. Ideology is not, in *The Rainbow*, set into conflictual relationship with history; ideology is, simply, offered as an alternative to history. Far from creating a progressive discontinuity with realism, *The Rainbow* surrenders literature almost completely to the domination of ideology.

The Rainbow (1915) is such a different kind of novel from *Sons and Lovers* that critical discussion has generally been conducted on a different terrain. Lawrence saw his more 'analytical' technique as a way of penetrating deeper into the lives of people than the realist novel – preoccupied with 'external' features of living, social existence and relationships, morals and manners – could ever hope to do. The method of *The Rainbow* certainly attempts this, and on the face of it such intensive 'depth psychology' must inevitably make the social world of the characters recede and diminish in importance. But the book is no 'stream-of-*un*consciousness' novel where individual characters are so detached from their society that it hardly seems to exist at all. On the contrary, as Eagleton points out, the form of the novel is, apparently, historical in a very large and impressive way: the three central figures, Tom, Anna and Ursula Brangwen, with their respective partners, Lydia, Will and Anton Skrebensky, represent three generations who live through a historically changing social world between 1840 and about 1905, and clearly the transition from the agricultural life of the Brangwen farmers to Ursula's life as a wage-earner in an industrial town is historically significant. At first glance *The Rainbow* seems to offer the ideal method for exploring human life in both its communal and individual dimensions: a form or structure which dramatises large-scale historical changes, and a manner or style which is able to explore very deeply the lives of the individuals living through this historical process.

This view of the novel is, of course, embodied in Leavis's study, where Lawrence appears as an 'incomparable' social historian with an unrivalled insight into individual life. And many other critics have been more than happy to accept the contention that these 'deeper', unconscious levels of experience are the more 'essential' reality of human existence. That kind of criticism we can leave to its own devices; it is the view (shared by both Leavis and Eagleton) that *The Rainbow* offers a significant attempt to interpret historical change that I wish to challenge.

'Where *Women in Love* has that astonishing comprehensiveness in the presentment of contemporary England (or the England of 1914), *The Rainbow* has instead its historical depth . . . As social historian, Lawrence, among novelists, is unsurpassed.'[2] Leavis's strategy is subtle but obvious: by concentrating on the *values*, the 'spiritual heritage' of a society, he is able to conflate individual with social existence and effectively negate history altogether. The essential aspects of a 'culture' and 'civilisation' are those values which live in the moral consciousness of individuals. But there can be little doubt that Leavis sees *The Rainbow* as a valid (and true) account of a society in transition, from 'organic' rural past to urban industrial present. Marvin Mudrick, arguing along similar lines, adds an important term to Leavis's analysis – the concept of 'community':

> In his historic moment, Lawrence has before him the life of the last English community . . . a life rich in productive labour and in continuity with the passing seasons . . . a life seemingly permanent yet fated to pass away in the general breakdown of codes and communities . . . It is this process, over three generations, which is the subject and theme of *The Rainbow*.[3]

This is the conventional view of *The Rainbow*, as a historical chronicle dramatising and enacting in its aesthetic form a transition from organic community to alienated individual; and I think Eagleton does little more than reproduce it in a different language. It is necessary therefore to examine more closely the novel's pretensions to a 'historical–chronicle' form, and to show how Lawrence's adaptation of that form provides an ideological basis for the assault on bourgeois society contained in the later stages of the novel: an ideology of individualism which contains the social criticism and draws its form into complicity with the very society it challenges.

The Rainbow is a radical novel of criticism and protest against the values of Lawrence's contemporary society; a protest launched, let us remember, in the early years of the 1914–18 war (the novel's suppression in 1915 was undoubtedly, in part at least, political). The common critical consensus that the later stages of the book are artistically weak no doubt has some connection with the concentrated and comprehensive assault against bourgeois society which they contain.

Ursula's experiences take her through a wide range of social realities, and gradually compose in her consciousness into a comprehensive view of industrial bourgeois society as a 'mechanised' system in which all institutions, practices and codes seem to have their subordinate function. Through her relationship with Skrebensky, Ursula develops a profound dissatisfaction with the ethics of bourgeois democracy, imperialism and war; teaching in a school, she finds a 'hard, malevolent system' (p. 377) which reproduces the general relations of society; at college she discovers education to be 'a warehouse of dead unreality', a 'little side-show to the factories of the town' (p. 434). Her major decision, made as the novel closes, involves the rejection of a bourgeois marriage. At the very heart of this system is industrial capitalism, and the primary image of that civilisation is a colliery town, Wiggiston.

Wiggiston is Lawrence's Eastwood, seen now from a radically alienated (indeed, by now, expatriate) perspective, and transmuted into symbol by the language and imagery of that 'organicist' tradition of social criticism studied by Raymond Williams in *Culture and Society*. Whereas the mining landscapes of *Sons and Lovers* and *Odour of Chrysanthemums* are always seen and known from within, here for the first time in Lawrence's work such a landscape is seen only from an external perspective (or rather two – that of the colliery manager, and that of the female dissident who attacks his values). Both perspectives are external: the system viewed cynically and irresponsibly from above; the system viewed passionately and antagonistically from outside.

The 'description' of the mining town is not at all realist in manner; it registers Ursula's point of view and reproduces terms familiar from the Romantics, Carlyle and Dickens: the town is uniform and monotonous ('homogeneous') shapeless ('amorphous') and 'rigid'. There is no concreteness or sensuous definition in the language; it is almost wholly analytical: 'abstract', 'sterile', 'meaningless', 'unreal'. The abstraction is itself a way of defining the nature of Wiggiston: the colliery is 'mathematical', another term from the vocabulary of Romantic social protest. Abstraction is also part of the method to indicate that Wiggiston is unreal, not amenable to realist presentation: it is a kind of dream or nightmare. It 'appears' like an apparition; it is inhabited by 'spectres'; it is a 'vision of pure ugliness', 'some gruesome dream'.

At the heart of the town there is a blank space, an 'absence': 'In the middle of the town was a large, open, shapeless space. . . . There was no meeting place, no centre, no artery, no organic formation' (p. 345). It is from that empty space, that social and human absence in the centre of industrial society, that the myth of pre-industrial society – the myth of Marsh Farm – is generated. Marsh Farm has no closer or more direct relation to history than that.

Wiggiston is the negation of community. It is dominated by the 'proud, demon-like colliery'; the miners are subdued to that dominion – they have to 'alter themselves to fit the pits'; each man is 'reified' to a function of the machine, one of Ruskin's 'unhumanised' labourers. Personal and social life are subordinated to the machine; the values of the community have disappeared. 'The pit was the great mistress.'

Ursula views the place with horror and distaste, from a carefully preserved distance. She also feels (in a passage which anticipates *Women in Love*) the powerful allurement of the system: 'There was a horrible fascination . . . human bodies and lives subjected in slavery to that symmetric monster of the colliery. There was a swooning, perverse satisfaction in it. . . . Hatred sprang up in Ursula's heart. If she could she would smash the machine' (p. 349–50).

That decision is defined as Ursula's 'growing-up'. She sees Wiggiston as a vision of unreality, recognises it as meaningless; and 'departs' from it – rejecting the machine, denying its power over her, and adopting a position of refusal, denial and resistance. The decision involves a comprehensive rejection of society as a whole: she enters a 'great loneliness, wherein she was sad but free' – the isolation of a life displayed and excluded from the social totality.

The style of presentation is now quite different from the realism of *Sons and Lovers* and *Odour of Chrysanthemums*. The industrial mining society is not a solid reality at all, but a kind of dream or nightmare. On the one hand there is a radical split between the conscious, perceiving subject and the external, objective society from which she excludes herself. On the other hand Wiggiston is Ursula's nightmare. The 'communal narrator', who in the realist *Sons and Lovers* assures the reader that the society is always more complex and comprehensive than any one character's perspective, has disappeared. Wiggiston is a record of Ursula's perceptions – not a social reality, but a bad dream. And, of course, from a dream one can always awake.

The posing of that contradiction – that bourgeois society is a subjective nightmare, which yet has an objective existence and a sinister and alien power over the individual who dreams it – is, of course, a valid and important revelation of a genuine social experience. It is a reflection of real historical contradictions – emerging in the intensification of human subjection to enormously violent and alien forces, industrial, imperialist and military, in the years immediately preceding the war. It also expresses an ideological crisis: 'the strange death of liberal England'; the ideological crisis of liberal humanism; the tortured conscience of an individualist society which has enslaved the individual and left him in possession only of a bad dream. But the reflection of real historical contradiction, and the expression of ideological crisis, are articulated into a specific aesthetic form; and this brings us to the real 'ideology' of *The Rainbow*.

If we measure the distance between this style and the realism of *Sons and Lovers*, we can see that although Lawrence is still here primarily concerned with the relation between individual and community, and although the image of community is still the mining town of his birth and upbringing, the vision of society is now both expanded and radically fractured. The colliery now holds sway over the whole of society; but the individual resists incorporation into that society, denies her own social existence, and therefore begins to see society as a dream, unreal, from which the sleeper can, by conscious effort and choice, awake. That is the contradiction. What *The Rainbow* does is to substitute a pleasant pastoral dream for the nightmare of bourgeois society. Into the blank space between living, conscious subject and alien, 'reified' society the novel inserts the organism of a myth which effectively seals that breach, ideologically resolving the glaring contradictions of historical reality. That myth is the myth of rural England: Marsh Farm.

I am proposing that we read *The Rainbow* backwards, from Wiggiston to Marsh Farm, rather than the other way round. We should see the novel not as a record of historical process, with Wiggiston as the culmination of a real history of social decline, but as mythology, where the 'history' is deduced from the present and cast backwards into the past. Marsh Farm is a myth created to fill that blank space in the centre of Wiggiston, that human absence at the heart of the modern community; a myth created to seal the painful breach between individual and community so clearly revealed in Ursula's vision of Wiggiston.

Marsh Farm – the first of the novel's three stages – is not an actual historical society at all, but a simple inversion of Wiggiston; a 'developing' of the photographic negative into colour and life. In Wiggiston society is mechanical and dehumanised; at Marsh Farm it is organic and human. In Wiggiston human beings are subdued to an impersonal collectivity; at Marsh Farm the individual is sovereign and autonomous (a clear distortion of history, which I will be discussing below). In Wiggiston labour is alienated and men reduced to industrial functions; at Marsh Farm work is creative and fulfilling, and although Tom Brangwen is not exactly the figure of the 'harmonious man',[4] he becomes a figure of organic harmony in his marriage to Lydia.

How, then, does the presentation of the mining town here compare with the realism of, say, *Odour of Chrysanthemums*? I have acknowledged that realism has its suppressions and absences; but I would wish to argue against Eagleton that there are *degrees* of suppression, and it is possible for art to reduce a social totality to such an extent that its contradictions are completely negated. In Wiggiston the working class is excluded as a dramatic presence, as an active agent, as a human force; the industrial system operates by its own laws, which deny and negate all value. Values can be introduced only from above or below within the system: either from the liberal paternalism of the owner, or from the struggle of the workers (such an interaction is explored very interestingly in the chapter 'The Industrial Magnate' in *Women in Love*). Where the bourgeoisie itself is excluded, and the managerial class is empty of value and devoid of humanity, and the working class is present only as passive and exploited victims – then the social totality appears, simply, as a myth of a negative kind, which drains a society of its contradictions, establishes it as a hollow deadness, and proceeds to fill its absences with retrospective and elegiac mythology. Contradiction can take place only between the society and a displaced individual; and Ursula, as we shall see, is actually rescued from that society and incorporated into the alternative myth.

I will now examine that alternative myth, the supposedly 'historical' society of the elder Tom Brangwen. The first image of society presented in *The Rainbow* (in the first part of Chapter 1) is, explicitly, not a realistic one at all: it is defined, in fact, as a 'poem'. There are no individuals here, but a collective 'race' of Brangwens. Only the sexes are differentiated: the men satisfied with their lives as agricultural producers, the women cherishing ambitions and aspirations extending beyond it. But these aspirations are actually fulfilled *within the rural community itself* – by the existence of a superior (gentry) class: 'The male part of the poem was filled in by such men as the vicar and Lord William . . . The wonder of the beyond was before them' (p. 11). The rural 'village' society is a 'poem' because within it imaginative needs are fulfilled; every part is organically articulated into a unified whole, and all contradictions are resolved. There is a complete circuit in which aspiration is automatically fulfilled, a complete harmony of parts corresponding to the bourgeois conception of aesthetic perfection: 'The lady of the Hall was the living dream of their lives, her life was the epic that inspired their lives. In her they lived imaginatively . . . they had their own Odyssey enacting itself' (p. 11). This model of society is a myth in the strictly philosophical sense: an ideological harmonising and resolution of real social contradictions. There is no conflict here between individual and community, because the Brangwen race is an unindividualised, collective entity; there is no conflict between 'society' and 'nature', because human life and the natural world are mediated by agricultural labour; there is no class conflict between gentry and yeomanry, no tension between human aspiration and an impoverished social environment.

The passage openly declares itself as myth, by its explicit self-definition as a 'poem' and by its declamatory rhetoric and biblical cadences, and it resists the temptation to site itself in real history. It is a deliberate evocation of an imaginary, pre-industrial, quasi-feudal organic community (the Brangwen women aspire to belong not to the cultured and educated bourgeoisie, but to a 'fighting host' – a touch of feudal romance). It makes no attempt to describe a society that ever existed, but presents itself as a myth constructed negatively in response to the conditions of Lawrence's own contemporary society. In keeping with the aestheticism which pervades Lawrence's earlier writing, it defines social harmony in terms of aesthetic completeness and perfection – poem, epic, Odyssey.

As the second part of Chapter 1 begins, myth gives way to 'historical-chronicle' ('About 1840, a canal was constructed across the meadows of the Marsh Farm . . .' (p. 11), and we are really entering a different world, a world of change and mobility. Early industrial developments – canal, railway, colliery – approach Marsh Farm. Tom's brother Alfred leaves the farm and works as a lace-designer in Nottingham, becoming a classic example of industrialised life. So Tom's decision to perpetuate the old agricultural life is made in a context of alternatives and possibilities; but the 'continuity' he chooses sets his own life into connection with that original myth rather than with history. The industrial world is sheared away, and Tom occupies a pastoral world irradiated by the illumination of that introductory social 'poem'.

There is actually no rural community at all in this earlier part of the novel: there is only a family. The family is, of course, as Eagleton says, 'at once social institution and domain of intensely interpersonal relationships';[5] but this family exists as an autonomous unit, with as little connection with a contingent or contextual community as a country house in Jane Austen – and without even other similar families to connect with. The elder Brangwen generation die, and all other members of the family move away, before the real beginning of Tom's history, his meeting with Lydia, at which point he stands completely alone, isolated in time and space.

Tom is presented as the only person who works the farm. We learn from a single reference that there are 'farm-hands' (p. 85), but these labourers have as little existence in the novel as servants in Jane Austen: they are simply not there. Tom's profitable farm could not be run without those absent people, but for Tom and Lydia they do not exist, and the narrator does not wish to accord them any more significance, or give them any more substance, than that. Lydia Lensky is scarcely aware of other people at all: she perceives 'people who passed around her, not as persons, but as looming presences' (p. 55); and Tom himself 'liked people, so long as they remained in the background' (p. 102). That is their privilege; but the novelist clearly shares and endorses their point of view. When Tom and Lydia marry, the wedding is pared right down to its 'core' of significance – the 'religious' binding of two people. As a social ritual or communal experience it has no existence; 'the guests' are shadowy presences whose 'being' both characters and novelist ignore (pp. 57–8).

Tom Brangwen's work is hardly ever given real substance, and there is certainly very little attempt to connect that aspect of social life with his emotional problems and crises. Leavis lights on a pair of examples from very few instances, notably the beautiful but 'set-piece' description of Tom taking the child Anna into the barn. Here a conflictual relation within the family is resolved in association with nature, the connection mediated by work. The dramatisation of this convergence is impressive, but 'community' exists only in Tom's recollections of childhood – 'community' is a function of the memory: 'He looked down at the silky folds of the paisley shawl. It reminded him of his mother. She used to go to church in it. He was back again in the old irresponsibility and security, a boy at home' (p. 79). Even the family (apart from its single-generation nucleus), which defines the range and limits of 'community', exists only in Tom's memory. The old rural society, then, exists only within the individual; 'community' has been internalised and embodied within the self. Tom is a model of pre-industrial society: 'organic' society is incorporated in the 'organic' individual. The marriage between Tom and Lydia forms an image of the original social 'poem': her 'foreignness' fulfils his aspiration, and the unified couple constitutes a symbol of wholeness and harmony (the arch) which stands for an 'organic' society. The family, whole and complete within itself, floats in a social vacuum free of the pressures and determinations of a real history: 'They were a curious family, a law to themselves, separate from the world, isolated, a small republic set in invisible bounds. The mother was quite indifferent to Ilkeston and Cossethay, to any claims made to her from outside . . . She was mistress of a little native land that lacked nothing' (p. 103). The form of the novel actually ratifies this isolation: it automatically negates 'claims from outside', suppresses Ilkeston and Cossethay, and detaches the family from its contingent socio-historical context. 'Community' is an absence, not a presence, in the text.

The novel's narrative technique works to confirm this abstraction of individual and family from community. Scenes of family life are narrated from a neutral point of view, dramatising the experience of several consciousnesses. In Chapter 3 a wider *social* life is evoked: the world of market town, inn, pub, cattle-yard and eating-house, where Brangwen's acquaintances became dramatic presences, and where a genuine world of work, commercial activity and sociable relationships is fully rendered. But the presentation is done from the point of view of the child, who is specifically alienated from that social world. Even at this early stage of the novel, and even though it is the pre-industrial, 'organic' community that is being dramatised, the 'privileged consciousness', the chosen viewpoint, is that of the outsider who looks at society as an external object from a radically alienated perspective.

Let me compare this first stage of *The Rainbow* with a more classically realist account of the life of an agricultural proprietor: that of Constantine Levin in Tolstoi's *Anna Karenina*. Naturally the differences between the life of a member of the Russian landed nobility and that of an English Midlands farmer obscure the comparison, but they do not adequately explain the difference of method. Levin's life on his estate is not at all individualised, and not at all reduced to a simple 'pastoral' setting. Levin lives in the midst of a busy and active network of social relationships: with members of his own family; with his servants; with other landowners; and, above all, with the peasants whose labour supports his life. It is the problem of relationship with them that preoccupies Levin as the most pressing problem of his life. And we actually see Levin (the aristocrat) working his farm more often than Tom Brangwen. All Levin's deep emotional problems (his marriage, his struggles with death and religion) are intimately connected with the lives of others in an effective working community. Of course, Tolstoi does not tell any 'whole truth', and *Anna Karenina* suppresses a great deal of Russian rural history. But the presentation has enough fullness and complexity to reveal a genuine alternative society, complete with its own contradictions, whereas Lawrence succeeds only in composing a myth.

In abandoning realism, Lawrence rejected more than 'the certain moral scheme' and 'the old, stable ego of the character' to which he objected in Tolstoi and the traditional novel. And it is not necessary to agree entirely with Lukács's conservative view of realism to want to withhold consent from Eagleton's argument that Lawrence's development beyond realism was 'progressive'. Considering what Lawrence lost in embarking on the experiment of *The Rainbow*, it is possible to conclude rather that the attempt was ultimately sterile and directionless. (For example, he lost the power to create an imaginative synthesis of individual life and actual history, such as that achieved in *Odour of Chrysanthemums*; he lost the power to present the complexity and contradiction of his own society and social existence, as in *Sons and Lovers*; and he lost the technique of the 'communal narrator' (derived from the realist novel and applied to a working-class community), which creates the necessary complexity of viewpoint and social experience – a method which is in *The Rainbow* replaced by a subjectivist narrator who constantly collapses into the immediate experience of individual character.) A historical criticism should surely take account of such losses before evaluating any specific example of the movement beyond realism.

The Rainbow does not, then, preserve the realist totality at all, since its 'evolving generational structure' has no realist or historical content. It merely presents three different settings for dramas of personal relationship: agricultural pastoral, rural village, and industrial city. Clearly, if the original rural society is mythical rather than historical, it cannot possibly contribute to an authentic presentation of historical evolution.

Neither does the novel 'explode' realism in a progressive way, exposing and calling into question the concealed ideology of the realist method. In fact its form and method amount to a denial of history and an affirmation of ideology. Its images of society are not the kinds of myth which balance, resolve and disclose contradictions; its form is rather a montage of myths, which never actually enter into dialectical conflict and connection, because they occupy different spaces, temporal and theoretical. The separate myths are organised loosely into a sequence corresponding to the theory of history sketched in *Lady Chatterley's Lover*: 'This is history. One England blots out another . . . The industrial England blots out the agricultural England. And the continuity is not organic, but mechanical' (p. 163). The myth of Marsh Farm *grows through* the solid nightmare of Wiggiston, in the presence of Ursula, as grass (to use one of Lawrence's favourite metaphors) grows through a concrete pavement, and effectively negates it.

The vision of society transformed which concludes *The Rainbow* is simply a substitution of pastoral dream for the myth of industrial nightmare. Ursula has rejected 'Skrebensky's world', all 'the old, dead things'; in her vision of the rainbow that world disappears, and she awakes into an alternative dream. The rainbow, symbol of organic social harmony, encompasses and unifies the regenerated society; beneath its arch symbols of organic growth ('fruition' and 'germination') stir into vitality. In structure and content the new society reproduces the old. Ursula is the organic descendant of the Marsh Farm myth, bearing its values within her as her grandfather did; her individual consciousness reaches out and embraces the real social world, transforming it, binding it around with the rainbow, fertilising its internal essence. The two meanings of 'organic' – unity of natural growth, and structural totality – here fuse into one. The novel's ideological images of social completeness, harmony and fulfilment – arch and rainbow – were offered as symbols of the old organic society, and were permitted, by the mythological mode, to stand unmolested by real history. They appear again in the novel's conclusion; and they are not set into conflict with real history at all. History, in fact, is explicitly cleared away, leaving ideology standing, firm yet evanescent, in a seductive nakedness of beauty. A completely unqualified ideology of individualism replaces the imagery of social harmony which was the pastoral ideology of Marsh Farm; the individualising, historically suppressive manner of the novel achieves, by an extraordinary ideological *tour de force*, a synthesis of those utterly contradictory structures: if the individual cannot be at one with society, then society will be incorporated into the individual and reproduced in her image.

This is the fundamental reason for Lawrence's abandoning, at this stage of his writing, not only of realism, but also of the tragic mode as a form for the novel. At precisely that moment, in 1914, when the tragic view of society should have appeared with new urgency and insistence, Lawrence's art denied and refused that recognition. In *The Rainbow* real historical forces are abstracted into separable myths, and the myths arranged into the sequence of an 'organic/mechanical' theory of history, while the organic continuity of the Brangwen race runs through Tom, Anna and Ursula in a *separate*, parallel evolution. The social tragedy enacted by the novel's mythological structure – from organic past to industrial present – is therefore in practice evaded by the characters. Tragedy is therefore never seen as a true historical process, and never really lived through, in *The Rainbow*. So the 'affirmative' conclusion is not an arbitrary note of optimism gratuitiously tacked on, as Leavis maintained, but the true consummation of the novel's form, the symbol for its explicit refusal of historical tragedy.

Powerful ideological images of social harmony and reconciliation are snatched from actual history and encoded within a specifically mythical context, where they can exist and flourish unmolested by the stubborn conflicts and contradictions of that actual history. It is hardly surprising that despite initial suppression and subsequent neglect, *The Rainbow* was incorporated very easily into the canon of 'classic' modern literature, its powerful social challenge already absorbed by its own ideology.

A text, according to Eagleton, produces ideology by setting it into conflict, not with itself (there can be no contradictions within ideology, since its precise function is to deny them), but with history. *The Rainbow* does not do this: it fills its absences with myth; and its individualist ideology is never exposed, as the unreality of the social world permits the individual consciousness to replace it. History disappears; ideology itself stands before us: 'And the rainbow stood on the earth . . .' History has to be 'swept away' before this vision can be achieved, a vision in which ideology, incarnate, descends from the heavens and unifies a fractured world.

Notes

(All page numbers in parentheses in the text refer to the Penguin edition of Lawrence's novels.)

1. TERRY EAGLETON, *Criticism and Ideology* (1976; London: Verso Editions, 1978), p. 160.

2. F.R. LEAVIS, *D. H. Lawrence/Novelist* (London: Chatto and Windus, 1955, repr. 1964), p. 151.

3. MARVIN MUDRICK, 'The Originality of *The Rainbow*', in Harry T. Moore (ed.), *A D.H. Lawrence Miscellany* (Carbondale: Southern Illinois University Press, 1959), p. 62.

4. See GEORGE LUKÁCS, 'The Ideal of the Harmonious Man in Bourgeois Aesthetics', in *Writer and Critic* (London: Merlin Press, 1970).

5. TERRY EAGLETON, *Myths of Power* (1975; London: Macmillan, 1988), p. 98.

5 Psychoanalysis (*Sons and Lovers*)*

Terry Eagleton

Please see the Headnote for Chapter 2 above and the Introduction, p. 14, for relevant information and comment. The present piece is a short excerpt from a much longer chapter introducing psychoanalytic approaches in criticism. As I have implied in the Introduction, it shows Eagleton attempting to weld together a Marxist criticism driven by the analysis of ideology and a critical perspective re-energised by the psychoanalytic dimension of post-structuralism.

Lacan himself is not much interested in the social relevance of his theories, and he certainly does not 'solve' the problem of the relation between society and the unconscious. Freudianism as a whole, however, does enable us to pose this question; and I want now to examine it in terms of a concrete literary example, D.H. Lawrence's novel *Sons and Lovers*. Even conservative critics, who suspect such phrases as the 'Oedipus complex' as alien jargon, sometimes admit that there is something at work in this text which looks remarkably like Freud's famous drama. (It is interesting, incidentally, how conventionally-minded critics seem quite content to employ such jargon as 'symbol', 'dramatic irony' and 'densely textured', while remaining oddly resistant to terms such as 'signifier' and 'decentring'.) At the time of writing *Sons and Lovers*, Lawrence, as far as we know, knew something of Freud's work at second hand from his German wife Frieda; but there seems no evidence that he had any direct or detailed acquaintance with it, a fact which might be taken as striking independent confirmation of Freud's doctrine. For it is surely the case that *Sons and Lovers*, without appearing to be at all aware of it, is a profoundly Oedipal novel: the young Paul Morel who sleeps in the same bed as his mother, treats her with the

---

* Reprinted from Terry Eagleton, *Literary Theory: an Introduction* (Oxford: Basil Blackwell, 1983), pp. 174–9; reference renumbered from the original.

tenderness of a lover and feels strong animosity towards his father, grows up to be the man Morel, unable to sustain a fulfilling relationship with a woman, and in the end achieving possible release from this condition by killing his mother in an ambiguous act of love, revenge and self-liberation. Mrs Morel, for her part, is jealous of Paul's relationship with Miriam, behaving like a rival mistress. Paul rejects Miriam for his mother; but in rejecting Miriam he is also unconsciously rejecting his mother in her, in what he feels to be Miriam's stifling spiritual possessiveness.

Paul's psychological development, however, does not take place in a social void. His father, Walter Morel, is a miner, while his mother is of a slightly higher social class. Mrs Morel is concerned that Paul should not follow his father into the pit, and wants him to take a clerical job instead. She herself remains at home as a housewife: the family set-up of the Morels is part of what is known as the 'sexual division of labour', which in capitalist society takes the form of the male parent being used as labour-power in the productive process while the female parent is left to provide the material and emotional 'maintenance' of him and the labour-force of the future (the children). Mr Morel's estrangement from the intense emotional life of the home is due in part to this social division – one which alienates him from his own children, and brings them emotionally closer to the mother. If, as with Walter Morel, the father's work is especially exhausting and oppressive, his role in the family is likely to be further diminished: Morel is reduced to establishing human contact with his children through his practical skills about the house. His lack of education, moreover, makes it difficult for him to articulate his feelings, a fact which further increases the distance between himself and his family. The fatiguing, harshly disciplined nature of the work process helps to create in him a domestic irritability and violence which drives the children deeper into their mother's arms, and which spurs on her jealous possessiveness of them. To compensate for his inferior status at work, the father struggles to assert a traditional male authority at home, thus estranging his children from him still further.

In the case of the Morels, these social factors are further complicated by the class-distinction between them. Morel has what the novel takes to be a characteristically proletarian inarticulateness, physicality and passivity: *Sons and Lovers* portrays the miners as creatures of the underworld who live the life of the body rather than the mind. This is a curious portraiture, since in 1912, the year in which Lawrence finished the book, the miners launched the biggest strike which Britain has ever seen. One year later, the year of the novel's publication, the worst mining disaster for a century resulted in a paltry fine for a seriously negligent management, and class-warfare was everywhere in the air throughout the British coalfields. These developments, with all their acute political awareness and complex organisation, were not the actions of mindless hulks. Mrs Morel (it is perhaps significant that we do not feel inclined to use her first name) is of lower-middle-class origin, reasonably well-educated, articulate and determined. She therefore symbolises what the young, sensitive and artistic Paul may hope to achieve: his emotional turning to her from the father is, inseparably, a turning from the impoverished, exploitative world of the colliery towards the life of emancipated consciousness. The potentially tragic tension in which Paul then finds himself trapped, and almost destroyed, springs from the fact that his mother – the very source of the energy which pushes him ambitiously beyond home and pit – is at the same time the powerful emotional force which draws him back.

A psychoanalytical reading of the novel, then, need not be an alternative to a social interpretation of it. We are speaking rather of two sides or aspects of a single human situation. We can discuss Paul's 'weak' image of his father and 'strong' image of his mother in both Oedipal and class terms; we can see how the human relationships between an absent, violent father, an ambitious, emotionally demanding mother and a sensitive child are understandable both in terms of unconscious processes and in terms of certain social forces and relations. (Some critics, of course, would find neither kind of approach acceptable, and opt for a 'human' reading of the novel instead. It is not easy to know what this 'human' is, which excludes the characters' concrete life-situations, their jobs and histories, the deeper significance of their personal relationships and identities, their sexuality and so on.) All of this, however, is still confined to what may be called 'content analysis', looking at what is said rather than how it is said, at 'theme' rather than 'form'. But we can carry these considerations into 'form' itself – into such matters as how the novel delivers and structures its narrative, how it delineates character, what narrative point of view it adopts. It seems evident, for example, that the text itself largely, though by no means entirely, identifies with and endorses Paul's own viewpoint: since the narrative is seen chiefly through his eyes, we have no real source of testimony other than him. As Paul moves into the foreground of the story, his father recedes into the background. The novel is also in general more 'inward' in its treatment of Mrs Morel than it is of her husband; indeed we might argue that it is organised in a way which tends to highlight her and obscure him, a formal device which reinforces the protagonist's own attitudes. The very way in which the narrative is structured, in other words, to some extent conspires with Paul's own unconscious: it is not clear to us, for example, that Miriam as she is presented in the text, very much from Paul's own viewpoint, actually merits the irritable impatience which she evokes in him, and many readers have had the uneasy sense that the novel is in some way 'unjust' to her. (The real-life Miriam, Jessie Chambers, hotly shared this opinion, but this for our present purposes is neither here nor there.) But how are we to validate this sense of injustice, when Paul's own viewpoint is consistently 'foregrounded' as our source of supposedly reliable evidence?

On the other hand, there are aspects of the novel which would seem to run counter to this 'angled' presentation. As H.M. Daleski has perceptively put it: 'The weight of hostile comment which Lawrence directs against Morel is balanced by the unconscious sympathy with which he is presented dramatically, while the overt celebration of Mrs Morel is challenged by the harshness of her character in action.'[1] In the terms we have used about Lacan, the novel does not exactly say what it means or mean what it says. This itself can partly be accounted for in psychoanalytical terms: the boy's Oedipal relation to his father is an ambiguous one, for the father is loved as well as unconsciously hated as a rival, and the child will seek to protect the father from his own unconscious aggression towards him. Another reason for this ambiguity, however, is that on one level the novel sees very well that though Paul must reject the narrowed, violent world of the miners for his venture into middle-class consciousness, such consciousness is by no means wholly to be admired. There is much that is dominative and life-denying as well as valuable in it, as we can see in the character of Mrs Morel. It is Walter Morel, so the text tells us, who has 'denied the god in him'; but it is hard to feel that this heavy authorial interpolation, solemn and obtrusive as it is, really earns its keep. For the very novel which *tells* us this also *shows* us the opposite. It shows us the ways in which Morel is indeed still alive; it cannot stop us from seeing how the diminishing of him has much to do with its own narrative organisation, turning as it does from him to his son; and it also shows us, intentionally or not, that even if Morel *has* 'denied the god in him' then the blame is ultimately to be laid not on him but on the predatory capitalism which can find no better use for him than as a cog in the wheel of production. Paul himself, intent as he is on extricating himself from the father's world, cannot afford to confront these truths, and neither, explicitly, does the novel: in writing *Sons and Lovers* Lawrence was not just writing about the working class but writing his way out of it. But in such telling incidents as the final reunion of Baxter Dawes (in some ways a parallel figure to Morel) with his estranged wife Clara, the novel 'unconsciously' makes reparation for its upgrading of Paul (whom this incident shows in a much more negative light) at the expense of his father. Lawrence's final reparation for Morel will be Mellors, the 'feminine' yet powerful male protagonist of *Lady Chatterley's Lover*. Paul is never allowed by the novel to voice the kind of full, bitter criticism of his mother's possessiveness which some of the 'objective' evidence would seem to warrant; yet the way in which the relationship between mother and son is actually dramatised allows *us* to see why this should be so.

In reading *Sons and Lovers* with an eye to these aspects of the novel, we are constructing what may be called a 'sub-text' for the work – a text which runs within it, visible at certain 'symptomatic' points of ambiguity, evasion or overemphasis, and which we as readers are able to 'write' even if the novel itself does not. All literary works contain one or more such sub-texts, and there is a sense in which they may be spoken of as the 'unconscious' of the work itself. The work's insights, as with all writing, are deeply related to its blindnesses: what it does not say, and *how* it does not say it, may be as important as what it articulates; what seems absent, marginal or ambivalent about it may provide a central clue to its meanings. We are not simply rejecting or inverting 'what the novel says', arguing, for example, that Morel is the real hero and his wife the villain. Paul's viewpoint is not simply invalid: his mother is indeed an incomparably richer source of sympathy than his father. We are looking rather at what such statements must inevitably silence or suppress, examining the ways in which the novel is not quite identical with itself. Psychoanalytical criticism, in other words, can do more than hunt for phallic symbols: it can tell us something about how literary texts are actually formed, and reveal something of the meaning of that formation.

Note

1. H.M. DALESKI, *The Forked Flame: A Study of D.H. Lawrence* (London: Faber, 1968), p. 43.

Part Two

Gender, Sexuality, Feminism

6 D.H. Lawrence (*Lady Chatterley's Lover*, *The Plumed Serpent*, 'The Woman Who Rode Away')*

KATE MILLETT

Kate Millett, writer, sculptor and film-maker, was a founding member in 1966 of the National Organisation of Women (NOW), and is one of the earliest and most trenchant of the new wave of feminist critics. *Sexual Politics*, her most famous work, was seminal both in the United States and Britain in putting feminism on the agenda, at least in the domain of literature and criticism. In addition to the chapter on Lawrence, it contains blistering attacks on Henry Miller and Norman Mailer (who responded with *The Prisoner of Sex* in 1971), and led to numerous controversies over the next decade. (Cf. Cora Kaplan's essay of 1979, 'Radical Feminism and Literature: Rethinking Millett's *Sexual Politics*', reprinted in Mary Eagleton's companion volume to this Reader, *Feminist Literary Criticism*. Eagleton also reproduces the passage on *Lady Chatterley's Lover*, and her comments in the Introduction and headnotes on Millett and Kaplan fill out several of the points made here.) As far as Lawrence is concerned (see Introduction, pp. 3, 14–15), Millett's essay helped prick the reputation he had acquired in the 1960s as the guru of sexual liberation by exposing his more obviously phallocratic and misogynistic tendencies to mockery and scorn. Often criticised by the squeamish for its crudity and its failure to engage the literary dimension of Lawrence's work, it is nevertheless a salutary reminder – in its demystifying frankness and radical debunking of literary idolatry – of just how partial and political literature and literary criticism must in fact always be.

* Reprinted from Kate Millett, *Sexual Politics* (1969; London: Rupert Hart-Davis, 1971), pp. 237–45, 283–93; footnotes in second excerpt renumbered from the original. (Note: there is some confusion as to the date of first publication of *Sexual Politics*. The English edition of 1971 used here gives the original copyright dates as '1969, 1970'; Cowan, Lawrence's chief bibliographer (op. cit., see Introduction, Note 6 for details), gives 1970, as does Mary Eagleton in *Feminist Literary Criticism*; Toril Moi in the bibliography to her *Sexual/Textual Politics* (1985) gives 1969; other English critics simply list the London edition of 1971. I think it is fair to take it, however, that the work does in fact belong to 1969, whatever the exact year of first publication.)

Millett's other written works include: (ed.) *The Prostitution Papers: A Candid Dialogue* (Paladin, 1975); an autobiography, *Flying* (Knopf, 1974); *Sita* (Virago, 1977); *The Basement: Meditations on a Human Sacrifice* (Simon and Schuster, 1979); and *Going to Iran* (Coward, McCann and Geoghegan, 1982).

Devotional

'Let me see you!'

He dropped the shirt and stood still, looking towards her. The sun through the low window sent a beam that lit up his thighs and slim belly, and the erect phallus rising darkish and hot-looking from the little cloud of vivid gold-red hair. She was startled and afraid.

'How strange!' she said slowly. 'How strange he stands there! So big! and so dark and cocksure! Is he like that?'

The man looked down the front of his slender white body, and laughed. Between the slim breasts the hair was dark, almost black. But at the root of the belly, where the phallus rose thick and arching, it was gold-red, vivid in a little cloud.

'So proud!' she murmured, uneasy. 'And so lordly! Now I know why men are so overbearing. But he's lovely, *really*. Like another being! A bit terrifying! But lovely really! And he comes to *me*! – ' She caught her lower lip between her teeth, in fear and excitement.

The man looked down in silence at his tense phallus, that did not change. . . . 'Cunt, that's what tha'rt after. Tell lady Jane tha' wants cunt. John Thomas, an' th' cunt o' lady Jane! – '

'Oh, don't tease him,' said Connie, crawling on her knees on the bed towards him and putting her arms round his white slender loins, and drawing him to her so that her hanging swinging breasts touched the top of the stirring, erect phallus, and caught the drop of moisture. She held the man fast.

'Lie down!' he said. 'Lie down! Let me come!'

He was in a hurry now.[1]

Lady Chatterley's Lover is a quasi-religious tract recounting the salvation of one modern woman (the rest are irredeemably 'plastic' and 'celluloid') through the offices of the author's personal cult, 'the mystery of the phallus'.[2] This passage, a revelation of the sacrament itself, is properly the novel's very holy of holies – a transfiguration scene with atmospheric clouds and lighting, and a pentecostal sunbeam (the sun is phallic to Lawrence's apprehension) illuminating the ascension of the deity 'thick and arching' before the reverent eyes of the faithful.

Lawrence's working title for the book was 'Tenderness', and although Oliver Mellors, the final apotheosis of Lawrentian man, is capable of some pretty drastic sexual animosities (he'd rather like to 'liquidate' all lesbians, and what Freudians would call 'clitoroidal' women, *en masse*, together with his own former wife), one still finds in this novel little of the sexual violence and ruthless exploitation so obtrusive in Mailer and Miller, nor, for that matter, the honest recognition of sexual caste one encounters in Genet. With *Lady Chatterley*, Lawrence seems to be making his peace with the female, and in one last burst of passion proposing a reconciliation for the hostilities embarked upon with the composition of *Aaron's Rod* in 1918, nearly ten years before. Compared with the novels and short stories which preceded it, this last work appears almost an act of atonement. And so Constance Chatterley is granted sight of the godhead,[3] which turns out to be a portrait of the creator himself, nude, and in his most impressive state. Whereas the mood of *Kangaroo*, *Aaron's Rod*, and *The Plumed Serpent* is homoerotic, here it is narcissistic.

In *Lady Chatterley*, as throughout his final period, Lawrence uses the words 'sexual' and 'phallic' interchangeably, so that the celebration of sexual passion for which the book is so renowned is largely a celebration of the penis of Oliver Mellors, gamekeeper and social prophet. While insisting his mission is the noble and necessary task of freeing sexual behaviour of perverse inhibition, purging the fiction which describes it of prurient or prudish euphemism, Lawrence is really the evangelist of quite another cause – 'phallic consciousness'. This is far less a matter of 'the resurrection of the body', 'natural love', or other slogans under which it has been advertised, than the transformation of masculine ascendancy into a mystical religion, international, possibly institutionalised. This is sexual politics in its most overpowering form, but Lawrence is the most talented and fervid of sexual politicians. He is the most subtle as well, for it is through a feminine consciousness that his masculine message is conveyed. It is a woman, who, as she gazes, informs us that the erect phallus, rising phoenix-like from its aureole of golden pubic hair is indeed 'proud' and 'lordly' – and above all, 'lovely'. 'Dark and cocksure' it is also 'terrifying' and 'strange', liable to give rise in women to 'fear' as well as 'excitement' – even to uneasy murmurs. At the next erection, Connie and the author-narrator together inform us the penis is 'overweening', 'towering' and 'terrible'.[4] Most material of all, an erection provides the female with irrefutable evidence that male supremacy is founded upon the most real and uncontrovertible grounds. A diligent pupil, Connie supplies the catechist's dutiful response, 'Now I know why men are so overbearing.' With the ecstasy of the devout, a parody of a loving

71

woman's rapture and delight, she finds the godhead both frightening and sublime. Lawrence's own rather sadistic insistence on her intimidation before biological event is presumably another proof of inherent female masochism. One cannot help admiring the technique: 'But he's lovely, *really* . . . A bit terrifying! But lovely really! And he comes to *me*!' – out of the mouth of the inamorata the most abject piety. It is no wonder Simone de Beauvoir shrewdly observed that Lawrence spent his life writing guidebooks for women.[5] Constance Chatterley is as good a personification of counter-revolutionary wisdom as Marie Bonaparte.

Even Mellors is impressed, pleased to refer to his penis in the third person, coyly addressing it in dialect: 'Ay ma lad! Tha'rt theer right enough. Yi, tha mun rear they head! Theer on thy own ey? an ta'es no count o' nob'dy . . . Dost want *her*? Dost want my lady Jane? . . . Say: Lift up your heads . . . that the king of glory may come in.'[6] John Thomas, this active miracle, is hardly matched by lady Jane, mere passive 'cunt'. Praise for this commodity is Mellors' highest compliment to his mistress: 'Th'art good cunt, though, aren't ter? Best bit o' cunt left on earth . . . Cunt! It's thee down theer; an' what I get when I'm i'side thee . . . Cunt! Eh, that's the beauty o' thee, lass.'[7] The sexual mystery to which the novel is dedicated is scarcely a reciprocal or co-operative event – it is simply phallic. Mellors' penis, even when deflated, is still 'that which had been the power': Connie moaning with 'a sort of bliss' is its 'sacrifice' and a 'newborn thing'.[8] Although the male is displayed and admired so often, there is, apart from the word cunt, no reference to or description of the female genitals: they are hidden, shameful and subject.[9] Male genitals are not only the aesthetic standard, '. . . the balls between his legs! What a mystery! What a strange heavy weight of mystery . . . The roots, root of all that is lovely, the primeval root of all full beauty',[10] they become a species of moral standard as well: 'The root of all sanity is in the balls.'[11] Yet all that is disreputable, even whole classes of society, are anathematised by the words 'female' or 'feminine'.

The scenes of sexual intercourse in the novel are written according to the 'female is passive, male is active' directions laid down by Sigmund Freud. The phallus is all; Connie is 'cunt', the thing acted upon, gratefully accepting each manifestation of the will of her master. Mellors does not even condescend to indulge his lady in foreplay. She enjoys an orgasm when she can, while Mellors is managing his own. If she can't, then too bad. Passive as she is, Connie fares better than the heroine of *The Plumed Serpent*, from whom Lawrentian man, Don Cipriano, deliberately withdraws as she nears orgasm, in a calculated and sadistic denial of her pleasure:

By a swift dark instinct, Cipriano drew away from this in her. When, in their love, it came back on her, the seething electric female ecstasy,

which knows such spasms of delirium, he recoiled from her . . . By a
dark and powerful instinct he drew away from her as soon as this
desire rose again in her, for the white ecstasy of frictional satisfaction,
the throes of Aphrodite of the foam. She could see that to him, it was
repulsive. He just removed himself, dark and unchangeable, away
from her.[12]

Lawrentian sexuality seems to be guided by somewhat the same
principle one finds expressed in Rainwater's study of the working class
(also the doctrine of the nineteenth-century middle classes) – 'sex is for
the man'.[13] Lawrence's knowledge of Freud was sketchy and
secondhand, but he appears to be well acquainted with the theories of
female passivity and male activity and doubtless found them very
convenient. Ladies – even when they are 'cunt' – don't move. In both
novels there are a number of severe reprimands delivered against
subversive female 'friction'.

The sexual revolution had done a great deal to free female sexuality.
An admirably astute politician, Lawrence saw in this two possibilities: it
could grant women an autonomy and independence he feared and
hated, or it could be manipulated to create a new order of dependence
and subordination, another form of compliance to masculine direction
and prerogative. The frigid woman of the Victorian period was
withholding assent, the 'new woman', could, if correctly dominated, be
mastered in bed as everywhere else. The Freudian school had
promulgated a doctrine of 'feminine fulfillment', 'receptive' passivity, the
imaginary 'adult' vaginal orgasm which some disciples even interpreted
as forbidding any penile contact with the clitoris. Notions of this kind
could become, in Lawrence's hands, superb instruments for the perfect
subjection of women.

In thanksgiving for her lover's sexual prowess, Lady Chatterley goes
out into the rain before their hut to dance what the reader recognises to
be a mime of King David's naked gyrations before the Lord. Watching
her, Mellors understands her to be performing a 'kind of homage toward
him', while 'repeating a wild obeisance'.[14] Such satisfaction as she is
granted by the lordly gamekeeper has converted her to a 'wonderful
cowering female' whose flashing haunches Mellors perceives in terms of
prey. Accordingly, he stirs himself to the chase. Having pursued and
caught her, 'he tipped her up and fell with her on the path, in the
roaring silence of the rain, short and sharp, he took her, short and sharp
and finished, like an animal.'[15]

Lawrence is a passionate believer in the myth of nature which has
ordained that female personality is congenital, even her shame not the
product of conditioning, but innate. Only the 'sensual fire' of the 'phallic
hunt' can rout this 'old, old physical fear which crouches in the bodily

roots'. On the occasion when Lady Chatterley submits to Mellors' anal penetration, we are told that 'She would have thought a woman would have died of shame. Instead of which the shame died . . . she had needed this phallic hunting out, she had secretly wanted it, and she had believed that she would never get it.' The 'phallus alone' is competent to explore the 'core of the physical jungle, the last and deepest recess of organic shame.'[16] Having reached the bedrock of her nature', the heroine breaks off momentarily to preach to the reader that the poets were 'liars': 'They made one think one wanted sentiment. When one supremely wanted this piercing, consuming, rather awful sensuality . . . The supreme pleasure of the mind! And what is that to a woman?'[17] Lawrence has killed three birds here, the bluestocking, the courtly pose, and it would seem, his own sodomous urges.[18] Although Constance Chatterley is more credibly a woman than most Lawrentian heroines (there are even casual references to her breasts and she becomes pregnant with the hero's child), the erotic focus of the novel is constantly the magnificent Mellors, 'remote', 'wild animal', with some superior and 'fluid male knowledge', the very personification of phallic divinity, described in caressing phrases which indicate Lawrence himself not only wishes to posses and partake of this power, but be possessed by it as well.

Lady Chatterley's Lover is a program for social as well as sexual redemption, yet the two are inextricable. Early in the novel, Tommy Dukes, one of the author's humbler mouthpieces, has deplored the fact that there are no 'real' men and women left in the world, predicting the fall of civilization on this account. We are all doomed unless the one hope of redemption is understood immediately: 'It's going down the bottomless pit, down the chasm. And believe me, the only bridge across the chasm will be the phallus.'[19] The metaphor is an unhappy one; in respect of penile length, the future hardly seems promising. Yet the program the novel offers against the industrial horrors it describes with such verve and compassion, is a simple matter: men should adopt a costume of tight red trousers and short white jackets and the working class should cease to desire money. In a single elaboration, Mellors suggests they busy themselves with folk art and country dances. This would be cruel, if it were not ridiculous. While a sexual revolution, in terms of a change in attitudes, and even in psychic structure, is undoubtedly essential to any radical social change, this is very far from being what Lawrence has in mind. His recipe is a mixture of Morris and Freud, which would do away with machinery and return industrial England to something like the middle ages. Primarily the thing is to be accomplished by a reversion to older sexual roles. Modern man is ineffectual, modern woman a lost creature (cause and effect are interchangeable in these two tragedies), and the world will only be put right when the male reassumes his mastery over the female in that total psychological and sensual domination which alone can offer her the 'fulfillment' of her nature.

This is why the novel concentrates on rehabilitating Constance Chatterley through the phallic ministrations of the god Pan, incarnated in Mellors. In the novel's early chapters we are instructed that her only meaningful existence is sexual and has been distorted by education and the indecent liberties of the modern woman. Married to an impotent husband, Connie mopes through some hundred and thirty pages of unfulfilled femininity. Neither a wife nor a mother, yearning for a child, her 'womb' contracting at certain stated intervals, she seeks her fleeting youth in unsatisfactory trips to the mirror, and endless visits to some hen pheasants, whose 'pondering female blood' rebukes 'the agony of her own female forlornness'[20] while affording her some solace by being 'the only things in the world that warmed her heart'.[21] In the presence of these formidable creatures she 'feels herself on the brink of fainting all the time,'[22] and the sight of a pheasant chick breaking its shell reduces her to hysterical weeping. In the best tradition of sentimental narrative we first see 'a tear fall on her wrist', followed by the information that 'she was crying blindly in all the anguish of her generation's forlornness . . . her heart was broken and nothing mattered any more'.[23] Thereupon Mellors intervenes out of pity ('compassion flamed in his bowels for her') and he invites her into the hut for a bit of what she needs.

He is characteristically peremptory in administering it: 'You lie there,' he orders. She accedes with a 'queer obedience'[24] – Lawrence never uses the word female in the novel without prefacing it with the adjectives 'weird' or 'queer': this is presumably done to persuade the reader that woman is a dim prehistoric creature operating out of primeval impulse. Mellors concedes one kiss on the navel and then gets to business:

> And he had to come into her at once, to enter the peace on earth of that soft, quiescent body. It was the moment of pure peace for him, the entry into the body of a woman. She lay still, in a kind of sleep, always in a kind of sleep. The activity, the orgasm was all his, all his; she could strive for herself no more.[25]

Of course Mellors is irreproachably competent and sexuality comes naturally to him. But the female, though she is pure nature to whom civilised thought or activity were a travesty, must somehow be taught. Constance has had the purpose of her existence ably demonstrated for her, but her conversion must take a bit longer:

> Her tormented modern-woman's brain still had no rest. Was it real? And she knew, if she gave herself to the man, it was real. But if she

kept herself for herself, it was nothing. She was old; millions of years old, she felt. And at last, she could bear the burden of herself no more. She was to be had for the taking. To be had for the taking.[26]

What she is to relinquish is self, ego, will, individuality – things woman had but recently developed – to Lawrence's profoundly shocked distaste. He conceived his mission to be their eradication. Critics are often misled to fancy that he recommends both sexes cease to be hard struggling little wills and egoists. Such is by no means the case. Mellors and other Lawrentian heroes incessantly exert their wills over women and the lesser men it is their mission to rule. It is unthinkable to Lawrence that males should ever cease to be domineering individualists. Only women must desist to be selves. Constance Chatterley was her husband's typist and assistant: she only ceases to serve this unworthy master when she becomes Mellors' disciple and farm wife. At no point is she given the personal autonomy of an occupation, and Lawrence would probably find the suggestion obscene. Even in the guise of a servant, Mellors has infinite assurance and a solid identity; Lady Chatterley appears an embarrassed impostor beside him.

Under the conventions of the eighteenth- and nineteenth-century novel, gentlemen entered into exploitative sexual liaisons with serving maids. Lawrence appears to have reversed this class relation by coupling the lady with her manservant, and his book is said to display an eloquent democracy by asserting that the class system is an 'anachronism'. Yet Mellors, a natural gentleman and therefore Lord Chatterley's superior, is just as great a snob as Connie, whose sermons mouth Lawrence's own disgust with the proletariat from whence he was saved by virtue of exceptional merit. Mellors also despises his own class. The lovers have not so much bridged class as transcended it into an aristocracy based presumably on sexual dynamism rather than on wealth or position. The very obnoxious Lord Chatterley represents the insufferable white male of the master caste, pretending to be worthy of the term 'ruling class'. Mellors and Lawrence are born outsiders to the privileged white man's general sway of empire, mine ownership, and the many other prerogatives of a male elite. But this has not persuaded them to overthrow so much as to envy, imitate, and covet. Rather in the manner of a black who is so corroded with white values that his grandest aspiration is sexual acceptance by the white woman, Lawrence's dark outsiders, whether Mexican Indian or Derbyshire collier, focus their ambition on the 'white man's woman' – the Lady. Women of his own class and kind are beneath his contempt; the cruelest caricatures in the novel are Bertha Coutts and Mrs Bolton, from whom Mellors withholds himself in rigid distaste – they are unbearably 'common'. Dissatisfaction with Clifford Chatterley's impersonation of the 'ruling class' has by no

means cured Lawrence of his allegiance to such a notion; to a large
extent, his wish is only to install himself in this position. His plan is to
begin by suborning the lady-class female, a feat which should give him
courage to subordinate other males. Then he may enter upon his
inheritance as natural aristocrat. Immersed in the ancient fantasy that he
had the wrong father, he has converted his own father into a god; for in
addition to being Lawrence himself and a desirable homosexual lover,
Mellors is also supposed to be the surly and unpleasant miner of *Sons and
Lovers*, Lawrence senior, rehabilitated and transformed into Pan. As it is
improbable Mellors can acquire the artistic prestige or political power of
other Lawrentian heroes, who are famous writers or generals, he is to be
exalted by purely religious means. And although he is a social prophet,
even this form of bettering his position is given little emphasis. Instead,
he bases his entire claim upon John Thomas. The possession of a penis is
itself an accomplishment of such high order (with the unimportant
exception of a Venetian laborer who appears on only one page, no other
male in the book gives any evidence of potency) that Mellors' divine
nature is revealed and established through this organ alone.

When he began to compose his last novel, Lawrence was suffering in
the final stages of tuberculosis. After *The Plumed Serpent* he admitted to
being weary of the 'leader cum follower' bit and had despaired of
political success.[27] All other avenues of grandeur appeared to be closed.
Public power was a delusion, only sexual power remained. If the last
Lawrentian hero is to have but one apostle to glorify him, let it be a
woman. Sexual politics is a surer thing than the public variety between
males. For all the excursions into conventional political fascism that
occupy the middle and late period of his work, it was the politics of sex
which had always commanded Lawrence's attention most, both as the
foundation and as a stairway to other types of self-aggrandisement. *Lady
Chatterley's Lover* is as close as Lawrence could get to a love story. It is
also something of a cry of defeat, perhaps even of remorse, in a man who
had aspired rather higher, but had to settle for what he could get. As a
handbook of sexual technique to accompany a mood of reaction in sexual
politics, it was not altogether a failure. . . .

Ritual

The Plumed Serpent records that moment when Lawrence was led to the
ultimate ingenuity of inventing a religion, even a liturgy, of male
supremacy. Theological underpinnings for political systems are an old
and ever-present need, and so in a sense, Lawrence is only being
practical. One of the pillars of the old patriarchy was its religion, and as

Lawrence was bored with Christianity, suspicious of its egalitarian potential, and quite uninterested in other established creeds, it was inevitable that he should invent one of his own. Yet as he requires only one service of the supernatural, he is content that it assume the blunt form of phallic worship: his totemic penis is alpha and omega, the word improved into flesh.

That there is a great deal of narcissism in all this was fairly obvious from the inception of the impulse, and a factor in many of the *Blutbruderschaft* relations described in earlier novels. His phallic cult enables Lawrence to achieve another goal: by investing the penis with magical powers (which might be slightly harder to substantiate without a religious aura) he has been able to rearrange biological fact. For in the new system, life arises by a species of almost spontaneous generation from the penis, bypassing the womb. Now the penis alone is responsible for generating all the vital forces in the world. When one remembers the powers the womb held for Lawrence in *The Rainbow*, it is perhaps not so surprising that he should have wished to effect such drastic alterations in the 'facts of life'.

The Plumed Serpent is the story of a religious conversion. A rather sensible Irish woman arrives in Mexico, falls in with two ambitious intriguers who wish to set themselves up as incarnations of the ancient Mexican gods in order to take over the country and establish a reactionary government, unmistakably fascist in character, and awkwardly neo-primitivist in program. Mrs Leslie is torn between her realisation that this is all 'high-flown bunkem', and the hypnotic masculinity of Don Ramon and Don Cipriano. At last she capitulates to the latter and stays on, married to one man and tempted by both to join the pantheon in the secondary capacity of a goddess.

The novel's point of view is the woman's; its point of interest is the two attractive males. The prose celebrates phallic supremacy continuously. Falling under Cipriano's spell, Kate Leslie is there to observe the 'living male power', the 'ancient phallic mystery', and the 'ancient god-devil of the male Pan', 'unyielding forever', 'shadowy, intangible, looming suddenly tall, and covering the sky, making a darkness that was himself and nothing but himself'.[28] The heroes, Ramon and Cipriano, are Lawrentian men and mouthpieces, intellectual and earthy respectively. Together with the heroine, they form a characteristic Lawrentian triangle. Cipriano and Kate Leslie appear to be in love with Ramon, who appears to be in love with himself. A very superior being, chief of the deities, the 'living 'Quetzalcoatl', brother and successor to Jesus Christ, Ramon is understandably self-sufficient. But in more relaxed moments, he enjoys some peculiarly erotic communions with Cipriano, as well as the pleasure of withholding himself from Kate, who is too imperfect to deserve him.

Leavis, and other critics, have remarked upon the impropriety of a heroine as the center of consciousness in this novel.[29] There is some truth in the objection, for Kate Leslie is a female impersonator, yet one cannot neglect her utility as an exemplary case of submission, and the model femininity she represents is surely part of her value. When presented with 'the old, supreme phallic mystery', her behaviour is unexceptional: after 'submitting' and 'succumbing', she abdicates self utterly and is 'swooned, prone beneath, perfect in her proneness'.[30]

> Ah! and what a mystery of prone submission, on her part, this huge erection would imply! Submission absolute, like the earth under the sky. Beneath an over-arching absolute. Ah! what a marriage! How terrible! and how complete! With a finality of death, and yet more than death. The arms of the twilit Pan. And the awful, half-intelligible voice from the cloud. She could conceive now her marriage with Cipriano; the supreme passivity, like the earth below the twilight, consummate in living lifelessness, the sheer solid mystery of passivity. Ah, what an abandon, what an abandon, what an abandon!'[31]

Overcome by the prospect of this supine future, the lady exclaims 'My demon lover!' this last epithet a sad instance of Coleridge fallen to the excited cliché of magazine prose.[32]

Kate Leslie is an exemplum, an object lesson placed so as to lead other women 'back to the twilight of the ancient Pan world, where the soul of woman was dumb, to be forever unspoken'.[33] Her vertiginous passivity is not only an admonition to her sex, but something the author appears to enjoy playing at himself. Through the device of the heroine, Lawrence has found a vehicle to fantasise what seems to be his own surrender to the dark and imperious male in Cipriano.

Throughout the novel, Kate Leslie is schooled in the author's notions of primeval truth. Learning that the salvation of the world lies in a reassertion of virility which will also make it possible for women to fulfill their true nature as passive objects and perfect subjects to masculine rule, she undergoes marriage in the new religion, devoutly kissing the feet of her new lord as the service commands her. She studies laboriously to relinquish her will and her individual selfhood, as Lawrence is very punctilious in assuring us female will is an evil and male will a blessing. Yet for all this, one can be fairly sure she won't last very long. Even within the novel it is predicted that she will end as some sort of human sacrifice, a repellent ritual to which the new order is given, described in shocking detail and with a complicity in its barbarism that makes the reader anxious for Lawrence's sanity. Ramon warns her, 'if you lived here alone . . . and queened it for a time, you would get yourself murdered – or worse – by the people who had worshipped you'.[34] Even as a member of the new regime, her status is so tenuous that her anxious premonitions carry great force: 'After all, she was a gringita, and she felt it. A sacrifice? Was she a sacrifice? . . . Now she was condemned to go through these strange ordeals, like a victim.'[35]

Lawrence wrote 'The Woman Who Rode Away' during the same period as *The Plumed Serpent*, and it is something of a sequel to it. The short story does accomplish the human sacrifice of the female to Lawrence's phallic sect and it is therefore a somewhat franker version of events than the novel. It is the story of a woman in an unhappy marriage, one Lawrence himself describes as an 'invincible slavery', which has left her 'conscious development . . . completely arrested'.[36] On an adventurous gamble, the woman, who significantly is never individualised by a name, rides away into the desert to join the Mexican Indians. She is clearly a woman who needs to run away – to something. What is curious is what Lawrence finds for her to run away to – a death which is astounding in the sadism and malice with which it is conceived.

The cult of primitivism, which provided Lawrence with so much aesthetic gratification, has its political side as well. Having seen in the feminist movement a surge toward the civilised condition which the male had enjoyed so long, Lawrence identified the female (at least his target, the New Woman) as a rather sophisticated enemy. This is quite the opposite tack from that taken by his contemporaries, Faulkner and Joyce, to name two examples, who were fond of presenting women as 'nature', 'unspoiled, primeval understanding', and the 'eternal feminine'. Even Freud, with whom Lawrence agrees so well on female character in the matters of passivity and masochism, imagined the female to be a fairly harmless savage. While Lawrence is determined to keep that part of civilisation he approves in male hands, he is also realistic enough to acknowledge that since the new breed have arrived, the female has actually escaped the primitive condition others assume to be her nature. Drastic steps must be taken if she is going to be coerced back into it: her will must be broken, her newly found ego destroyed. That is why the heroines of Lawrence's novels spend each book learning their part as females. Indeed, so little can one trust to nature in these matters, that very severe measures must occasionally be taken. 'The Woman Who Rode Away' is just this sort of measure. Critics fudge the meaning of this story by mumbling vaguely that it is all allegorical, symbolic.[37] Of course it is – symbolic in the same sense as a head exposed on London Bridge.

The idea of leaving the emancipated woman to the 'savage' to kill, delegating the butchery as it were, is really an inspiration; sexism can appear thereby to be liberal and anti-colonialist. Lawrence is able to relish the beauty of dark-skinned males, while congratulating them on what, despite his usual fastidious distaste for non-Aryans, he regards as their stellar virtue – they 'keep their women in their place'. This is a common fantasy of the white world, the favorite commodity of western movies and the Asian–African spectaculars. Such epics follow a well-paved story line which satisfies a host of white male expectations: the white woman is captured by 'savages' – and 'we all know how they treat their women'; she is forced to live in a state of utter humiliation and abjection, raped, beaten, tortured, finally stripped and murdered.[38] Such little comedies serve to titillate the white male, intimidate 'his woman', and slander the persons upon whom the white male has shifted the burden of his own prurient sadism.

Lawrence has improved upon the rape fantasy by sterilising the story – removing all traces of overt sexual activity and replacing them with his home-made mythology – the woman is sacrificed to the sun. But there is a sincere 'religious impulse' in the tale, apart from the inanities of the pseudo-Indian legend, for the story is Lawrence's most impassioned statement of the doctrine of male supremacy and the penis as deity. The fraudulent myth also prevents the story from appearing as the pandering to pornographic dream that it is. On one level of intention, 'The Woman Who Rode Away' would reward a careful comparative reading with *The Story of O*; in a number of ways it resembles commercial hard core.

The office of sexual avenger is of course left in the hands of the dark male. Non-Aryan females, like proletarian women, held no interest whatsoever for Lawrence, and never appear in the story. Psychologically, the very pattern of the tale cleverly provides satisfactions for the white male's guilt feelings over the dark peoples and 'primitives' whom he exploits. He will atone by throwing them his woman to butcher, advancing his dominion over her in the process, and substituting his own rival as the scapegoat for imperialist excesses. And the liberal, the humanistic, and the well meaning among his numbers are satisfied with the fable at its surface level, while the aggressive, and malign and the sadistic are provided with greater sustenance below the surface. . . .

Lawrence's cautionary tale for white women has odd assumptions common to the white mind: that the dark peoples of the world are fascinated and arrested by yellow hair, an axiomatic assumption of those white fairy tales like *Lord Jim*. It is a common white fancy that when one of the blond folk go to the dark peoples the latter are so overawed, they make him god or king, an event highly satisfactory to his vanity. Lawrence makes this old chestnut do service again while punishing the white woman in the process. The following passage works on both assumptions, and while it humiliates the woman, flatters white egocentricity at the same time:

There was now absolute silence. She was given a little to drink, then two priests took off her mantle and her tunic, and in her strange pallor

she stood there, between the lurid robes of the priests, beyond the
pillar of ice, beyond and above the dark-faced people. The throng
below gave the low, wild cry. Then the priest turned her round, so she
stood with her back to the open world, her long blond hair to the
people below. And they cried again.[39]

The scene is shot in MGM technicolor, the whole story reeks of
Hollywood, but it also satisfies voyeurism, a sadistic sort of buggery, and
the white dream of being uplifted and proclaimed.

One is always struck by the sexual ambiguity in Lawrence. The woman
of the fable is bent on going toward death like a bird hypnotised by the
eye of a snake. But her fatalism is never explained, save in Lawrence's
obsessive wish to murder her. There is a strange quality about this
fatalism: while it is supposed to represent the decline of the West or
some other abstraction, the narrative derives its power from a
participation on the part of the author himself which appears to derive
from perverse needs deep in Lawrence's own nature. There is as much
attention lavished upon the masochistic as upon the sadistic, and one
perceives a peculiar relish for the former in the author, a wallowing in
the power of the Indian male, his beauty and indifference and cruelty,
exerted not only on the silly woman, his victim, but on Lawrence too. It
is the author himself standing fascinated before this silent and darkly
beautiful killer, enthralled, aroused, awaiting the sacrificial rape.

Yet the real interest in the story is in the crushing of the woman's will,
of which the murder is merely a consummation. As with the *Story of O*,
or much of 'exotic' pornography (e.g. that set in Near and Far Eastern or
in primitive cultures, where a real or assumed contempt for women
rationalises the large dose of sexual sadism which caused the author to
choose such a locale to begin with), the interest is not in the physical
pain inflicted but in the damage done to will and spirit, the humiliation
of the human claim or dignity of the victim. Progress is measured in
hundreds of phrases like this: '. . . she was very tired. She lay down on a
couch of skins . . . and she slept, giving up everything'[40] . . . 'she was
utterly strange and beyond herself, as if her body were not her own'.[41]
Imprisoned in a little hut, drugged day after day as the torture drags on,
vomiting continuously, she is reduced to a phenomenal despair and
passivity 'as if she had no control over herself'.[42] Lawrence lingers over
her gradual relinquishment of selfhood:

She was not in her own power, she was under the spell of some other
control. And at times she had moments of terror and horror . . . the
Indians would come and sit with her, casting their insidious spell over
her by their very silent presence . . . As they sat they seemed to take

her will away, leaving her will-less and victim to her own
indifference.[43]

The message – for this story has a message – is revealed at last in a
central passage, when the author delivers a formal lecture to the modern
woman:

> In the strange towering symbols on the heads of the changeless,
> absorbed women, she seemed to read once more the Mene Mene
> Tekel Upharsin. Her kind of womanhood, intensely personal and
> individual, was to be obliterated again, and the great primeval
> symbols were to tower once more over the fallen individual
> independence of women. The sharpness and the quivering nervous
> consciousness of the highly-bred white woman was to be destroyed
> again, womanhood was to be cast once more into the great stream of
> impersonal sex and impersonal passion. Strangely, as if clairvoyant,
> she saw the immense sacrifice prepared, and she went back to her
> little house in a trance of agony.[44]

Well she might. With bemused pity one contemplates those women of
Africa, Asia, and South America, lobbying in the United Nations for civil
rights. Sadly misled, they have failed to grasp Lawrence's wise
understanding of the impropriety in their hope of sexual revolution – and
their own importance as models to the rest of their sex.

Now that the sermon has been delivered, the proceedings may
continue: 'She felt always in the same relaxed, confused, victimised state
. . . This at length became the only state of consciousness she really
recognised, this exquisite sense of bleeding out into the higher beauty
and harmony of things.'[45] The last phrase is pure gas, but there is no
mistaking its intention. Of course, much is made of the masochistic
nature of the female, called on to justify any ghastliness perpetrated
upon her: 'She knew she was a victim, that all this elaborate work upon
her was the work of victimising her. But she did not mind. She wanted
it.'[46] Of all masculine fantasies, this is perhaps the most revered; not only
does it rationalise any atrocity, but even more to the point, it puts such
action beyond the moral pale – all these enormities only satisfy her
inherent nature. Freud had provided the scientific justification for
sadism; Lawrence was not slow to buy the product.

Every effort is made to humiliate her. Since Lawrence's notion of *hubris*
is a woman who exhibits any self-assurance, she is rewarded for
speaking to the Indians who capture her with cuts at the horse she rides,
throwing her painfully in the saddle at every step. Later Lawrence has
her dismount and crawl. Other details savored are the gratuitous insult
of the animal she shares her prison with, 'a little female dog', and her

rabbit-like terror as she is carried to her death; 'she sat looking out of her litter with her big transfixed blue eyes . . . the wan markings of her drugged weariness'.[47]

Her captors, who are the embodiment of an idea, and bear no resemblance to living beings of any race whatsoever, are supernatural males, who are 'beyond sex' in a pious fervour of male supremacy that disdains any genital contact with women preferring instead to deal with her by means of a knife. These are the final priests of Lawrence's phallicism: 'There was nothing sensual or sexual in [their] look. It had a terrible glittering purity'[48] . . . 'there was not even derision in the eyes. Only that intense, yet remote, inhuman glitter which was terrible to her. They were inaccessible. They could not see her as a woman at all.'[49] We are informed incessantly that they are 'darkly and powerfully male',[50] yet paradoxically, we are told of their 'silent, *sexless*, powerful, physical presence'.[51] There is no real contradiction here for in this apotheosis of puritanical pornography, Lawrence has separated sexuality from sex. The ersatz Indians are ultimate maleness and therefore can have no relationship with the female, as they are entirely beyond trucking with her. By 'male', Lawrence simply means oppressive force, a charisma of mastery, 'something primevally male and cruel',[52] 'the ancient fierce human male'.[53] Naturally, this is incompatible with any sexual activity, for such might introduce the danger of communicating with or even gratifying a woman. Their relations with their female victim are of an antiseptic antisexual quality which is remarkably obscene, both in its arrogance and in its deliberately inhuman quality:

'You must take off your clothes, and put these on.'
'If all you men will go out', she said.
'No one will hurt you', he said quietly.
'Not while you men are here', she said.
He looked at the two men by the door. They came quickly forward and suddenly gripped her arms as she stood, without hurting her, but with great power. Then two of the old men came, and with curious skill slit her boots down with keen knives, and drew them off, and slit her clothing so that it came away from her. In a few moments she stood there white and uncovered. The old man on the bed spoke, and they turned her round for him to see. He spoke again, and the young Indian deftly took the pins and comb from her fair hair, so that it fell over her shoulders in a bunchy tangle.
Then the old man spoke again. The Indians led her to the bedside. The white-haired, glassy-dark old man moistened his finger-tips at his mouth, and most delicately touched her on the breasts and on the body, then on the back. And she winced strangely, each time, as the finger-tips drew along her skin, as if Death itself were touching her.[54]

It is by no means incongruous that the victim feels the touch of death – this is how Lawrence's male supremacy manifests itself at last – lethal, an utter denial of sexuality, of life, and of fertility. One cannot become more sterile than this. The final rites take place before a phallic totem of ice, and there is wonderful propriety in the detail that this penis is an icicle:

Facing, was a great wall of hollow rock, down the front of which hung a great dripping fang-like spoke of ice. The ice came pouring over the rock from the precipice above, and then stood arrested, dripping out of high heaven, almost down to the hollow stones where the stream-pool should be below. But the pool was dry . . . They stood her facing the iridescent column of ice, which fell down marvellously arrested.[55]

In the images of genital topography the reader may perceive the supernatural origin of the penis (dropping out of high heaven), the miracle of an erection (marvellously arrested), and the negation of the womb (a dry pond). The ice-pick is Lawrence's god, an idol, his image of the holy. This is what phallic consciousness can accomplish.

Before the penetration of death, the victim is to be purified, 'fumigated', mauled, rubbed, and the reader stimulated through a method possibly the most frankly auto- or perhaps anti-erotic in pornographic literature. These bits are generally quoted on the flyleaf of cheap paper editions as sex bait – the attraction is obvious.

In the darkness and in the silence she was accurately aware of everything that happened to her: how they took off her clothes, and standing her before a great, weird device on the wall, colored blue and white and black, washed her all over with water . . . Then they laid her on a couch under another great indecipherable image of red and black and yellow, and now rubbed all her body with sweet-scented oil, and massaged all her limbs, and her back, and her sides, with a long, strange, hypnotic massage. Their dark hands were incredibly powerful, yet soft with a water softness she could not understand. And the dark faces, leaning near her white body, she saw were darkened with red pigment, with lines of yellow round the cheeks. And the dark eyes glittered absorbed, as the hands worked upon the soft white body of the woman.

When she was fumigated, they laid her on a large flat stone, the four powerful men, holding her by the outstretched arms and legs. Behind her stood the aged man, like a skeleton covered with dark glass, holding the knife and transfixedly watching the sun and behind him was another naked priest with a knife.[56]

All sadistic pornography tends to find its perfection in murder. Lawrence's movie priests themselves seem to understand the purpose of the rites and are 'naked and in a state of barbaric ecstasy',[57] as they await the moment when the sun, phallic itself, strikes the phallic icicle, and signals the phallic priest to plunge the phallic knife – penetrating the female victim and cutting out her heart – the death fuck.[58]

With elaborate care, Lawrence has plotted the sexualised landscape to coincide with the sexual scenario – as his victim lies poised and waiting, he works up suspense:

> Turning to the sky she looked at the yellow sun. It was sinking. The shaft of ice was like a shadow between her and it. And she realised that the yellow rays were filling half the cave though they had not reached the altar where the fire was, at the far end of the funnel shaped cavity. Yes, the rays were creeping round slowly. As they grew ruddier, they penetrated farther. When the red sun was about to sink, he would shine full through the shaft of ice deep into the hollow of the cave to the innermost. She understood now that this was what the men were waiting for . . . And their ferocity was ready to leap out into a mystic exultance of triumph . . . Then the old man would strike, and strike home, accomplish the sacrifice and achieve the power.[59]

This is a formula for sexual cannibalism: substitute the knife for the penis and penetration, the cave for a womb, and for a bed, a place of execution – and you provide a murder whereby one acquires one's victim's power. Lawrence's demented fantasy has arranged for the male to penetrate the female with the instrument of death so as to steal her mana. As he supposes the dark races envy the white, who in his little legend, have 'stolen their sun', Lawrence himself seems envious, afraid – murderous.

The act here at the centre of the Lawrentian sexual religion is coitus as killing, its central vignette a picture of human sacrifice performed upon the woman to the greater glory and potency of the male. But because sexual potency could accomplish little upon a corpse, it is painfully obvious that the intention of the fable is purely political. The conversion of human genitals into weapons has led him from sex to war. Probably it is the perversion of sexuality into slaughter, indeed, the story's very travesty and denial of sexuality, which accounts for its monstrous, even demented air.

Notes

1. D.H. LAWRENCE, *Lady Chatterley's Lover* (1928). (New York: Random House, 1957), pp. 237–8.

2. Ibid., p. 238.

3. It had been Lawrence's consistent practice to veil the sanctities of sex in vague phrases about cosmic flight, movement into space, and so forth, while the trademark adjective droned its tedious 'deep, deep, deep' refrain at the reader. *Lady Chatterley* contains the only wholly explicit sexual descriptions in his work.

4. D.H. LAWRENCE, *Lady Chatterley's Lover*, p. 238.

5. SIMONE DE BEAUVOIR, *The Second Sex* (New York: Knopf, 1953), p. 209.

6. Lawrence, op. cit., p. 237.

7. Ibid., p. 201.

8. Ibid., p. 197.

9. This is true, despite the great insight Lawrence displays about the nature of sexual inhibition and prurience, brutality and shame in 'A Propos of *Lady Chatterley's Lover*' and in his other critical essays on sex and censorship. Here, too, he is busy affirming that the phallus is not only the bridge to the future, but the very essence of marriage and life itself. His silence as regards to female genitals is most remarkable, and evidence, I believe, of considerable inhibition and very probably of strongly negative feelings. In Henry Miller one encounters the same phenomenon in a more severe form.

10. Ibid., p. 197.

11. Ibid., p. 246.

12. D.H. LAWRENCE, *The Plumed Serpent* (1923; New York: Knopf, 1951), p. 463.

13. LEE RAINWATER, *And the Poor Get Children* (Chicago: Quadrangle, 1960).

14. LAWRENCE, *Lady Chatterley's Lover*, p. 250.

15. Ibid., pp. 250–1.

16. Ibid., pp. 280–1.

17. Ibid., p. 281.

18. One remembers that Mellors' first love was his colonel. With the exception of *Sons and Lovers* and *The Rainbow*, every Lawrence novel includes some symbolically surrogate scene of pederasty: the rubdowns in *The White Peacock* and *Aaron's Rod*, the consecration scene in *The Plumed Serpent*, the kiss denied in *Kangaroo* and the wrestling scene in *Women in Love*.

19. LAWRENCE, *Lady Chatterley's Lover*, p. 82.

20. Ibid., p. 127.

21. Ibid., p. 126.

22. Ibid., p. 127.

23. Ibid., p. 129.

24. Ibid., p. 130.

25. Ibid., p. 130.

26. Ibid., pp. 130–1.

27. D.H. LAWRENCE, *The Letters of D.H. Lawrence*, edited by Aldous Huxley (New York: Viking, 1932), p. 719. To Witter Bynner, 13 March 1928:

> I sniffed the red herring in your last letter a long time: then at last decided it's a live sprat. I mean about *The Plumed Serpent* and 'the hero'. On the whole, I think you're right. The hero is obsolete, and the leader of men is a back number . . . the leader-cum-follower relationship is a bore. And the new relationship will be some sort of tenderness, sensitive, between men and men and men and women, and not the one up, one down, lead on I follow, *ich dien* sort of business . . . But still, in a way, one has to fight . . . I feel one still has to fight for the phallic reality . . .

28. D.H. LAWRENCE, *The Plumed Serpent* (1926). (New York: Viking, 1951), p. 342.

29. See F.R. LEAVIS, *D.H. Lawrence, Novelist* (New York: Knopf, 1956), p. 70.

30. LAWRENCE, *The Plumed Serpent*, p. 341.

31. Ibid., p. 342.

32. Ibid.

33. Ibid.

34. Ibid., p. 478.

35. Ibid., p. 369.

36. D.H. LAWRENCE, *The Woman Who Rode Away* (1928; New York: Knopf, 1928, Berkeley Medallion Edition), p. 8.

37. Both Leavis and Tindall take this line. See Leavis' *D.H. Lawrence, Novelist*, and William York Tindall, *The Later D.H. Lawrence* (New York: Knopf, 1952).

38. Lawrence has a number of stories like this: 'None of That' is a grim little piece of hate about an American woman who is gang-raped by a group of shoddy toreadors in gratitude for the fortune she wills to one of them; 'The Princess' gives an account of a Mexican guide who rapes and imprisons an American in the mountains – a story done with infinite malice and sexual enmity. There is a premonition of the Lawrence who wrote 'The Woman Who Rode Away' as early as *Sons and Lovers*, when little Paul Morel performs strange rites upon his sister Annie's doll. Having broken her 'accidentally', he suggests 'Let's make a sacrifice of Arabella . . . Let's burn her.' Having found her face 'stupid' he stands by, watching with satisfaction while the figure melts, then takes the charred remains and smashes them with stones. Annie, whose only toy this had been, stands by helpless and understandably disturbed while Paul shouts, 'that's the sacrifice of Misses Arabella . . . And I'm glad there's nothing left of her' (*Sons and Lovers*, pp. 57–8).

39. LAWRENCE, *The Woman Who Rode Away*, p. 39.

40. Ibid., p. 24.

41. Ibid., p. 24.

42. Ibid., p. 25.

43. Ibid., p. 27.

44. Ibid., p. 29. Needless to say, the 'symbol' which will tower over the fallen freedom of women is none other than the phallus.

45. Ibid., p. 31.

46. Ibid., p. 36.

47. Ibid., pp. 37–8.

48. Ibid., p. 20.

49. Ibid., p. 18.

50. Ibid., p. 27.

51. Ibid. (italics added).

52. Ibid., p. 35.

53. Ibid., p. 29.

54. Ibid., pp. 23–4.

55. Ibid., pp. 38–9.

56. Ibid., pp. 36, 39.

57. Ibid.

58. Curiously enough, Lawrence has created a realisation of the popular equation of sexuality and violence one finds, for example, in street language, where our obsessive cultural habit of sexual loathing causes 'fuck' to become synonymous with kill, hurt, or destroy.

59. Ibid., pp. 39–40.

7 Lawrence, Feminism and the War ('Tickets, Please', *The Lost Girl*)*

Hilary Simpson

Hilary Simpson took her BA at York University and her PhD at Reading in the seventies. For the last thirteen years she has worked in local government, where she has pioneered a number of policies to improve the position of working women. As I have indicated in the Introduction (see p. 15), *D.H. Lawrence and Feminism* has been widely respected for its painstaking historical and cultural situating of Lawrence's changing attitudes to women and the contemporary women's movement. Its title, then, does not imply a feminist critique of Lawrence: as Marion Shaw remarked in reviewing it (op. cit., see Introduction, Note 4, for details), it does not 'politicise' him, *à la* Millett, but 'historicises' his work 'in the context of the feminism he experienced and responded to'. Simpson's own Introduction explicitly announces an attempt to redirect feminist criticism away from partisan posturing, and to find 'a new basis' in women's history for considering Lawrence's work. The book as a whole is a revealing account of Lawrence's shift – as part of a general tendency in male ideology and culture – from a liberal, pro-feminist position before the First World War to the rabid post-war vision of women as the destructively dominant sex, and of programmes for masculinist revolution. (Particularly good is Simpson's thesis in Chapter 6 that Lawrence's later fiction has much in common – *pace* F.R. and Q.D. Leavis – with the sensationalist romances of the twenties, best exemplified by Edith Maud Hull's *The Sheik*.) The chapter included here (from which some pages dealing with 'Monkey Nuts' and 'The Fox' are cut) focuses on the pivotal role of the war itself in Lawrence's responses.

Hilary Simpson continues to study and teach Lawrence, and

---

* Reprinted from Hilary Simpson, *D.H. Lawrence and Feminism* (London: Croom Helm, 1982), p. 62–9, 73–80; references renumbered from the original.

recently contributed to the Open University course on Literature in
the Modern World.

With an incongruous irony seldom equalled in the history of
revolutions, the spectacular pageant of the woman's movement, vital
and colourful with adventure, with initiative, with sacrificial emotion,
crept to its quiet, unadvertised triumph in the deepest night of war-
time depression.[1]

The First World War brought women the vote, the struggle for which
had been the predominant symbol of feminist enterprise in the pre-war
years. But the war also brought about more fundamental and spectacular
changes in women's lives, some temporary, others more lasting. A
highly industrialised nation faced with mass conscription of its active
men had no choice but to look for an alternative labour force, and the
employment of women was the obvious answer. The large-scale entry of
women into the labour market did not take place overnight, and there
was considerable hostility to it. But the exceptional requirements of the
war economy swept aside some of the conventional notions about
women's place in society. The movement of women into jobs previously
held by men proved to be the crucial factor in their changing status
during the war. It gave them new social freedoms and a staggering new
financial independence. For example, before the war the average weekly
wage for women in paid employment had been 11s 7d; but a war-time
bus conductress, like those in Lawrence's story 'Tickets, Please', started
on a wage of £2 5s per week.[2]

As Sheila Rowbotham has pointed out, it would be naïve to see the
work in itself as particularly emancipating for women.[3] It was frequently
hard, dangerous and monotonous, especially in the munitions factories
which came to employ large numbers of the new female work-force.
Obviously, only a small number of the women doing war-work were
motivated by an overt political commitment to feminism; most wanted to
do their bit to help their country, or sought escape from a repressive
family or the rigours of domestic service. There was in any case no single
feminist policy on the war. Emmeline and Christabel Pankhurst became
fervent patriots, and there was talk of 'women's right to serve', while
other women considered pacifism to be more in line with feminist
principles. Although the basis for most of the social and economic
changes that affected women had been laid by the pre-war feminist
campaigns, when the changes actually came they were dictated more by
economic necessity and the exigencies of war than by any conscious
ideology. The number of women employed in industry in Britain

increased by more than a million during the war, with about seven hundred thousand directly replacing men. Other women moved into a large number of other traditionally male occupations, and many whose husbands or fathers had run small businesses took these over. Others joined the new women's services such as the WAAC, or semi-official organisations like the Women's Land Army, while thousands more worked voluntarily in relief organisations. It was a remarkable show of strength by the female population which succeeded in dispelling many myths about women's role.

One of the most important by-products of the war for women was the way in which it changed attitudes to sexuality in a direction that was generally in their favour. The new freedom that women derived from war-work, and the casting aside of conventional restraints in the highly charged emotional atmosphere of war, contributed to this. Extra-marital sexual relationships were less harshly looked upon, conventional expectations about chastity were relaxed and the unmarried mother was more sympathetically treated. An official report stated that men and women were 'so thrown into daily contact with each other that conventional notions of a certain reserve as between the sexes have been very largely modified'.[4] In such circumstances some of the repressions and taboos which had surrounded female sexuality were bound to be removed, and this shift in sexual *mores* naturally caused some alarm. A worried lady wrote towards the end of the war of 'the alarming rapidity with which the women of the country are accepting the laxer standard of morality', blaming it on 'a short-sighted system of education, the excitement inherent in war conditions, [and] the emancipation of women, immediately followed by the economic independence of very large numbers under conditions removed from home influences'.[5] There is no doubt that the war *was* an emancipating experience for most women. It changed their image of themselves, and the public's image of them, from decorative but largely useless creatures with their own sphere of trivial interests and duties, to people of resourcefulness, strength and capability who differed from men much less than had been imagined.

That the experience of the war also marked a turning-point in Lawrence's life and work has, of course, been widely acknowledged and discussed. It set him off on his 'savage pilgrimage', and, as Neil Myers has written, transformed him 'from a symbolist experimenter in the traditional novel into the compulsive, chaotic, half-comic propagandist of the popular imagination'.[6] Myers argues convincingly that the post-war Lawrence deserves as much attention as the more accessible author of *Sons and Lovers* or *The Rainbow*.

If one takes World War I and its aftermath seriously, one must take seriously the Lawrence who spilled his awesome energy in reaction to

it. One must take seriously precisely what alienates so many readers –
the restless, angry disorder, and the interest in the kinds of savage
energies that would fill the sudden chasm that the war had opened.[7]

In Lawrence's post-war exploration of power relationships and 'savage
energies', male dominance plays a crucial part. Lawrence develops in the
twenties an explicit anti-feminism which is of a different quality from the
more open-ended probings of love and power to be found in his earlier
work. Even in, say, *Women in Love* (written largely during the war), the
notion of male supremacy is only one of a whole range of controversial
subjects discussed, often in a spirit of intellectual play, by the central
characters. Ultimately, the reader of *Women in Love* feels that Lawrence
has no one axe to grind; in a complex presentation of possibilities and
potentialities we are not forced to take sides. This poise certainly
vanishes to a large extent in the post-war works, and anti-feminism,
along with other notions which had earlier been only possibilities,
becomes an imperative. Yet the very explicit historical relationship
between the changing position of women in the war years and
Lawrence's launching on his career as the prophet of male supremacy
has rarely been discussed.

During the first part of the war Lawrence continued to insist on the
need for women's voices to be heard and on the necessity for the
feminine side of experience to be brought into prominence. A month
after the outbreak of hostilities he wrote to Gordon Campbell: 'The war
doesn't alter my beliefs or visions . . . I believe there is no getting of a
vision, as you call it, before we get our sex right: before we get our souls
fertilised by the *female*.'[8] This attitude is reflected in the emphasis on
balance and relationship in the *Study of Thomas Hardy*, written around
this time. In the autumn of 1915 he wrote to Cynthia Asquith, 'If only the
women would get up and speak with authority.'[9] 'I very much want you
to tell me what you think, because it is a question for the *women* of the
land now to decide: the men will never see it. I don't know one single
man who would give the faintest response to this. But I still have some
hope of the women.'[10] On the same note he wrote to Hugh Meredith, 'I
can make nothing of the men, they are all dead . . . Perhaps the
women – .'[11] During the various stages of his war-time dabbling in
revolutionary political theory with Bertrand Russell, he continued to
envisage a crucial role for women in the reconstruction of the state.

It is all the more surprising, then, to discover an abrupt espousal of
male supremacy which coincides with the end of the war. In a letter to
Katherine Mansfield in November 1918 Lawrence writes: 'I do think a
woman must yield some sort of precedence to a man, and he must take
this precedence. I do think men must go ahead absolutely in front of
their women, without turning round to ask for permission or approval

from their women. Consequently the women must follow as it were unquestioningly.'[12] This assertion has the air of a discovery newly formulated, and Lawrence adds as if in apology, 'I can't help it, I believe this.' Frieda, he says, thinks his attitude 'antediluvian'. It was shortly after this crucial letter to Katherine Mansfield that Lawrence wrote 'Tickets, Please', 'Monkey Nuts' and 'The Fox', three stories dealing explicitly with the overturning of traditional sexual roles and relationships as a result of the war.[13] It is as if, at this time, Lawrence suddenly consolidated a whole new set of attitudes on the relationship between the sexes. What women had proved during the war was that they were capable of doing men's work and of assimilating themselves into the man's world. This was not the sort of revolution that Lawrence had hoped for: he had urged the 'feminisation' of experience, the necessity for men to take women, and the feminine side of their own natures, seriously. He had never argued that women should enter the masculine world of industry and technology which he hated. In 1917, when he was asked to write an article on the recruitment of women into traditional male occupations, Lawrence had replied that he hadn't 'the guts' to write it.

> All I can say is, that in the tearing asunder of the sexes lies the universal death, in the assuming of the male activities by the female, there takes place the horrid swallowing of her own young, by the woman . . . I am sure woman will destroy man, intrinsically, in this country. But there is something in me, which stops still and becomes dark, when I think of it . . . I am sure there is some ghastly Clytemnestra victory ahead, for the women.[14]

When the war ended, the great social upheaval which Lawrence had hoped for did not materialise; rather, he found most of the things he detested about pre-war society left intact. In particular, he must have felt that the women in whom he had placed much of his hope for the future had merely become more like men. In 1914 Lawrence had written approvingly of woman 'becoming individual, self-responsible, taking her own initiative'.[15] The three stories about the war which I discuss in this chapter show a tremendous unease about the directions which that initiative had taken.

Lionel Trilling has written that 'Tickets, Please' 'exemplifies the drastic revision of the notion of womanliness'[16] which was brought about by the First World War. The story concerns a group of tram conductresses who unite to humiliate their womanising inspector, John Thomas Raynor.

> The girls are fearless young hussies. In their ugly blue uniform, skirts up to their knees, shapeless old peaked caps on their heads, they have

all the *sang-froid* of an old non-commissioned officer. With a tram packed with howling colliers, roaring hymns downstairs and a sort of antiphony of obscenities upstairs, the lasses are perfectly at their ease. They pounce on the youths who try to evade their ticket-machine. They push off the men at the end of their distance. They are not going to be done in the eye – not they. They fear nobody – and everybody fears them.[17]

The presentation of the tram conductresses works on both a realistic and a symbolic level. Such women were among the élite of the new female work-force, earning over £2 a week at a time when the Lawrences could rent a Cornish cottage for £5 a year. Their fighting spirit is reflected in their pseudo-military uniforms; it was one of the great culture-shocks of the war for women to be seen in this kind of uniform, but it does give them 'all the *sang-froid* of an old non-commissioned officer'. And it is as warriors, combatants, Amazons, that they feature in this tale. Their fight is against men, or against man's representative, the phallic male himself, John Thomas. So it is apt that from the start the women are in authority over their male passengers. A tram conductor does not *serve* the public in the same way that, say, a shop assistant does, which is possibly one of the reasons why it was a traditionally male job. Having boarded the tram the passenger is obliged to pay, and the job of the conductor is almost to extort the money. So the girls 'pounce on' those who try to avoid payment, and the whole story is, on one level, a kind of extended pun on the notion of 'making men pay'.

The theme of battle is reinforced by the mock-heroic tone in which Lawrence describes Annie Stone, who leads the other women into the fight. 'She is peremptory, suspicious, and ready to hit first. She can hold her own against ten thousand. The step of that tram-car is her Thermopylae.'[18] Rejected by John Thomas for demanding more from their relationship than his mere 'nocturnal presence', Annie enlists the help of his other former sweethearts, 'the half dozen girls who knew John Thomas only too well'.[19] Trapped by the girls in a room at the depot on a Sunday evening, John Thomas is first subjected to friendly taunts and humiliating games. But the mock-heroism of the first part of the story gives way to real violence, graphically described.

She had taken off her belt, and swinging it, she fetched him a sharp blow over the head with the buckle end. He sprang and seized her. But immediately the other girls rushed upon him, pulling and tearing and beating him. Their blood was now thoroughly up. He was their sport now. They were going to have their own back, out of him. Strange, wild creatures, they hung on him and rushed at him to bear him down. His tunic was torn right up the back. Nora had hold at the back of his collar, and was actually strangling him. Luckily the button burst. He struggled in a wild frenzy of fury and terror, almost mad terror. His tunic was simply torn off his back, his shirt-sleeves were torn away, his arms were naked. The girls rushed at him, clenched their hands on him and pulled at him: or they rushed at him and pushed him, butted him with all their might: or they struck him wild blows. He ducked and cringed and struck sideways. They became more intense.

At last he was down. They rushed on him, kneeling on him. He had neither breath nor strength to move. His face was bleeding with a long scratch, his brow was bruised.[20]

The persistent theme in the attack on John Thomas is to force him to choose one of the women, to distinguish between them as individuals. But when he finally capitulates they each in turn reject him, although their renunciation costs an effort, so integral to the mythology of femininity is the dream, here parodied, of being chosen from amongst others by the handsome male.

The feeling that prevails at the end of the story is that something stupendous has happened, that things have got out of hand, that the women have gone further than they intended. By bonding together to humiliate the promiscuous male the women have indeed broken several taboos of patriarchy, and their sense of the enormity of what they have done is justified. They have attacked the double standard and their own status as sexual objects; attacked the notion that women are incapable of solidarity and must always compete with each other when a man is at stake; and shown themselves capable of violent action. It is partly because of this breaking of taboos that the story has a powerful and shocking quality. It is also Lawrence at his technical best, the build-up of tension as friendly revenge turns to actual physical assault being particularly well handled; and the various elements – realism, symbolism, mythology, psychological observation – are painlessly integrated.[21] . . .

To survey the changes in his attitude in one volume, one cannot do better than look at *The Lost Girl*, a perfect transition-piece clearly spanning Lawrence's pre- and post-war concerns, moving as it does from woman's revolt to woman's submission. It was begun, as *The Insurrection of Miss Houghton*, in 1913, at the same time as *The Sisters* (the first draft of *The Rainbow/Women in Love*). The manuscript was left in Germany during the war, with the story 'three parts done'.[22] Lawrence retrieved it at the beginning of 1920, started it again, and had completed the novel by May of that year.[23]

The main part of the novel, describing Alvina's progressive revolt against the conventions and expectations of provincial life, takes its starting-point very much from the realist tradition. *The Insurrection of Miss Houghton* was partly inspired by Lawrence's reading of Arnold Bennett's *Anna of the Five Towns* (1902) in October 1912. This tightly controlled realist novel describes the narrow life of a young woman in a strict Wesleyan community in the Potteries, over a short period during which she comes of age, inherits property and its responsibilities, and is engaged to be married. Lawrence was fascinated by the book's Midland setting and its evocation of a community similar to the one in which he had grown up, but he hated what he called Bennett's resignation. He felt that strict realism all too often constituted a pessimistic acceptance of what it described – in this case, the 'oldness and grubbiness and despair'[24] of ordinary English life. It was in connection with Bennett's novel that Lawrence made his famous pronouncement, 'Tragedy ought really to be a great kick at misery.'[25]

The published version of *The Lost Girl* has some noticeable affinities of plot not only with *Anna of the Five Towns* but with the novel that in turn inspired Bennett, George Moore's *A Mummer's Wife* (1885), part of which is also set in the Potteries. This tells the story of a young woman who leaves her invalid husband and his draper's shop to elope with an actor from a variety troupe; after some success as a variety star herself, she is ruined by alcoholism. Christopher Heywood has discussed the relationship of *The Lost Girl* to these two novels,[26] which are part of a realist tradition focusing on the cramped and restricted lives of bourgeois women which may be said to go back to *Madame Bovary* (1857). Lawrence takes the same basic theme of a young woman imprisoned within a constricting routine from which there seems no escape, but Alvina neither submits to convention, as Anna Tellwright does, nor rebels only to suffer worse miseries, like Kate Ede in *A Mummer's Wife*. In fact, Lawrence's determination to portray a successful rebellion (as indicated in the original working title *The Insurrection of Miss Houghton*), would seem to align him also with the writers of the 'problem novel' who dealt rather more specifically with some of the social and economic causes of the heroine's position. There is something about the jaunty tone of *The Lost Girl* which recalls the Wells of *Ann Veronica* (1909), and the very first page of the novel makes reference to Gissing's *The Odd Women* (1893), which Lawrence read in 1910 and which combines realism with the more sociological perspective of the 'problem novel' by introducing characters who are trying to change the conditions that produce their oppression.

> 1913 . . . A calm year of plenty. But one chronic and dreary malady: that of the odd women. Why, in the name of all prosperity, should every class but the lowest in such a society hang overburdened with Dead Sea fruit of odd women, unmarried, unmarriageable women,

called old maids. Why is it that every tradesman, every schoolmaster, every bank-manager, and every clergyman produces one, two, three or more old maids? Do the middle-classes, particularly the lower middle-classes, give birth to more girls than boys? Or do the lower middle-class men assiduously climb up or down, in marriage, thus leaving their true partners stranded? Or are middle-class women very squeamish in their choice of husbands?

However it be, it is a tragedy. Or perhaps it is not. Perhaps these unmarried women of the middle-classes are the famous sexless Workers of our ant-industrial society, of which we hear so much. Perhaps all they lack is an occupation: in short, a job. – But perhaps we might hear their own opinion, before we lay the law down.[27]

The writing here shows no genuine concern with the socio-economic causes of the so-called 'woman surplus', although in bringing out *The Lost Girl* as 'a perfect selling novel'[28] in 1920 Lawrence may well have been influenced by the fact that the existence of a large proportion of unmarried women, a topical subject in 1913, was even more of a pertinent issue after the war. Women were ejected from their temporary war-work to make room for homecoming soldiers, yet so many men had been wiped out that marriage was a realistic proposition for only a limited number of them. But the passage above shows no clear engagement with the 'problem'. The rambling style, full of 'perhaps's and qualified statements and swift changes of mind, is a sort of empty thinking aloud, frequently used by Lawrence in discussing social questions, which often merely leads to the conclusion that his preoccupations are elsewhere. It represents a kind of parody of the tone adopted by writers like Wells.

Lawrence is interested in the *theme* of a young woman's revolt, but he cares little for either the sociological analysis of the problem novel or the meticulous factual accumulation of realism. Embarking, then, on a novel in the realist mode – a mode which he could, of course, handle more than adequately when he chose – he treats the tradition in which he is writing with scant respect, complaining, for example, that 'it is wearying to repeat the same thing over and over'.[29] *The Lost Girl* is full of authorial comment undercutting the realist pretensions of the style – 'but why drag it out?', 'now incredible as it may seem', and so on. Faced with the prospect of describing Alvina's period of training as a midwife in London, Lawrence simply gives up – his readers, he says, have heard it all before. 'Surely enough books have been written about heroines in similar circumstances. There is no need to go into the detail of Alvina's six months in Islington.'[30] He is determined to offer a positive alternative to what he saw as the dreary pessimism of the conventional realist novel.

Now so far, the story of Alvina is commonplace enough. It is more or
less the story of thousands of girls. They all find work. It is the
ordinary solution of everything. And if we were dealing with an
ordinary girl we should have to carry on mildly and dully down the
long years of employment; or, at the best, marriage with some dull
school-teacher or office-clerk.

But we protest that Alvina is not ordinary . . . we are not going to
follow our song to its fatal and dreary conclusion.[31]

Despite these reservations, *The Lost Girl* may still be regarded in its initial
conception as a 'woman-question' novel. This was recognised by the
reviewers, for reviews appeared under such titles as 'The Surplus
Woman' and 'Frustrate Ladies'.[32] The pre-war Lawrence was intensely
interested in the theme of a young woman breaking out from the
conventional life prescribed for her (one should remember that *The
Rainbow* was taking shape at around the same time as *The Insurrection of
Miss Houghton*), even though he was dissatisfied with the traditional
methods of portraying such a rebellion and with its traditional fictional
conclusions. Lawrence represents Alvina's revolt as the triumph of a
kind of healthy vulgarity over an outdated, false refinement. She escapes
from 'the beautiful, but unbearable tyranny' of 'purity and high-
mindedness',[33] as represented by Miss Frost, into the vulgarity of being a
midwife, a cinema pianist and a member of a variety troupe. Unlike Kate
Ede in *A Mummer's Wife*, her espousal of this kind of life does not lead to
tragedy; rather, Alvina's insurrection is essentially a comedy.

The latter part of the novel, dealing with Alvina's marriage to Ciccio, is
much more recognisably the work of the post-war Lawrence in its
depiction of her submission to a man of another race and another class.
For example, the contrast between vulgarity and refinement is replaced
by the more radical division between nature and artifice. Alvina's
willingness to yield to Ciccio in a passivity tempered by nonchalance and
indifference is contrasted with the attitude of Mrs Tuke, an advanced and
artistic young woman whom Alvina is attending in childbirth when
Ciccio seeks her out for the second time. Mrs Tuke refuses to accept the
natural processes that condition her pregnancy, and considers Ciccio's
love for Alvina to be just as 'animal' and irrational as her own labour
pains. She warns Alvina that what she feels for the Italian is simply
atavism – following 'at a man's heel just because he's a man . . . like
barbarous women, a slave'.[34] Alvina realises the truth of these
accusations – 'I wish he didn't attract me'[35] – but for the first time in her
life she is powerless to revolt. 'Why didn't she revolt? Why couldn't she?
She was as if bewitched. She couldn't fight against her bewitchment.
Why? Because he seemed so beautiful, so beautiful. And this left her
numb, submissive. Why must she see him beautiful? Why was she will-

less?'[36] Ciccio's power over Alvina does not touch her conscious mind. She is quite capable of seeing him as a common, rather flashy Italian with whom she has virtually nothing in common. 'Her mind remained distinctly clear. She could criticise him, find fault with him, the things he did. But *ultimately*, she could find no fault with him.'[37] We see realised in her the state that Henry had demanded of March in 'The Fox'.

> His love did not stimulate or excite her. It extinguished her. She had to be the quiescent, obscure woman: she felt as if she were veiled . . . Was it atavism, this strange, sleep-like submission to his being? Perhaps it was . . . But it was also heavy and sweet and rich. Somewhere, she was content. Somewhere even she was vastly proud of the dark veiled eternal loneliness she felt, under his shadow . . . a nonchalance deep as sleep, a passivity and indifference so dark and sweet she felt it must be evil.[38]

Only two things temper the novel's exaltation of this trance-like state. The first is that the real hero of the book turns out to be not so much Ciccio as the primitive but breathtakingly beautiful landscape to which he transports her. The writing in the final few chapters set in Italy is of a different order to that in the rest of the book, which increases the reader's conviction that it is the stark but liberating quality of the life encountered by Alvina in Pescocalascio which effects the really radical change in her. 'She had gone beyond the world into the pre-world, she had reopened on the old eternity.'[39] It is in this remote part of Italy that Alvina is finally 'lost – lost – lost utterly',[40] possessed by a 'savage hardness' which issues in terrible despair and wild happiness. The second point which qualifies Alvina's 'atavism' is her feeling that it is a temporary state, something which she must experience for a while but which is not necessarily her final destiny: 'she could never endure it for a life-time. It was only a test on her.'[41] Because of the intricate connection of her state of mind with the Italian landscape, she feels that 'Ciccio must take her to America, or England – to America preferably.'[42]

The last chapter of the novel is called 'Suspense' and the ending is left open, as in so many of Lawrence's novels – Ciccio leaving for the war, Alvina pregnant, the future uncertain; a situation very like that at the end of *Lady Chatterley's Lover*. The distance traversed by Alvina from her upbringing in Woodhouse to her isolation in primitive Italy is immense, and critics have commented on the book's disjointed quality, as if it begins as one novel and ends as another. This can be accounted for not solely by the circumstances of its composition but also by the significant changes that occurred in Lawrence's thinking between the conception of *The Insurrection of Miss Houghton* in 1913 and the final writing of *The Lost Girl* in 1920. It is of course most unlikely that Lawrence ever intended to conclude his heroine's insurrection with, say, a successful career or a conversion to feminism. From the start the emphasis is on the finding of a suitable mate. But the particular form of mating which Lawrence eventually envisages for Alvina, with its insistent emphasis on submission and passivity, is a product of his post-war thinking and his growing anti-feminism.

Notes

1. VERA BRITTAIN, *Testament of Youth* (London: Victor Gollancz, 1933), p. 405.

2. RUTH ADAM, *A Woman's Place 1910–1975* (London: Chatto and Windus, 1975), p. 46.

3. SHEILA ROWBOTHAM, *Hidden from History* (London: Pluto Press, 1973), p. 110.

4. Quoted in DAVID MITCHELL, *Women on the Warpath* (London: Jonathan Cape, 1966), p. 241.

5. MRS NEVILLE-ROLFE, 'The Changing Moral Standard', *The Nineteenth Century and After*, **84** (1918): 725.

6. NEIL MYERS, 'Lawrence and the War', *Criticism*, **4**, no. 1 (1962): 44.

7. Ibid., p. 45.

8. Letter to Gordon Campbell, 21 September 1914, *Letters*, vol. 2, p. 218.

9. Letter to Lady Cynthia Asquith, 21 October 1915. Ibid., p. 415.

10. Letter to Lady Cynthia Asquith, 2 November 1915. Ibid., p. 425.

11. Letter to Hugh Meredith, 2 November 1915. Ibid., p. 426.

12. Letter to Katherine Mansfield, 21 November 1918. *Collected Letters*, p. 565.

13. 'Tickets, Please' and 'The Fox' were written in November 1918, at almost exactly the same time as the letter to Katherine Mansfield; 'Monkey Nuts' was written in May 1919. See Keith Sagar, *D.H. Lawrence: A Calendar of his Works* (Manchester University Press, Manchester, 1979), pp. 90, 94.

14. Unpublished letter to Robert Mountsier, 20 January 1917 (The University of Texas at Austin: Humanities Research Center).

15. Letter to Edward Garnett, 22 April 1914. *Letters*, vol. 2, p. 165.

16. LIONEL TRILLING, *Prefaces to the Experience of Literature* (Oxford: Oxford University Press, 1981), p. 124.

17. *England, My England*, p. 42.

18. Ibid., p. 43.

19. Ibid., p. 48.

20. Ibid., p. 51.

21. The myth of the death of Pentheus at the hands of the Bacchantes has been

suggested as a possible source for the story; see George H. Ford, *Double Measure* (New York: Holt, Rinehart and Winston, 1965), p. 94. It has also been conjectured that Lawrence may have been drawing on his own experience as a youth at the hands of the women workers in the surgical goods factory where he was briefly employed; they are said to have humiliated him by cornering him and forcibly exposing his genitals. See Harry T. Moore, *The Priest of Love* (revised edn, London: Heinemann, 1974), p. 43.

22. Letter to Martin Secker, 27 December 1919. *Collected Letters*, p. 602.

23. SAGAR, D.H. *Lawrence: A Calendar of his Works*, pp. 99–101.

24. Letter to Arthur McLeod, 4 October 1912. *Letters*, vol. 1, p. 459.

25. Ibid.

26. CHRISTOPHER HEYWOOD, 'D.H. Lawrence's *The Lost Girl* and its Antecedents by George Moore and Arnold Bennett', *English Studies*, **47**, no. 2 (1966), pp. 131–4. Another possible antecedent for Lawrence's novel is E.M. Forster's *Where Angels Fear to Tread* (1905), in which an English widow marries an Italian inferior to her in social status and many years her junior. The contrast between English suburban existence and the romantic yet vulgar life of an Italian hill town is central to both novels, as is the attraction which the Latin male holds for Englishwomen.

27. *The Lost Girl*, pp. 1–2.

28. Letter to Martin Secker, 27 December 1919. *Collected Letters*, p. 602.

29. *The Lost Girl*, p. 18.

30. Ibid., p. 32.

31. Ibid., pp. 83, 85.

32. FRANCIS HACKETT, 'The Surplus Woman', *New Republic*, (16 March 1921): 77–8; 'Frustrate Ladies' (unsigned), *Nation* (New York), (7 September 1921): 269.

33. *The Lost Girl*, p. 36.

34. Ibid., p. 286.

35. Ibid., p. 283.

36. Ibid., p. 288.

37. Ibid.

38. Ibid.

39. Ibid., p. 316.

40. Ibid., p. 313.

41. Ibid., p. 320.

42. Ibid.

8 The Symbolic Father and the Idea of Leadership ('Sun', *Aaron's Rod*, *Kangaroo*, *The Plumed Serpent*)*

Judith Ruderman

Judith Ruderman is Director of Continuing Education, and Adjunct Faculty in English, at Duke University, North Carolina, where, amongst other courses, she teaches American–Jewish literature. She is immediate past president of the D.H. Lawrence Society of North America and longtime member of the editorial board of *The D.H. Lawrence Review*. As I have implied in the Introduction (see pp. 15–16), Ruderman is no more polemically engaged with Lawrence from a feminist perspective than is Hilary Simpson (see Chapter 7), although where the latter 'historicises' him, the present author seeks to 'psychologise' him. Her book as a whole reads Lawrence's *oeuvre* in terms of a governing psycho-term, 'the Devouring Mother', and his love/hate relationship to what it implies; the present uncut Chapter 12 focuses on its reflex in the so-called 'leadership novels' of the early twenties where Lawrence's masculinist obsessions become most evident. Characteristic of Ruderman's (and other) post-feminist criticism is the dispassionate exegesis of Lawrence's work in the light of a particular psycho-sexual theory, and the absence, by and large, of either social or formal analysis of ideology and text. In a way, what Eagleton is attempting in the brief passage on *Sons and Lovers* (Chapter 4), is to integrate Ruderman's kind of criticism with a broader (and not specifically gendered) political perspective.

Ruderman has also written books on William Styron (Ungar, 1987) and Joseph Heller (Ungar, 1991), as well as articles on these and other modern writers. She is currently working on a full-length assessment of Lawrence's attitudes toward the Jews.

---

* Reprinted from Judith Ruderman, *D.H. Lawrence and the Devouring Mother: The Search for a Patriarchal Ideal of Leadership* (Durham N.C.: Duke University Press, 1984), pp. 173–87, 202–3; a number of parenthetical references to Lawrence's works in the text have been omitted.

Although the works of D.H. Lawrence's leadership period are commonly read in terms of the political power of superior male individuals, the central character in these works is the same domineering mother who figures so importantly in *Sons and Lovers*. The antagonistic female, opposed to her husband's search for a male leader, plays such a prominent role in the fiction published between 1922 and 1926 that all critics must deal with her; and in fact, almost in spite of themselves, many of the critics who eschew the biographical approach to Lawrence's works do suggest the overwhelming importance of biographical matters, especially those concerning Lawrence's wife and mother, for understanding Lawrence's ideal of leadership. For example, by way of explaining Aaron Sisson's attitude toward his predatory wife in *Aaron's Rod*, Mary Freeman, who disdains biography, notes in passing that 'Lawrence's mother, having been dominant, predisposed him to see all women as dominant, insidiously if not overtly.'[1]

Ernest Tedlock establishes the female's opposition – in *Aaron's Rod* and elsewhere – as Frieda Lawrence's, and sees it as 'the major challenge' to Lawrence's urge toward leadership. That this opposition may have originated with Lawrence's mother, and that it may have been the source of that urge as well as the challenge to it, is suggested by Tedlock's remark that 'the conflict of the boy's dependence with the man's independence', and the guilt over betrayal of mother-love, are implicit in all of Lawrence's work.[2] This assumption of a mother fixation is at the center of a frankly biographical study, Daniel Weiss's *Oedipus in Nottingham* (1962). But Weiss's strictly oedipal approach, in the tradition of Murry's *Son of Woman*, is used mainly to explain *Sons and Lovers*. In contrast, the comprehensive study by John Stoll entitled *The Novels of D.H. Lawrence: A Search for Integration* (1971) attempts to combine and transform the Freudian approach (exemplified by Weiss) and the Jungian, or vitalist, approach (exemplified by Tedlock). Biographical and psychological matters are not brought in to 'explain away' Lawrence's ideas. Yet underlying this study is an assumption of Lawrence's conflicting attitudes toward woman in her *Magna Mater* role, and this assumption places the contradictions inherent in Lawrence's 'leadership phase', to use Stoll's term, in the continuum of Lawrence's life.

The assumption behind the present work is that D.H. Lawrence's ambivalence toward the 'devouring mother' was the prime motivating factor behind the works of his leadership period. *Fantasia of the Unconscious* most clearly identifies the relationship between Lawrence's fear of woman and his strictures about leadership by man; every other work of the period is likewise concerned with the question not of which man is to lead the masses, but of whether man has the courage to lead woman. In the Eden that Lawrence's works tentatively define or suggest, man fulfills his 'primal need, the old-Adamic need' (as Lawrence expresses it in *Apocalypse*) to be the master. This need may conflict with Lawrence's deeply held conviction that man and woman must maintain their integrity in the love relationship, but it is nevertheless present at the same time.

The effect of Rupert Birkin's famous description in *Women in Love* of the ideal marriage as a star polarity is counteracted in that novel by the stress on male dominance. The same contradiction can be found in the novels on leadership, although the male–female issue is masked by the sociopolitical concerns and by a general misanthropy that were characteristic of these years in Lawrence's life. In *Aaron's Rod*, Rawdon Lilly speaks of the masses as insects to be exterminated and then immediately extols the worth of the individual soul. While this contradiction has stimulated commentary on Lawrence's ambivalence toward humanity,[3] what frequently passes notice is that Aaron Sisson's flight from his wife is directly connected with his search for the superior male leader, and that the only such leader offered by this novel is continually engaged in warfare with his own wife. Lawrence himself was in constant conflict with, and flight from, the *Magna Mater*, and his embrace of the dark gods at this time signifies not so much an acceptance of his own coalmining father as it signifies a last-ditch effort, through acceptance of a fantasy father, to escape the smothering embrace of woman.

Certain features common to the fiction of the leadership period combine to suggest a pattern of pre-oedipal concerns and conflicts:

- the male protagonists are often smaller and/or younger than their female lovers or antagonists;
- attention is drawn to the disparity in size by repetition of the words *small* and *little* in reference to the man;
- attention is drawn to the disparity in age by such devices as repetition of the phrase 'old enough to be your mother';
- the women are potential or actual mothers, narcissistically absorbed in their pregnancies or children;
- the women demand the men's acknowledgment of dependency on them, yet they often chafe at the burden of this dependency;
- when crossed or left out, the women refer to their lovers/antagonists as babies or children and characterise their behaviour as willful, obstinate, or perverse;
- the women attempt to make the men feel small;
- they manipulate and force allegiance, by playing on guilt or making subtle threats to cut off sustenance;
- the men wish to establish a homeplace and to connect with nurturing women;
- the men also chafe at their dependence upon women since it makes them vulnerable to domination and bullying;

- emphasis is placed on the men's stiffening their backbones in opposition, or generating power 'at the tail';
- the men subjugate the women or attempt to do so;
- the reversal of power roles is often indicated by a change in physical position: the men stand erect, the women kneel;
- the men decide that the women are bad and must die if the men are to live;
- a turn toward violence is taken;
- animal images connect the human and non-human realms and give sanctions for violence;
- there is a recoil from connection into separation, singleness and aloneness;
- the men pledge allegiance to a nurturant male as an escape from the domination of women.

Many of the above motifs, it should be noted, are to be found as well in works with female protagonists, like *The Lost Girl*, a fact suggesting that Lawrence saw the struggle for independence as a universal rather than a gender-specific phenomenon.

That Lawrence himself had difficulty separating from the mother-figure is evidenced by the tension between the desire for merger and the need for independence that informs all his work; this difficulty was a wound that stimulated his art but that also resulted in the shrill excesses of his leadership period. Lawrence's relations with Lydia Beardsall Lawrence were no doubt troubled and even pathologised; the almost hysterical stress on singleness in his leadership period suggests an unresolved conflict over this issue of separation. His treatises on psychology reveal that Lawrence was well aware of the connection between his feelings of having been smothered as a child and his battle cry for space and fresh air as an adult. In fact, the developmental process that he sets forth in these treatises, and the crises in this process that he records throughout his writings, are in accord with the almost three decades of work on the 'separation–individuation' phase of psychological growth conducted by psychoanalyst Margaret Mahler and her associates, mainly through observation of children. Mahler's findings shed light on the excesses of Lawrence's leadership period.

In *The Psychological Birth of the Human Infant*, Mahler delineates the phases constituting the child's growth into what might be called personhood. The first birth experience is the obvious one, the biological. The second birth experience occurs in stages between five and thirty-six months, when the child separates from the mother and achieves a sense of self. This psychological birth is the separation–individuation phase of personality development. Separation refers to the child's awareness of differentiation from the mother; individuation refers to his or her feelings of autonomy. The phase succeeds and grows out of the symbiotic phase, in which the relationship of dual unity with the mother is 'the primal soil from which all subsequent human relations form'.[4]

Within a certain range, there are several potential children within each child; the child is to a degree created out of the mother's own psychological makeup and therefore reflects her personality. If a mother's attachment to her baby in the very earliest stages is formed primarily out of her own narcissistic, parasitic needs rather than out of regard for her child, then differentiation – the first subphase of separation–individuation – can set in almost vehemently, with the child's pushing and arching away from the mother. Conversely, if the mother overvalues the child's sedentary, vegetative behavior, the child may fail to invest libidinally in motor functions, in order to remain dependent and hence rewarded; the differentiation subphase will in this case be delayed.

The development of motor functions, culminating in the ability to stand and walk, allows the child a great step forward psychologically as well as physically. In the so-called practising subphase of separation-individuation, occurring from ten to twelve months to sixteen to eighteen months of age, the child's point of view changes, literally and figuratively. The world lies open before him or her, and the threats of object loss – the disappearance of the mother – are compensated for by the pleasures of discovery and mastery as well as of escape from engulfment by the mother. The child still needs the mother, and she the child, but both must let go if the child is to become an individual. Not coincidentally, 'it is the rule rather than the exception that the first unaided steps taken by the infant are in a direction away from the mother or during her absence' (Mahler, p. 73.).

In the third, *rapprochement* subphase, the child fears being left too much on his or her own and makes great demands on the mother to restore the symbiotic status quo. Having already witnessed the child's movements toward separation, the mother may become confused by these demands and resentful, or she may more actively resist separation. This crisis in the child's development, like all such crises, requires great adaptiveness and sensitivity on the part of the mother. The end of the *rapprochement* subphase, at around eighteen months of age, is characterised by the rapidly alternating or even simultaneous desires to push the mother away and to cling to her. Observers of child behavior can see in this ambivalence the 'roots of many uniquely human problems and dilemmas – problems that sometimes are never completely resolved during the entire life cycle' (Ibid., p. 100).

The last subphase, occurring in roughly the third year, is the consolidation of individuality and the beginning of object constancy. The mother is kept in mind even when absent; and her 'good' and 'bad' elements are united into one image. In a state of object constancy, the mother is not rejected or supplanted by another if she is not providing satisfaction. This fourth subphase is also marked by the development of such complex cognitive functions as speech, fantasy-making, and reality-testing. Each child shows his or her distinctive way of adapting to problems and crises in this period, depending upon the nature of the mother–child relationship, the innate endowment, and the accidents and circumstances of life.

Lawrence clearly delineates these crises in the practising and *rapprochement* subphases of the psychological birth process in his short story called 'Sun', written in late 1925, thirty years before the stages were officially observed and named. At the beginning of the story, Juliet is an inadequate mother, one who keeps her child dependent upon her and then chafes at his dependence: 'The child irritated her, and preyed on her peace of mind. She felt so horribly, ghastly responsible for him: as if she must be responsible for every breath he drew. And that was torture to her, to the child, and to everyone else concerned.' After only a few hours in the sun, however, Juliet begins to change her ideas about mothering and comes home from sunbathing in the nude with a different attitude toward her child:

> 'Mummy! Mummy!' her child came running toward her, calling in that peculiar bird-like little anguish of want, always wanting her. She was surprised that her drowsed heart for once felt none of the anxious love-anguish in return. She caught the child up in her arms, but she thought: He should not be such a lump! If he were in the sun, he would spring up.
>
> She resented, rather, his little hands clutching at her, especially at her neck . . .
>
> She had had the child so much in her mind, in a torment of responsibility, as if, having borne him, she had to answer for his whole existence . . .
>
> Now a change took place. She was no longer vitally interested in the child, she took the strain of her anxiety and her will from off him. And he thrived all the more for it.

Juliet has learned how *not* to be a 'devouring mother'. She is capable of protecting and sheltering her son when he needs her, as when she prevents him from falling against the thorns. But otherwise she leaves him to his own devices, to grow apart from her. At first the child is afraid, having come to depend upon his mother: Juliet must firmly loosen his grasp upon her neck – and his grasp upon her own life – and urge him into independence by such devices as rolling an orange away from her across the tiled terrace; she rewards the boy for toddling after the fruit, and eases his fear in doing so, by calling him in to the safety of her presence with the orange as a token of his courageous effort.

Eventually, like his mother, the boy becomes 'another creature, with a peculiar, quiet, sun-darkened absorption. Now he played by himself in silence, and she hardly need notice him. He seemed no longer to know when he was alone'. Even the presence of a snake in their Eden cannot disrupt their idyllic relationship with the cosmos or each other: 'Some stillness of the sun' in Juliet keeps panic at bay and puts the incident in perspective. As the story progresses, the child moves, with Juliet's encouragement, physically and emotionally farther away from his mother, while still maintaining a connection with her; when he needs to run back to her for momentary support, she is there for him. And she, in turn, has no need to find emotional fulfillment in her child. Although her marriage is a failure, she finds sexual stimulation in a vital, animalistic Italian peasant.[5]

In short, Juliet lets go of her role as the smothering, overprotective mother and allows her boy successfully to undergo what Mahler, years later, would call the separation–individuation phase of childhood. The story is almost a textbook case of a turning point in a child's psychological development.

According to Mahler, conflicts over separation and separateness throughout the first few years of life are so crucial and intense that they can be 'reactivated (or can remain peripherally or even centrally active) at any and all stages of life'. In Lawrence's case, the conflicts were probably always peripherally active. The facts of Lawrence's earliest years provide some clues as to the origins of his pre-oedipal conflicts. Mrs Lawrence was disappointed in her husband and found little satisfaction in her marriage. She looked to her sons for emotional – and later, even financial – sustenance. Lawrence was sickly from birth, and his mother did not expect him to live three months; as an adult he stated that he had nearly died of bronchitis barely two weeks after he was born. His eldest brother, George, has reported that Lawrence was petted and spoiled from the beginning, and that their mother 'poured her very soul into him'.[6] Obviously the young Lawrence required and received a great deal of maternal care. Evidence suggests, however, that the robust second brother, Ernest, and not the sickly 'Bert', was the mother's favorite child. One can only speculate on the development of self-esteem by the youngest boy, who continually looked to his mother for bolstering and who may have found that bolstering inadequate to his needs for both nurturance and independence. Early on, Lawrence may well have developed a rage against his mother and, in defence against his aggressive impulses, split the love object into 'good' and 'bad' mother, reserving his hostility for the latter. This rage against the 'bad' mother lasted well beyond the period when object constancy might be expected to have been achieved. Indeed, it appears in one guise or another throughout the Lawrence canon, as well as in biographical accounts of Lawrence's stormy existence with Frieda and others, with its abrupt transitions of mood.

By his adult years Lawrence was convinced that women tend to engulf or devour their loved ones. His logic faltered when he placed woman securely in the domestic realm (as in the essay 'Matriarchy') and then blamed her for becoming overly involved in her children; or when he attributed to woman the innate, biological urge toward connection (as in his treatises on psychology) and then blasted her for her unwillingness to let go. Yet Lawrence had a clear desire to merge with the caretaker mother himself. On the one hand he extolled the value of intimacy in his works; on the other he saw intimacy as a life-threatening merger and was driven to extoll separation and even the violence he saw as necessary to attain it.

During the leadership period, this conflict between the desire for merger and the need for separation moved to center stage in Lawrence's life and art. At this time Lawrence was especially vulnerable and powerless: feeling his autonomous self threatened by the exigencies of illness, war, and indebtedness, he lashed out at those within easy reach – his physical battles with Frieda are legendary – and took revenge in his art on those whom he could or would not touch in life, achieving a kind of separation in the process and, paradoxically, maintaining a kind of dependency. Henry Grenfel feels caught in Jill Banford's web in the first versions of *The Fox*, the image being particularly apt in terms of what Lawrence saw as the female's stress on interconnectedness;[7] the final version of *The Fox* shows Grenfel's dubious (even to Lawrence) solution to the problem of entrapment: killing off Banford to restore autonomy to the self and a hierarchical order to the world. The same repulsion from the female web is found to underlie the three so-called leadership novels – *Aaron's Rod*, *Kangaroo*, and *The Plumed Serpent* – as well as the Lawrence corpus as a whole.

Lawrence's ideal of leadership, developed in reaction to the female web, can be defined as the domination of the male as symbolic father. In this metaphor of paternalism, *father* is aggrandised beyond his natural role in the family, and *leader* is likewise imbued with a greater emotional power than he normally possesses.[8] Intimacy and distance are thereby combined in one figure. Lawrence's urge toward the paternalistic leader may be attributed partly to the economic conditions in which he grew up, with his father absent from the home during the day working in the coal mines (and during most evenings drinking in the pubs with his cronies), and partly to the emotional climate in which he was raised, with the mother effectively eliminating the father as a presence in the family and taking sole charge of the home and of her sickly youngest son. Early in Lawrence's search for the ideal society he was extremely wary of the charismatic, paternalistic leader: in a 1915 letter to Ottoline Morrell he wrote of the organisation of their Rananim and warned,

> We must go very, very carefully at first. The great serpent to destroy, is the Will to Power: the desire for one man to have some dominion over his fellow man. Let us have *no* personal influence, if possible – nor personal magnetism, as they used to call it, nor persuasion – no 'Follow me' – but only 'Behold'.

By the time of the leadership period, however, Lawrence had committed himself to the idea if not to the reality of a man of personal magnetism who calls others to follow him. Lilly and Count Dionys articulate this ideal in *Aaron's Rod* and *The Ladybird*, calling it the power mode of relationships; Ben Cooley offers himself as such a leader in *Kangaroo* but is ultimately repudiated by the Lawrence character as being too smothering – that is, maternal; finally, Don Ramón incarnates the paternalistic ideal of leadership in *The Plumed Serpent*, a mystical novel about a fantasy Mexico.

Although Lawrence never found a leader in contemporary life worth attaching himself to – for what leader could measure up to Lawrence's demands for him to be an idealised father – he certainly had aggrandised notions of his own wisdom and leadership abilities. Many have remarked that the notion of Lawrence attaching himself to a group as either leader or follower is ridiculous, given his iconoclastic, cranky personality; Paul Delany states that Lawrence never sought 'to assemble any body of initiates over whom he might exercise total control. His temperament was too open and volatile for him to become the master of a cult.' But Delany overstates his case, for if Lawrence did not try to exercise total control he certainly did try to assemble a body of initiates whose disagreements with him he tended to regard as betrayals. Here is Delany himself on this subject:

> When he found . . . disciples he became euphoric, convinced that they would be 'unanimous' with him in action; but his elation would be replaced by an equally profound rage and depression when the views of his followers diverged in any way from his own. Those who were acclaimed as disciples were, before too long, anathematised as heretics and cast forth . . . [W]hen he quarreled with one intimate, he was led to demand more support and sympathy from each of those who remained – who were then all the more likely, under this increased strain, to draw the line against his encroachments.[9]

Cecil Gray, a musician friend of the Lawrences during the last years of the war, argued that Lawrence shared with Hitler 'the same dark, passionate, fanatical power, the same capacity for casting spells',[10] and Bertrand Russell went so far as to declare that Lawrence's ideas about blood-consciousness led 'straight to Auschwitz'.[11]

D.H. Lawrence never actually attached himself to real-life dictators nor became a dictator himself. But he sought and created fantasy leaders in his fiction. His antidemocratic notions link him with other, widely disparate British and American writers of the period – Yeats, Lewis, Eliot, and Pound[12] – and place him in a certain intellectual tradition originating, perhaps, with the ancient Greeks. In July 1915 Lawrence read a book on early Greek philosophy and wrote to Bertrand Russell, who had lent him the book, 'You must drop all your democracy. You must not believe in "the people" . . . There must be an aristocracy of people who have wisdom, and there must be a Ruler: a Kaiser: no Presidents and democracies. I shall write out Herakleitos, on tablets of bronze.' Of course Lawrence was familiar with similar nineteenth- and twentieth-century thinkers: among them, Carlyle, with his cult of the hero; Ruskin, with his idea of the paternal state; Nietzsche, with his Superman (the emblem of Zarathustra, prophet of the Superman, is a plumed serpent). With such thinkers Lawrence believed that the hero is the chief determinant of the course of history. He wrote to Dollie Radford, in late 1916, 'I firmly believe that the pure desire of the strong creates the great events, without any action: like the prayer of the saints . . . What the world needs to learn, today, is to give due honour to those who are finer in spirit, and to know the inferiority of those who are mean and paltry in spirit.' Eric Bentley states that Carlyle and Nietzsche, in their later work, 'shriek, bully, and exaggerate because no one will listen'.[13] So, too, Lawrence in his leadership period harangued and assaulted his readers and produced the works for which he earns no laurels. At times the carelessness, even disorder, of his language seems symptomatic of a psychological breakdown. The subject matter makes many readers uncomfortable, especially as it gives voice to antisocial urges that Lawrence expressed as early as 1915, when he wrote, 'Sometimes I wish I could let go and be really wicked – kill and murder – but kill chiefly. I do want to kill. But I want to select whom I shall kill. Then I shall enjoy it.'[14] Surely Lawrence had been driven bellicose, if not mad, by the banning of *The Rainbow* and the wartime persecution perpetrated on him by what he saw as mob rule and mass taste.

Gradually Lawrence carried his ideal of male leadership to an extreme in the decade between 1915 and 1925; it was from this extreme, and not from the basic issue, that Lawrence later turned away. The extreme is human sacrifice. What one finds in the leadership works, time and time again, are ruminations about the dark gods' requirements of blood. In

The Lost Girl, Lawrence states that 'the gods who had demanded human sacrifice were quite right, immutably right. The fierce, savage gods who dipped their lips in blood, these were the true gods'. And in *Kangaroo* he adds, 'to be pure in heart, man must listen to the dark gods as well as to the white gods, to the call of blood-sacrifice as well as to the eucharist.' Human sacrifice of one sort or another occurs in *The Fox*, *The Captain's Doll*, *The Plumed Serpent*, and 'The Woman Who Rode Away'. But psychic as well as physical sacrifice occurs just as frequently, and the misogyny implicit in both kinds of sacrifice is emphasised in *The Plumed Serpent*, when Kate Leslie is instructed to submit totally to her husband Cipriano: 'Was this the knife to which she must be sheath?' Keith Sagar notes that Kate's 'marriage to Cipriano is seen by the novel as equivalent to the death of the woman who rode away'.[15] In *The Lost Girl*, too, Alvina's sexual contact with Ciccio spells her annihilation: 'And he killed her. He simply took her and assassinated her.' Later, as Mrs Marasca, Alvina realises that 'it was *his* will which counted. Alvina, as his wife, must submit'. Ultimately she makes the firmest possible commitment when she says to her husband, 'I love you, even if it kills me.'

In his later works Lawrence renounced the call to blood-sacrifice; the phallus as the source of regeneration replaces the dark gods, and erection equals resurrection in such stories as 'Sun', *Lady Chatterley's Lover*, and *The Man Who Died*. But the basic, even desperate, belief in male dominance occupied him to the very last. Although after 1925 Lawrence no longer embodied either his destructive urge or his leadership ideal in sanctioned religious or political systems, in his fiction the phallus always demands annihilation in the sense of complete capitulation of woman to man. Lawrence did not repudiate the 'lead on I follow, *ich dien* sort of business' in 1927, his statement notwithstanding. He had let go of the quasi-religious, philosophical, and political belief in the necessity for death before resurrection, emphasising instead the physical cycle of tumescence and detumescence; but this emphasis on the life force cannot quite overshadow the same urge to destroy the Magna Mater that had marked – and marred – his earlier works.

One factor militating against acceptance of Lawrence's tribal partiarchy is his arbitrary distinction between 'bullying' and power or leadership. His use of animals is intimately associated with this distinction. As early as 1915, in the posthumously published essay 'The Crown', Lawrence had set up a dichotomy between wild, often dangerous, animals and domesticated animals, assigning to them the respective modes of power and love. Animals appear continually in the fictional works, as trope and as symbol; in fact, the first novel is entitled *The White Peacock*, the bird figure embodying the vanity and spirituality of modern woman. But the peacock itself plays a small part in this early novel, and Lawrence makes it carry a symbolic burden too great for it to support. Not until 1921 did animals become the controlling symbols in Lawrence's fiction, and accordingly he then gave his works animal titles. Especially in *The Fox*, *Kangaroo*, and *The Plumed Serpent*, human power struggles seem to gain the sanctions of the wild state, in which animals kill – but do not murder. Similarly, male dominance is seen as the 'natural' state; often what females do is 'bully' – that is, self-consciously exert their wills – and what males do is 'lead'. And the feminine, bullying will, for all Lawrence's talk of a rainbow reconciliation of opposites, or a star polarity, needs to be eliminated.

Lawrence confuses the issue when he assigns the wolf as totem to Gerald Crich in *Women in Love*, for although Gerald recognises the need for a man of new values to save the modern world, he is himself a bully with a machine mentality. Yet Lawrence's ultimate judgment is against that form of bullying accomplished through the ideal of love, or 'spiritual incest' as he calls it. Women do not alone ascribe to this ideal – Walt Whitman, with his 'merging', refutes such a simpleminded notion – but they are the primary offenders. The Eden that Lady Chatterley and her lover enjoy in the woods is not only a paradise of uninhibited sexuality; it represents an escape for Connie from 'the strange dominion and obsession of *other women*. How awful they were, women', and an escape for Mellors from the 'ghastly female will' of Bertha Coutts. The animal of Lawrence's last two novels – the cock – is as little a real animal as the peacock of the first: it is clearly the phallus, liberated from the demands of spiritual love and ready to conquer the world.[16]

In the fiction of his leadership period, and even afterward, Lawrence's overreaction to the 'devouring mother' caused him to create leaders who themselves act as 'devouring mothers', fostering their followers' dependence upon them and tolerating no deviation from strict adherence to their tenets. In the heterosexual love relationship, the capacity for intimacy as Lawrence depicts it leads most often not to mutuality but to exploitation of one by the other, a situation that he deplored in the mother–child relation. Occasionally Lawrence does portray a strong (as opposed to domineering) mother – Juliet in 'Sun' comes to mind – but it is the sun, the male principle of 'father-spark', that has taught Juliet how to parent. Instinctual good mothering seems to abound for Lawrence only in the wild animal kingdom, among she-wolves, for instance. The one human mother who seems to live by she-wolf principles is Mrs Barlow in the play *Touch and Go* (1920), but she is too sketchily drawn, and her son too weak, for her to exemplify model motherhood. On the whole the animal kingdom provided Lawrence with role models for fathers rather than for mothers, especially in his leadership period, with its foxes and plumed serpents (its kangaroo, large of foot and thigh, shows promise of wise fatherhood, but its smothering pouch is suspiciously maternal). Although Lawrence credited both male and female children with a 'father-spark', he was largely unwilling to credit females with the ability to use theirs wisely. Unfortunately, the rigidity of Lawrence's mother–father roles led to a dangerous idealisation of particular males.

Yet if Lawrence's solution to the problem of maternal domination is suspect, his analysis of the problem is no less significant and the problem itself is no less real. Because of his particular family constellation in its particular Victorian setting, Lawrence was preoccupied with the parent–child relation. Indeed, it is more central to his canon that the male–female sexual relation for which he is commonly known. But Lawrence's statements on good parenting have value beyond autobiography or cultural biography. As we have seen, psychoanalytic thinking since Freud has emphasised the early dependence of the child upon the mother and the centrality of the pre-oedipal conflict between dependency and autonomy to the child's psychological development. Although the extremes of father worship to which Lawrence was led are abnormal, the basic urge toward the father is normal indeed. Margaret Mahler's work with children suggests that during the practicing subphase of separation–individuation, the child's world expands to include other people besides the mother, most notably the father. When the mother is overprotective and unable to let go, the father is in an ideal position to 'rescue' the child, for the father stands outside the mother–child symbiosis but not so far outside as to be unfamiliar and frightening. Even if the mother does not feel the need to live through her children, having enough life and independence of her own, a strong father figure is still desirable – in fact, necessary – in providing the child a way to get beyond the primary caretaker: he aids the child in achieving a sense of autonomy. Sensing the difference between the parents, very young children (so Mahler has found) often show fear at their mothers' playful attempts to seize them for games or fondling, yet will seek and enjoy similar romping with and handling by their fathers. The object of the fear is interpreted as engulfment by the 'devouring mother' (Mahler, *The Psychological Birth of the Human Infant*, p. 118). Some children resolve the *rapprochement* crisis not so much by coming to terms with the mother as by turning to the father, who is less ambivalently loved; this solution is only temporary, however, since the relationship with the mother must eventually be faced and separation struggles with her resolved (Ibid., p. 129).

Research into the role of the father in the pre-oedipal years is relatively recent, but it demonstrates conclusively the importance of the father to early childhood development. In Ernest Abelin's terms, children possess a 'father thirst'[17] – a desire and need for connection with their fathers. Lawrence terms this psychological reality the 'father-spark' and gives it a physical basis in *Fantasia of the Unconscious*. The movement in Lawrence's writing culminating in the patriarchal ideal of leadership shows what can happen when the father thirst is not slaked early in life: the thirst may be quenchable only by a flood that threatens the very life it is supposed to save. The matter of a father's role in the child's early development and subsequent life course bears as well on the controversial issue of D. H. Lawrence's homosexual tendencies (as suggested in the suppressed prologue to *Women in Love*[18] and certain remarks of Frieda Lawrence and others).[19] One psychoanalyst, Charles Socarides, pinpoints the nuclear conflict of homosexuality as the wish to merge with the mother versus the dread of ego dissolution that this merger signifies; the homosexual has never progressed adequately from the mother–child symbiotic unity to separation–individuation. Socarides states that

> . . . [i]n all homosexual cases [female as well as male] there is an insatiable yearning for the father which the patient may have suppressed or repressed for years . . . This yearning is a plaintive cry for the father whom the patient unconsciously feels to be his only source of help in his fight against the phenomenon of engulfment and merging with the mother. The importance of the father to the child's psychological development cannot be overestimated.[20]

Lawrence's letters and literature, the memoirs about him by friends and enemies, and psychological studies of the mother–child relation in general – all of these underscore the importance of the 'devouring mother' figure for understanding D.H. Lawrence's life and art. Because the connection between this figure and Lawrence's patriarchal ideal of male leadership is most clearly manifested in the works of Lawrence's middle years – his leadership period – these works offer important keys to the Lawrence canon; far from being anomalies, they are as deeply concerned with personal power relationships as the earlier and later works. The urge to leadership and the eventual embrace of the dark gods may be seen as facets of Lawrence's pre-oedipal, ambivalent relationship with his mother, which Joseph Rheingold terms 'the most basic of all human conflicts'.[21]

In a sense, Lawrence demythologises the institution of motherhood by debunking the notion of unadulterated and wholly beneficial maternal devotion. His demythologising of motherhood leads naturally to a reassessment and revaluation of fatherhood, freeing the male to assume parenthood of his children and to show his nurturant side without being considered 'womanish'. Lawrence's own tender yet firm ways with children have been documented by many who knew him, but Tom Brangwen's relationship with his stepdaughter Anna, in *The Rainbow*, stands out as perhaps the single depiction of a meaningful father–child relationship in Lawrence's fiction. In his leadership period, Lawrence stressed the importance of the father in the family constellation, as an alternative to the mother and her smothering love. Readers who wish to make instructive use of Lawrence's rage against women may view his homicidal fantasies as symbolic murder of the 'bad' or 'devouring' mother,[22] and his worship of the dark gods as recognition of the father's importance in the child's development of an autonomous self.

For both the mother and the father, good parenting as Lawrence forcefully and helpfully defines it includes the wisdom and the self-control to leave the child adequate space or growing room, while still providing nurturance. Lawrence's lifelong emphasis on striking the proper balance between protectiveness and respect for the integrity of each individual tempers somewhat the shrill excesses of his leadership period, and remains the emphasis that ensures his works' lasting value.

Notes

1. MARY FREEMAN, *D.H. Lawrence: A Basic Study of His Ideas* (Gainesville: University of Florida Press, 1955), p. 253, n. 5.

2. ERNEST TEDLOCK, *D.H. Lawrence: Artist and Rebel* (Albuquerque: University of New Mexico Press, 1963), pp. 128, 166.

3. See, for example, KEITH SAGAR, *The Art of D.H. Lawrence* (Cambridge: Cambridge University Press, 1966), p. 109.

4. MARGARET S. MAHLER, FRED PINE, and ANNI BERGMAN, *The Psychological Birth of the Human Infant* (New York: Basic Books, 1975), p. 48.

5. It is interesting to speculate about the extent to which the characters in the story 'Sun' are modeled on the family of Martin Secker, Lawrence's British publisher at the time. From the Villa Bernarda Lawrence wrote to Secker about Secker's wife Rina and his eighteen-month-old son Adrian, who were visiting in Sportorno:

   > Rina usually comes with Adrian in the afternoon. She is much better now, was very *nervosa* at first . . . Adrian is not 'in the pink' but the scarlet. He is very bonnie, and growing fast, and perfectly happy and chirpy here . . . When Rina can leave the boy for a few hours with her mother, and get a good walk in the hills with us all, she will be perfectly happy all right.

   These remarks suggest at least a partial resemblance between Rina and Adrian and the mother and child in 'Sun'; by extension, the implied comparison between Secker himself and the character of the husband, Maurice, is distinctly unflattering. But – had he been asked – Lawrence probably would have explained patiently to Secker, as he had explained about Compton Mackenzie's relationship to Lawrence's story 'The Man Who Loved Islands', that Secker's family 'only *suggests* the idea – it's no portrait'. Lawrence obviously had an interest in these people and inquired about 'Rina and the boy' to the end of his life. See D. H. Lawrence, *Letters to Martin Secker, 1911–1930* (Buckingham: Martin Secker, 1970), pp. 68, 88.

6. HARRY T. MOORE, *The Priest of Love: a Life of D.H. Lawrence* (New York: Farrar, Straus, & Giroux, 1974), p. 12.

7. The female web is discussed by CAROL GILLIGAN in *In a Different Voice: Psychological Theory and Women's Development* (Cambridge, Mass.: Harvard University Press, 1982).

8. For a discussion of paternalism see RICHARD SENNETT, *Authority* (New York: Knopf, 1980). Technically Lawrence's ideal of leadership should be termed paternalistic rather than patriarchal, since in a patriarchy the leader is related to his followers by blood ties.

9. PAUL DELANY, *D.H. Lawrence's Nightmare: the Writer and His Circle in the Years of the Great War* (New York: Basic Books, 1978), pp. 301, 205.

10. CECIL GRAY, *Musical Chairs* (London: Home and Van Thal, 1948), pp. 130–1.

11. BERTRAND RUSSELL, *Autobiography*, 2 vols (Boston: Little, Brown, 1951), vol. 2, p. 13.

12. See JOHN HARRISON, *The Reactionaries: Yeats, Lewis, Pound, Eliot, Lawrence, A Study of the Anti-Democratic Intelligensia* (New York: Schocken, 1967).

13. ERIC BENTLEY, *A Century of Hero-Worship*, 2nd edn (Boston: Beacon Press, 1957), p. 162.

14. D.H. LAWRENCE, *Letters*, ed. Aldous Huxley (London: William Heinemann, 1932), p. 237.

15. SAGAR, *Art of D.H. Lawrence*, p. 167.

16. The poetry of Lawrence's leadership period, collected in *Birds, Beasts and Flowers*, by and large escapes the onus of being an inferior Lawrence production, even though the work concerns the nonhuman realm that usually allowed Lawrence the freedom to act less than human. Sandra Gilbert explores the connection between the ideal of leadership and the overall success of this poetry in *Acts of Attention: the Poems of D.H. Lawrence* (Ithaca: Cornell University Press, 1972), pp. 128–9.

17. See 'The Role of the Father in the Preoedipal Years', report of the annual meeting of the American Psychoanalytic Association, April 1977, in the *Journal of the American Psychoanalytic Association*, **26** (1978): 143–61.

18. In *Phoenix II: Uncollected, Unpublished, and Other Prose Works by D.H. Lawrence*, ed. Warren Roberts and Harry T. Moore (New York: Viking Press, Compass Books, 1970), pp. 92–108.

19. MOORE, *Priest of Love*, pp. 59–63.

20. CHARLES W. SOCARIDES, *The Overt Homosexual* (New York: Grune & Stratton, 1968), p. 226.

21. JOSEPH C. RHEINGOLD, *The Mother, Anxiety, and Death: the Catastrophic Death Complex* (Boston: Little, Brown, 1967), p. 18.

22. CAROLYN G. HEILBRUN reinterprets the murder of Clytemnestra in this fashion in *Reinventing Womanhood* (New York: W.W. Norton, 1979), p. 154. Marina Warner demythologises the Virgin Mary in a similar fashion and for similar reasons in *Alone of All Her Sex: The Myth and Cult of the Virgin Mary* (New York: Knopf, 1976).

9 Lawrence, Foucault, and the Language of Sexuality (*Lady Chatterley's Lover*)*

LYDIA BLANCHARD

Lydia Blanchard is Associate Professor of English at South-West Texas State University where she has served as Director of Women's Studies and Acting Director of the Centre for the Study of the South-West. She is a member of the editorial board of *The D.H. Lawrence Review* and President Elect of the D.H. Lawrence Society of North America. Whilst herself clearly influenced by feminist thought, Blanchard wrote the 1975 essay, 'Love and Power: a reconsideration of sexual politics in D.H. Lawrence' (see Introduction, Note 17, for details), which sought to rescue Lawrence and his treatment of women from the wilder excesses of the post-Millett debates. Like Judith Ruderman (see Chapter 8), she has also approached Lawrence from a psychoanalytic perspective ('Women in Love: Mourning Becomes Narcissism', *Mosaic: A Journal for the Interdisciplinary Study of Literature* (winter 1982): 105–18), and in the piece reproduced here, she draws on and partly rebuts Michel Foucault's comments on Lawrence (see Introduction, pp. 16, 21). In her continuous attempt to deploy feminist, psychoanalytic and post-structuralist approaches to Lawrence's fiction, Blanchard seeks positively to enhance our understanding of its depth and complexity.

Lydia Blanchard has published extensively on Lawrence in journals and collections of essays, as well as on feminist literary criticism and on other British writers such as George Orwell and Virginia Woolf. Her current research interests include Lawrence and *l'écriture feminine*, and Lawrence's experiences in the American South-West.

* Reprinted from Michael Squires and Dennis Jackson (eds), *D.H. Lawrence's 'Lady': a New Look at Lady Chatterley's Lover* (Athens, Georgia: University of Georgia Press, 1985), pp. 17–35; a number of parenthetical references to Lawrence's works in the text have been omitted.

And I, who loathe sexuality so deeply, am considered a lurid sexuality specialist.

(D.H. Lawrence to Dr Trigant Burrow, 1926)

Near the end of 'A Propos of *Lady Chatterley's Lover*', D. H. Lawrence recounts the story of the timid Florentine critic who cautioned him about the novel, 'I don't know – I don't know – if it's not a bit too strong. . . . Listen, Signor Lawrence, you find it really necessary to *say* it?' Lawrence records his characteristically testy response, 'I told him I did', and the Florentine's reaction, 'he pondered' (*Phoenix II*, p. 515).

Ponder he should. If more than fifty years after the publication of *Lady Chatterley* the critic's question no longer interests us, if it appears not only timid but ingenuous, the reason is that we rest in a false complacency, assuming that we have been freed from the repression felt by the Florentine. Fearing neither pornography nor censorship, we discount the question's obvious concern with both, cheer Lawrence for helping us overcome the 'censor-morons', and look no further. But in the first volume of *The History of Sexuality* (1978), French philosopher Michel Foucault has also quoted from 'A Propos' Lawrence's argument that it is 'now our business . . . to realise sex. Today the full conscious realisation of sex is even more important than the act itself' – and Foucault has pondered, like the Florentine critic, the significance of Lawrence's decision. For Foucault the necessity that Lawrence found to *say* it is central to a preoccupation of the modern world which, Foucault predicts, will surely puzzle future generations.

> Perhaps one day people will wonder at [Lawrence's concern]. They will not be able to understand how a civilisation so intent on developing enormous instruments of production and destruction found the time and the infinite patience to inquire so anxiously concerning the actual state of sex; people will smile perhaps when they recall that here were men – meaning ourselves – who believed that therein resided a truth every bit as precious as the one they had already demanded from the earth, the stars, and the pure forms of their thought; people will be surprised at the eagerness with which we went about pretending to rouse from its slumber a sexuality which everything – our discourses, our customs, our institutions, our regulations, our knowledges – was busy producing in the light of day and broadcasting to noisy accompaniment. And people will ask themselves why we were so bent on ending the rule of silence regarding what was the noisiest of our preoccupations.[1]

For Foucault, Lawrence is an example, perhaps the paradigmatic example, of those who have misunderstood the nature of discourse, of those who have misunderstood the relationship between the language in which we talk about sex and the repression of sexuality. In the essay 'A Preface to Transgression', which first appeared in 1963, Foucault challenges the modern wisdom that by bringing sexuality into discourse we have regained for it 'full truth as a process of nature, a truth which has long been lingering in the shadows and hiding under various disguises – until now, that is, when our positive awareness allows us to decipher it so that it may at last emerge in the clear light of language'.[2] By bringing sexuality into the clear light of language, Foucault argues, we have succeeded only in controlling and thus repressing it. Like the inspector in one of Foucault's favourite images, the Panoptican of Jeremy Bentham, we have been made prisoner by what we bring under our gaze; our sexuality is trapped by the language meant to free it; rather than liberating sexuality we have 'carried it to its limits: the limit of consciousness, because it ultimately dictates the only possible reading of our unconscious . . . the limit of language, since it traces that line of foam showing just how far speech may advance upon the sands of silence'.[3] Repression created our modern understanding of sexuality, and without repression sexuality loses rather than gains power.

And yet Foucault underestimates Lawrence – if not Lawrence's readers. It is true that *Lady Chatterley's Lover* remains fixed in the public mind with the battle against prudery and censorship, with the fight both to destroy the sexual restrictions of the Victorian age and to affirm the phallic reality of the body – readings of the novel certainly strengthened by the recent film *Priest of Love*. But for a novel associated in the public mind almost exclusively with sexuality, *Lady Chatterley's Lover* has also seemed, for many of its critics, curiously unsatisfactory on the subject of sex. If this dissatisfaction has manifested itself in different ways, underlying them all is uncertainty about how to read the work as a *whole* – about how to integrate the passages describing intercourse into the rest of the novel. As Scott Sanders has argued, 'The insistent realism of the sexual descriptions prevents us from reading *Lady Chatterley* simply as a fable. Yet read as realism the novel appears either trivial or simply wrong-headed.'[4]

Trivial, wrongheaded, quaint, silly, embarrassing – the negative litany voiced by the novel's critics is long. Certainly the passages descriptive of intercourse must be confusing, or why else the critical debates about what Lawrence is describing, much less advocating? The best-known criticism of the novel is still the attempt to determine the exact positions of the lady and her lover in the dark mysteries of the novel's final night of lovemaking. Although engaging some of our most astute critics in not one but three of our finest journals, the question of what the lady was up to remains unanswered – a failure of criticism that must come as a surprise to a general public who, even if they do not approve of the novel, certainly think they know what it is about.[5]

If the intensity of the critical debate on what is happening has led to some quite uncollegial name-calling, how much more angry we have become with each other about what we think Lawrence (or at least the novel) is advocating about sex. Is the emphasis on the importance of male sexuality, 'those modes of belief and manners of sex which men display in their various ways of "loving"'? Or is Lawrence rather interested in 'the imaginative rendering of a woman's sexual experience'? Does the novel advocate a passive woman or mutual orgasm? the 'apocalyptic possibility of conception' or the Italian way?[6]

Such difficulties with understanding and explaining the passages of intercourse are so great, in fact, that many readers have chosen to ignore the novel's treatment of sex altogether, a critical evasion that would surely have puzzled the novel's early censors. Numerous studies of the work either do not discuss or else minimise the importance of the sections that describe intercourse, instead treating *Lady Chatterley's Lover* as a version of the utopian or the pastoral, as a retelling of myth or medieval romance, as a philosophical tract concerned with epistemology – treating the novel, in other words, as if it were a discourse on anything but sexuality, as if (reversing the nineteenth-century convention) sexuality were itself metaphor.[7] Given the general success of these readings – they are for the most part lucid, convincing, internally consistent, compatible – even Lawrence's most sympathetic critics have concluded that *Lady Chatterley's Lover* as a whole is a failure; that because its passages of sexuality are not integrated into the rest of the novel, it falls short of the earlier works, in particular *The Rainbow* and *Women in Love*; that these passages can most generally be explained as Lawrence's attempt to reconcile himself with Frieda and to deal with his own impotence; that Lawrence fails in his attempt, however admirable, to create a language of the feelings, to achieve the full conscious realisation of sex.

In fact, many critics argue that Lawrence would have done well to listen to himself, to his own bitter indictment of a sterile Wragby that destroyed sex by talking about it; that he should have heeded his own indictments about the life of the mind, surely some of the most bitter in his canon: 'don't, with the nasty, prying mind, drag [sex] out from its deeps / and finger it and force it, and shatter the rhythm it keeps / when it's left alone, as it stirs and rouses and sleeps' – or more briefly, 'sex, alas, gets dirtier and dirtier, worked from the mind'.[8] These critics see the failure of the novel, as Sanders argues, in the fundamental contradiction implicit in Lawrence's use of 'tools of consciousness to define and defend the unconscious'.[9] Given Lawrence's attitude about the mental life, how could the novel be a 'declaration of the phallic reality'? How indeed can one declare that which loses force as it is declared?

How much better, these critics seem to say, if Lawrence had restricted himself to the conventions of his earlier works in which, operating in the tradition of the romantic novel, he drew on metaphor, imagery, even apparently asexual dialogue and plot to suggest both the experience of and the response to sex, the artistic decision informing such scenes as Miriam on the swing, the flowers crushed in Paul's meeting with Clara, the sheaf-gathering of *The Rainbow*, and the brutal passion of horse and rabbit in *Women in Love* – brilliant passages affirming Lawrence's ability to re-create the power of sexuality without submitting it to the cold light of explicit description.

Such reactions to those very passages that have brought *Lady Chatterley* much of its fame and many of its readers might well be attributed to the general perversity of critics. But as attractive as such an explanation might be (what adolescent ever had trouble with *Lady Chatterley*?), it does little to solve the very real tensions involved in the novel and, in fact, in all of Lawrence's work. Even the most casual readers of Lawrence, even careful readers of only this last novel, are aware that Lawrence has a fundamental interest in the relationship between language and sexuality that goes far beyond fighting the 'censor-morons'. Indeed, Lawrence would have condemned readers like Gay Talese who praise the novel for freeing us from our Victorian repression to enjoy the world of *Thy Neighbor's Wife*. Lawrence lashed out at the censors, but he did not write *Lady Chatterley's Lover* to open literature to Erica Jong and *The Executioner's Song*. Many readers, including Foucault, underestimate Lawrence's interest in the relationship between language and sexuality.

Lawrence was certainly interested in the full conscious realisation of sex, but that interest was, for him as for Foucault, part of a broader concern with what it means to bring sexuality into discourse, part of a broader interest in the relation between language, sexuality, power and knowledge. If Lawrence's thinking on these subjects is presented in a way less systematic than that of French critics like Foucault and Roland Barthes, Lawrence's work, in particular *Lady Chatterley's Lover*, not only addresses the same concerns but also clarifies much of what we now understand about language and its pecular relation to sexuality.

Recent French criticism has argued the centrality of language to human communication, maintaining 'that no other meaning-system can manage without its aid' and 'that human beings organise virtually all their experiences along linguistic lines', but the work of Barthes and Foucault in particular has suggested a more complex relationship of language to sexuality.[10] If, as in other meaning systems, the experience of sexuality must be understood through language structures, the rhythm of sexuality itself also underlies these structures – as the rhythm of life underlies Lawrence's argument in 'A Propos'. Robert Scholes has maintained, 'It is in . . . the various periodicities of sperm production, menstruation, courtship, and coitus, that our sense of narrative structure is itself generated.'[11]

In his recent writing, therefore, Foucault has shifted from a vocabulary centering on the *episteme*, a discursive concept, to an approach centering on the *apparatus*, a concept both discursive and nondiscursive, a system of relations that Foucault maintains goes beyond discourse and that reflects a new recognition of structures that are outside of language.[12] Arguing that '*I-love-you* belongs neither in the realm of linguistics nor in that of semiology', Barthes has suggested music as its occasion ('the point of departure for speaking it'),[13] and both he and Foucault echo Lawrence's warnings of the dangers of bringing sexuality into language. 'To try to write love is to confront the *muck* of language: that region of hysteria where language is both *too much* and *too little*, excessive . . . and impoverished', Barthes writes, and if he can regard the situation with some good humor (in intercourse 'the Image-repertoire goes to the devil'),[14] Foucault in his word choice more closely approaches the frequent bitterness of Lawrence: for Foucault, language has 'absorbed' our sexuality, 'denatured' it, 'cast [it] into an empty zone'.[15]

Lawrence's understanding of the relationship between sexuality and language is complex. Often he simply rejects the structuralist emphasis on language (as, for example, in the late poem 'If ever there was a beginning / there was no god in it / there was no Verb / no Voice / no Word').[16] On occasion he also considers how the loss of language is related to the loss of emotion. In the short story 'The Man Who Loved Islands', for example, Lawrence portrays a hero who increasingly withdraws from language and thus from his humanity. Because Cathcart is unable to register his own feelings, his feelings cease to exist: 'He looked stupidly over the whiteness of his foreign island, over the waste of the lifeless sea.'[17] Most frequently, however, Lawrence recognises that the sexual rhythms of the body underlie language; these rhythms, when they are brought into discourse, are controlled rather than freed.

Indeed, part of Lawrence's increased absorption in painting in the last years of his life may stem from the terrible risks he saw in bringing sexuality into discourse, risks made clear in the sterile intellectual discussions at Wragby. His letters about the progress of *Lady Chatterley* are filled with references to his simultaneous attempts to capture the phallic self on canvas. 'It is fun to paint', he affirms, even though in their portrayal of sexuality his paintings are 'worse' (more shocking to the public) than his writing. In May 1928, while working on the last proofs of *Lady Chatterley*, he told Mark Gertler, 'One's got to get back to the live, really lovely phallic self, and phallic consciousness. I think I get a certain phallic beauty in my pictures too. I know they're rolling with faults . . .' But there's something *there*'.

Why then, we must surely ask (but not as timidly as the Florentine critic), why *did* Lawrence say it in *Lady Chatterley*? Or, of more recent writers, why did Barthes write *A Lover's Discourse*? And Foucault enter into a six-volume *History of Sexuality*? Why bring into discourse an experience that will presumably lose from its expression in language? Why study the effects of such a discourse? 'O know yourself, O know your sex!' Lawrence affirmed. 'You must know sex in order to save it, your deepest self, from the rape / of the itching mind and the mental self, with its pruriency always agape.'[18] As Barthes uses the language of eroticism to describe the pleasure of the text, and Foucault traces the history of sexuality to rescue it from its history, so Lawrence exhausts the language of sexuality to return that language to the area where he had always argued it belonged – to the darkness, to silence, to oblivion. 'Man knows nothing / till he knows how not-to-know. / . . . The end of all knowledge is oblivion / sweet, dark oblivion, when I cease / even from myself, and am consummated.'[19] And so Mellors writes in his final letter to Lady Chatterley, in the ignored last pages of the novel, 'So many words, because I can't touch you. If I could sleep with my arms round you, the ink could stay in the bottle'.

Lawrence then is as interested as Foucault in the question of why sexuality has been brought into discourse, and the effect that such bringing of sexuality into the language has on its control; and like Foucault he has traced – though not so extensively – the cultural reasons that underlie this change in Western consciousness. Arguing that ideas of sexuality and sex are historically recent (before the eighteenth century flesh alone mattered), Foucault poses the question, 'What had to happen in the history of the West for the question of truth to be posed in regard to sexual pleasure?'[20] Cultural institutions themselves created the need for the discourse, developing a vocabulary by which sexuality could be controlled. For Foucault the emphasis – at least in the work to date – is on the role of the confessional ('all those procedures by which the subject is incited to produce a discourse of truth about his sexuality which is capable of having effects on the subject himself');[21] for Lawrence the emphasis is on medicine, and he argues in 'Introduction to These Paintings' that the growth of the spiritual–mental consciousness of sexuality came through fear of syphilis, which entered the blood and then the consciousness during the Renaissance, hitting the vital imagination and turning man into an 'ideal being' (*Phoenix*, pp. 551–9).

Both Lawrence and Foucault see the bringing of sexuality into discourse as contemporaneous with the death of the religious feeling: 'The language of sexuality has lifted us into the night where God is absent', Foucault writes. 'On the day that sexuality began to speak and to be spoken, language no longer served as a veil for the infinite; and in the thickness it acquired on that day, we now experience finitude and being.'[22] Sexuality is one of the areas of darkness that the Enlightenment brought into the light; to do so meant not only to create a language through which a variety of institutions – for example, the church (through the confessional), medicine (through textbook descriptions of treatment), the law (through a definition of the illegal) – could control sexuality, but also to create, through that repression, a recognition of sexuality itself, giving to sexuality a power that it did not have before the discourse of repression. 'Sexuality, through thus becoming an object of analysis and concern, surveillance and control, engenders at the same time an intensification of each individual's desire, for, in and over his body.'[23] We have failed to see the positive effects of repression, Foucault argues; just as madness must exist for reason to exist, so repression must exist for sexuality to have power. And so Lawrence writes that one result of freeing sexuality from repression is chastity: 'Great is my need to be chaste / and apart, in this cerebral age.'[24]

Lady Chatterley's Lover thus becomes an important fictional treatment – perhaps our most important fictional treatment – of the relationship between power, language and sexuality. To deal with this relationship Lawrence had to develop formal innovations in *Lady Chatterley* as significant as those in *The Rainbow* and *Women in Love*, innovations that make special demands on the reader who tries to naturalise the text (that is, to bring it within conventions which, as Jonathan Culler has explained, enable the writing 'to speak to us').[25] Striving for *vraisemblance*, the 'principle of integration between one discourse and another or several others',[26] we are constantly dislocated by *Lady Chatterley*, in particular by the passages of explicit sex. But this is because we are reading the novel within the wrong conventions, trying to naturalise it in relation to Lawrence's earlier fiction as well as to what we understand as the mimetic quality of the novel of realism. To naturalise *Lady Chatterley* as a text, however – 'to bring it into relation with a type of discourse or model which is already, in some sense, natural and legible'[27] – is to see the novel as drawing simultaneously on a variety of genres.

A choice of genre is, of course, one way to naturalise the text, establishing a tacit contract between writer and reader 'to make certain relevant expectations operative and thus to permit both compliance with and deviation from accepted modes of intelligibility'.[28] Nearly all criticism that has found *Lady Chatterley's Lover* flawed as a novel has argued the lack of *vraisemblance* on the level of genre, but Culler points out that generic *vraisemblance* is only one way to naturalise a text; a text may also be read as an exposing of 'the artifice of generic conventions and expectations'.[29] On such a level the text finds 'its coherence by being interpreted as a narrator's exercise of language and production of meaning. To naturalise it at this level is to read it as a statement about the writing of novels, a critique of mimetic fiction, an illustration of the production of a world by language.' To introduce opposing conventions of genre is to bring about 'a change in the mode of reading' and to look for a synthesis at a higher level.

It is a process of naturalisation in that what seemed difficult or strange is made natural (a blur so natural as to pass unnoticed) by locating a proper level of *vraisemblance*. And this level is a repertoire of projects. Even the most radical readings of literary works propose a project from whose vantage point the blur becomes clear or natural: the project of illustrating or enacting the practice of writing.[30]

It is to this project – the illustration and enactment of the practice of writing – that Lawrence addresses himself in *Lady Chatterley's Lover*, in particular to the practice of writing about sexuality, and in the process he makes extraordinary demands on the reader.

In part, Lawrence makes these demands through his use of language play and parody, perhaps most noticeably in the extensive allusions in dialogue to a variety of writers (Whitman and Shakespeare, for example) and forms of writing (for example, poetry, the Bible, hymns, and other novels). If *Lady Chatterley* in its close attention to detail often is within the tradition of the nineteenth-century novel, its traditional passages are also interspersed, unpredictably, with parody of the literary tradition. We are reminded of the courtly tradition through references to Sir Malcolm's knighthood when Sir Malcolm is at his lewdest, talking about his daughter with Mellors. We are reminded of the limits of modern theater through Michaelis and of modern fiction through Clifford Chatterley himself. Mellors is equated in village gossip to the Marquis de Sade, undermining the significance of both men; Clifford writes letters that Lady Chatterley finds uninteresting because they are good, thus questioning the value of the epistolary tradition. The examples abound, as George Levine has argued, calling *Lady Chatterley's Lover*, not surprisingly, a novel that is 'importantly about novel writing': 'In *Lady Chatterley's Lover*, [Lawrence] creates a work that resonates parodically with the now dead traditions of realism. . . . It stands in parodic relation to the tradition of moral–aesthetic realism, while itself (good parody that it is) belonging to that tradition.'[31] But there is more. For while Lawrence was creating a language for the feelings through the passages of lovemaking, he was also using those passages to parody not only traditional forms but also his own earlier works – to question through imitation (so that he can later reaffirm) the power of those works.

Read within the context of Lawrence's earlier fiction, for example, the first passage in which Lady Chatterley and Mellors have intercourse suggests a novel like *Women in Love* in which Lawrence creates the experience of sexuality through animal imagery: as horse and rabbit suggest the brutality and cruelty of the love that Gerald and Gudrun will experience with each other, so the newborn chick suggests the tenderness of the love that will be manifested between Lady Chatterley and Mellors. But in *Women in Love* Lawrence separated the animal scenes from the lovemaking of Gerald and Gudrun, and the different scenes gain power from the suggestions that they carry back and forth. In *Lady Chatterley* Lawrence brings the two together and the power of both is significantly different. While the chick retains its brilliance as an image of the new birth that will come through love, the language through which Lady Chatterley's 'tormented modern-woman's brain' tries to understand the significance of the experience is lugubrious and ponderous: 'Why was this necessary? Why had it lifted a great cloud from her and given her peace? Was it real? Was it real? . . . Was it real?' Similarly, on their second occasion of intercourse, Lady Chatterley's will keeps her detached from Mellors, and she articulates the experience for herself as 'a little ridiculous . . . supremely ridiculous . . . intensely ridiculous'.

As the first two occasions of intercourse are set within the context of the young chicks but question their meaning, so the third is occasioned by Lady Chatterley's holding of the young Flint child and is the time she first feels the possibility of conception. After the experience 'it feels like a child . . . it feels like a child in me'. Again, however, there is the sense of the ridiculous, Mellors being likened, after all, to Balaam's ass, although the parody, the imitation, does not recall Lawrence's earlier work so much as it comments on *Lady Chatterley* itself. While the passage contains one of the lines often quoted to praise Lawrence's ability to capture the experience of a woman's orgasm (the sentence that begins 'She clung to him unconscious in passion, and he never quite slipped from her', a sentence which re-creates the rhythms of intercourse in a truly brilliant way), within the same paragraph are parodies of that sentence: 'Rippling, rippling, rippling, like a flapping overlapping of soft flames, soft as feathers . . . melting her all molten inside'. Not only does the passage parody itself, it challenges the convention of narrative structure, for this is the conclusion toward which the sense of the novel has been leading. It is the experience of sexuality that Mellors recommends ('It's good when it's like that' – coming off together), and it is the experience that Lady Chatterley believes may lead to pregnancy; the narrative structure suggests that it is here the novel should end. But, of course, it does not. The novel is concerned not only with a realisation of the phallic reality but with the way in which that realisation is re-created in language, and Lawrence has not yet exhausted the possibilities.

In the next passage the word 'ridiculous' reappears, but here in connection with the many literary allusions that fill the work: Lady Chatterley thinks of the poets who have said that 'the God who created man must have had a sinister sense of humour, creating him a reasonable being, yet forcing him to take this ridiculous posture'. Caught in language that describes love in terms of the ridiculous, Lady Chatterley is divorced from the act and calls Mellors, to herself, a clown, but having done so, she is also able to lose herself, forgetting Maupassant and creating a woman's language for the description of female orgasm: 'And it seemed she was like the sea.'

Even here, however, the language draws on the imagery of the popular sex manuals of the period, manuals that Lawrence objected to (for example in 'Pornography and Obscenity'). Arguing the necessity for doing away with the secrecy surrounding sex, Lawrence also criticised the work of 'idealists' like Marie Stopes, a pioneer in the study of female sexuality and an advocate of birth control ('How to get out of the dirty little secret! . . . You can't do it by being wise and scientific about it, like Dr Marie Stopes' [*Phoenix*, p. 182]), but in fact the language with which Stopes describes female sexuality, drawing on 'the tides of the sea' and its 'ebb and flow', contains imagery not significantly different from Lawrence's to describe orgasm from the point of view of the woman. Indeed, the Stopes program for married love, stressing the importance of the woman and her satisfaction, is re-created, often ironically, by the lady and the gamekeeper, Stopes even referring in her 1918 work, *Married Love*, to 'flower-wreathed love-making'.[32]

Having drawn on language similar to that of *Married Love* – language still used by women to describe the experience of orgasm (for example in the Hite report) – Lawrence returns to his argument that the experience exists beyong language, in touch:

What a mystery! . . . such as no consciousness could seize. Her whole self quivered unconscious and alive, like plasm. She could not know what it was. She could not remember what it had been. Only that it had been more lovely than anything ever could be. Only that. And afterwards she was utterly still, utterly unknowing, she was not aware for how long. And he was still with her, in an unfathomable silence along with her. And of this, they would never speak.'

But the novel moves forward, in an even more dramatic way, to do precisely that, to speak of the experience of love – when it has not been satisfactory.

The next episode, in fact, is preceded by the novel's most detailed talk about intercourse. Of all the passages dealing with lovemaking, Mellors's discussion here of his previous unsatisfactory experiences presents the most extensive preliminary dialogue and the briefest description of the act itself. 'He lay with her and went into her there on the hearthrug, and so they gained a measure of equanimity', as if the talk about intercourse eliminated the need for the experience of it. 'And then they went quickly to bed, for it was growing chill, and they had tired each other out.'

In still another pattern, using language in still another way, on the next morning Mellors expands the use of dialect to introduce John Thomas and Lady Jane, but the allusions parody: 'Say: Lift up your heads o' ye gates, that the king of glory may come in . . . Blest be the tie that binds our hearts in kindred love.' Similarly, much talk precedes the scene of the dance in the rain, talk about the condition of England that makes Lady Chatterley uneasy, for as Mellors talks, 'despair seemed to come down on him completely'. In the weaving of flowers that follows, again there is a parody not only of Stopes but also of the earlier Lawrence, for the significance of the bouquets that Lady Chatterley and Mellors bring to each other to accompany their love is essentially different from the significance of flowers in, for example, *Sons and Lovers*, a significance shattered by Mellors's sneeze which causes him to forget what he started to say: '"Ay, what *was* I going to say?" He had forgotten. And it was one of the disappointments of her life, that he never finished.'

And so, after drawing on a variety of earlier conventions for the descriptions, frequently to parody them, Lawrence abandons language as a tool to re-create the experience of intercourse, abandons dialect, abandons talk about sex and use of imagery to suggest the experience itself, and turns instead to the emphasis of most of his earlier work, shifting from what happened to its effect. If the experience on the night before Lady Chatterley leaves for Italy is unclear, if the 'sensuality sharp and searing as fire' is not described clinically, the effect on Lady Chatterley, her rejection of the pleasure of the mind, *is* clear. Similarly, the reader is also led to understand the importance of touch – no new idea in Lawrence – and also to a recognition that one can best approach true touch through rejection of the ways in which language may be used in making love. When Lady Chatterley and Mellors are together for the last time, in Mellors's room in London, the act itself is only briefly described, accompanied by the realisation that 'this was the thing he had to do, to come into tender touch'.

Clifford Chatterley clings to the power of language – it is his wife's going back on her word that most incenses him, and he insists that she fulfill her commitment in language, her promise that she return to Wragby, before he will divorce her. But both Mellors and Lady Chatterley understand the life that underlies the language in which they have tried to speak, and in his final letter to her, Mellors writes that he does not 'like to think too much about you, in my head, that only makes a mess of us both'. That Lawrence is using the novel to investigate the relation between language and sexuality is made clear in this final letter, a recapitulation of the novel's concerns with novel-writing that serves as the epilogue Victor Shklovsky suggests we need to show us how to read the strange and unfamiliar.[33]

As the story of two lovers, *Lady Chatterley's Lover* is curiously unfinished. The future of Mellors and Lady Chatterley is unresolved, and in 'A Propos' Lawrence makes clear the uncertainty that the two will ever be freed from their previous marriages to come together again. But as a novel about the relation between language and sexuality, Mellors's final statement is clear. Like the novel as a whole, the letter moves through a variety of approaches to novel-writing – opening with a gossipy realism concerned with money and the precise details of Mellors's job; moving into a middle section that recalls the didactic preaching of Lawrence as Victorian sage, here arguing for an approach to life that Mellors believes will bring renewed spirit to the colliers; shifting from realism and didacticism to the importance of symbol and image (the forked flame, the crocus, the great grasping white hands), as Lawrence was so effectively to use image and symbol himself in his own greatest novels; re-creating in words the act of love itself, the great attempt of *Lady Chatterley's Lover*; finally recognising that such re-creation is inadequate, for if Lady Chatterley and Mellors were together, the ink could stay in the bottle: 'So many words, because I can't touch you.' It is to a different system of signs, to the forked flame, to a world in which there is no need for a mediating language that Mellors and Lady Chatterley move, and it is small wonder that Lawrence's letters and discursive prose during this period also show much interest in the story of Adam and Eve, before the fall, in a time before consciousness and language.

Readers have tended to ignore this concern with the limits of language, unless to criticise or to see it as paradoxical, perhaps from fear that it will somehow lessen the significance of Lawrence's role as priest of love. But to see that Lawrence is both creating a language of the feelings and simultaneously calling into question the adequacy of that language is to see the very brilliance of the novel. Lawrence has not only created a language of love, a lover's discourse, but has also shown the limits of such a discourse, even at its most eloquent and persuasive. In addition to freeing us from the repression of sexuality, *Lady Chatterley's Lover* also frees us from the constraints of language itself. The novel achieves its brilliance through the tension it creates by drawing on traditional genres at the same time it calls those forms into question; the novel builds on the tension created by the simultaneous use of a variety of conventions.

Lawrence's use of four-letter words in a dialect his early audiences found uncomfortable, his explicit description of the body and its use in intercourse, were shocking to readers who assumed such material belonged only within the conventions of the pornographic, and in the subsequent dislocation readers attempted to naturalise the novel in its entirety within the conventions of earlier fiction, conventions used by Lawrence and in the tradition of the realistic novel; such readings, as they became acceptable, were initially freeing for many who saw the novel as a way to escape the repression of sexuality. Only recently have we begun to see how much more sophisticated and profound is the novel's treatment of sexuality and its relation to language. To understand a text, as Barthes has pointed out, 'is not only to pass from one word to another, it is also to pass from one level to another'; to do so with *Lady Chatterley* is to experience *jouissance*, the 'rapture of dislocation produced by ruptures or violations of intelligibility'.[34] While *Lady Chatterley's Lover* utilises parody, it is not itself parody; it is in the tradition of realism but does not take realism too seriously – it cannot, after all, adequately convey the experience of sexuality, which underlies the rhythms of language itself.

Alan Sheridan has pointed out, in considering Foucault, that when one can '*say* things in a new way', one can 'see things in a new way'.[35] It is this attempt to see sex in a new way that underlies Lawrence's desire to *say* it in a new way – but not because one must or should talk about sex. Lawrence knew, as Foucault has argued, that sex loses its power in language – even though we must use language to explain that loss. Jacques Derrida has written:

> We must . . . try to free ourselves from . . . language. Not actually *attempt* to free ourselves from it, for that is impossible without denying our own historic situation. But rather, to imagine doing so. Not actually *free* ourselves from it, for that would make no sense and would deprive us of the light that meaning can provide. But rather, resist it as far as possible.[36]

Mellors attempted to be silent, by withdrawing from the world of men, but without touch he was drawn back into the world, into language. At the same time, in the most simple and direct way, his final letter affirms that he and Lady Chatterley cannot truly be together as long as they are dependent solely on language. Like the novel itself they must both resist the historic situation which makes them dependent on language and simultaneously imagine what they might be without language. 'Books are not life. They are only tremulations on the ether', Lawrence wrote, but we *can* listen to the 'low, calling cries of the characters, as they wander in the dark woods of their destiny' (*Phoenix*, pp. 535, 760). When we are truly together, the ink *can* stay in the bottle.

Foucault is right, of course, that Lawrence did not want to realise sex; Lawrence, after all, maintained that the point of *Lady Chatterley's Lover* was 'to think sex, fully, completely, honestly, and cleanly' (*Phoenix II*, p. 489). But Lawrence also argued that 'in [man's] adventure of self-consciousness [he] must come to the limits of himself and become aware of something beyond him. A man must be self-conscious enough to know his own limits, and to be aware of that which surpasses him' (*Phoenix*, p. 185). *Lady Chatterley's Lover* is a study of the tension between these two ideas, between the need to rescue sexuality from secrecy, to bring it into discourse, and the simultaneous recognition that the re-creation of sexuality in language must always, at the same time, resist language.

Notes

1. MICHEL FOUCAULT, *The History of Sexuality*, vol. I, trans. Robert Hurley (New York: Pantheon Books, 1978), pp. 157–8.
2. MICHEL FOUCAULT, 'A Preface to Transgression', in *Language, Counter-Memory, Practice: Selected Essays and Interviews*, ed. Donald F. Bouchard, trans. Bouchard and Sherry Simon (Ithaca: Cornell University Press, 1977), p. 29.
3. Ibid., p. 30.
4. SCOTT SANDERS, *D.H. Lawrence: The World of the Five Major Novels* (New York: Viking, 1974), p. 195. Sanders is only one of a number of critics who have found Lawrence's treatment of sex in some way inadequate. See, for example, Julian Moynahan, *The Deed of Life: The Novels and Tales of D.H. Lawrence* (Princeton, N.J.; Princeton University Press, 1963), pp. 140–72; David Parker, 'Lawrence and Lady Chatterley: the Teller and the Tale', *Critical Review*, **20** (1978): 31–41; and Kingsley Widmer, 'The Pertinence of Modern Pastoral: the Three Versions of *Lady Chatterley's Lover*', *Studies in the Novel*, **5** (Fall 1973): 298–313. Moynahan, although admiring Lawrence, argues that the reader of *Lady Chatterley* 'fails to achieve any deep realisation of the sexual mystery' (p. 163); Parker faults the third version of the novel for its 'narrow didactic preoccupation with sex' (p. 34); Widmer maintains that the novel's 'reduction of erotic fulfillment and conversion to a highly specific, and quite likely idiosyncratic, sexuality may weaken the larger theme and exemplary role of the lovers' (p. 300).
5. See, for example, G. Wilson Knight, 'Lawrence, Joyce and Powys', *Essays in Criticism*, **11**, no. 4 (October 1956): 403–17, and the subsequent debate in the same journal, **12**, nos. 2 and 4; **13**, nos. 1–3; Mark Spilka's review of Colin Clarke's *River of Dissolution* in 'Lawrence Up-Tight, or the Anal Phase Once Over', *Novel*, **4**, no. 3 (Spring 1971): 252–67, and the subsequent replies by George Ford, Frank Kermode, and Colin Clarke in *Novel*, **5**, no. 1; and John Sparrow, 'Regina v. Penguin Books Ltd.', *Encounter*, **13**, no. 2 (February 1962): 35–43.
6. For two different emphases on the novel's treatment of sexuality, representative of the divided approaches, see the recent collection *D. H. Lawrence: the Man Who Lived*, ed. Robert B. Partlow, Jr. and Harry T. Moore (Carbondale: Southern Illinois University Press, 1980): Mark Spilka, 'Lawrence Versus Peeperkorn on Abdication; or *What Happens to a Pagan Vitalist When the Juice Runs Out?*' and Peter H. Balbert, 'The Loving of Lady Chatterley: D.H. Lawrence and the Phallic Imagination', in particular pp. 143, 116 and 156.
7. Readings of the novel which are not centrally concerned with its language of sexuality include but are certainly not restricted to the following: Joseph C. Voelker, 'The Spirit of No-Place: Elements of the Classical Ironic Utopia in D. H. Lawrence's *Lady Chatterley's Lover*', *Modern Fiction Studies*, **25**, no. 2 (Summer 1979): 223–39; Michael Squires, *The Pastoral Novel: Studies in George*

Eliot, Thomas Hardy, and D. H. Lawrence (Charlottesville: University Press of Virginia, 1974), pp. 196–212; Dennis Jackson, 'The "Old Pagan Vision": Myth and Ritual in *Lady Chatterley's Lover*', *D.H. Lawrence Review*, **11**, no. 3 (Fall 1978): 260–71; Jerome Mandel, 'Medieval Romance and *Lady Chatterley's Lover*', *D.H. Lawrence Review*, **10**, no. 1 (Spring 1977): 20–33.

8. D.H. Lawrence, 'Sex Isn't Sin', in *The Complete Poems of D.H. Lawrence*, ed. Vivian de Sola Pinto and F. Warren Roberts (New York: Viking, 1971), p. 464.

9. SANDERS, *The World of the Five Major Novels*, p. 182.

10. ROBERT SCHOLES, *Structuralism in Literature: an Introduction* (New Haven: Yale University Press, 1974), pp. 16 and 150.

11. Ibid., p. 197.

12. See, for example, the discussion in 'The Confession of the Flesh', in Michel Foucault, *Power/Knowledge: Selected Interviews and Other Writings, 1972–1977*, ed. Colin Gordon, trans. Gordon et al. (New York: Pantheon Books, 1980).

13. ROLAND BARTHES, *A Lover's Discourse*, trans. Richard Howard (New York: Hill and Wang, 1978), p. 149.

14. Ibid., p. 99 and p. 104.

15. FOUCAULT, 'A Preface to Transgression', p. 50 and pp. 29–30.

16. 'Let There be Light!' in *The Complete Poems of D.H. Lawrence*, p. 681.

17. D.H. Lawrence, *The Complete Short Stories*, vol. 3 (New York: Viking, 1961), p. 746.

18. 'Sex Isn't Sin', in *The Complete Poems of D.H. Lawrence*, p. 465.

19. 'Know-All', in *The Complete Poems of D.H. Lawrence*, p. 726.

20. FOUCAULT, 'The Confession of the Flesh', p. 209.

21. Ibid., pp. 215–16.

22. FOUCAULT, 'A Preface to Transgression', p. 31, p. 51.

23. FOUCAULT, 'Body/Power', in *Power/Knowledge*, pp. 56–7.

24. 'Noli me Tangere', in *The Complete Poems of D.H. Lawrence*, p. 469.

25. JONATHAN CULLER, *Structuralist Poetics: Structuralism, Linguistics and the Study of Literature* (Ithaca: Cornell University Press, 1975), p. 134.

26. G. GENOT, quoted in Culler, *Structuralist Poetics*, p. 139.

27. CULLER, *Structuralist Poetics*, p. 138. Culler writes, 'Actions are plausible or implausible with respect to the norms of a group of works, and reactions which would be thoroughly intelligible in a Proustian novel would be extremely bizarre and inexplicable in Balzac' (p. 145).

28. Ibid., p. 147.

29. Ibid., p. 148.

30. Ibid., pp. 150–2.

31. GEORGE LEVINE, *The Realistic Imagination: English Fiction from Frankenstein to Lady Chatterley* (Chicago: University of Chicago Press, 1981), pp. 323–4. In a related argument, Evelyn J. Hinz writes, 'Lawrence's own criticisms of various types of fictional practices and attitudes in the final version of the work and in "A Propos of *Lady Chatterley's Lover*" are as much directed against his own practice in the first two versions as they are against any other examples'. See 'Pornography, Novel, Mythic Narrative: the Three Versions of *Lady Chatterley's Lover*', *Modernist Studies*, **3**, no. 1 (1979): 36.

32. MARIE CARMICHAEL STOPES, *Married Love: a New Contribution to the Solution of Sex Difficulties* (London: A.C. Fifield, 1918), pp. 19–20.

33. CULLER, *Structuralist Poetics*, p. 223.

34. Quoted in Culler, *Structuralist Poetics*, p. 192.

35. ALAN SHERIDAN, *Michel Foucault: the Will to Truth* (London: Tavistock Publications, 1980), p. 58.

36. Quoted in Culler, *Structuralist Poetics*, p. 252.

Part Three

Post-Structuralist Turns

10 Taking a Nail for a Walk: on Reading *Women in Love**

GĀMINI SALGĀDO

Gāmini Salgādo, Professor of English at Exeter University at the time of his death in 1985, was one of the generation of talented textual critics who emerged in the late fifties and sixties in Britain, but who were not party to the Marxist-structuralist theoretical developments of the post-1968 period. The essay from which this excerpt derives is an excellent example of Salgādo's critical practice of close, complex reading of the text, which, in this instance, brings out the contradictory and irresolute nature of the novel in question (see Introduction, p. 20, for further comment on the proto-deconstructive orientation of this essay). In the early pages (not included here) Salgādo indicates how plural and uncertain most criticism of *Women in Love* had been to date, and he goes on to account for this by way of the novel's own 'radical indeterminacy': first, in its structure, second, in its symbolism, and third – in what follows here – in its language.

Salgādo's work on Lawrence included *Sons and Lovers: A Selection of Critical Essays* (Macmillan, 1978); *A Preface to Lawrence* (Longman, 1982); and (with G.K. Das) *The Spirit of D.H. Lawrence* (Macmillan, 1988). His other main scholarly interests were Shakespeare and Elizabethan drama.

Women in Love is not merely a novel that accommodates contradictory readings, it positively invites and even compels them. It beckons us towards both sorts of reading and frustrates both, and it does this on such a scale and with such 'consistency' that we are justified in calling it the novel's intention. It is, to use a recent critic's useful term, a Janiform novel, that is 'a two-faced novel: morally it seems to be centrally or

---

* Reprinted from Gabriel Josipovici (ed.), *The Modern English Novel: the Reader, the Writer and the Work* (London: Open Books, 1976), pp. 97, 102–12; references renumbered from the original.

importantly paradoxical or self-contradictory. Not merely ambiguous or complex, but paradoxical or self-contradictory.'[1] . . .

There seem to me to be three aspects of Lawrence's language which point to the radical indeterminacy which is the novel's principal effect. All of them are in some degree characteristics of Lawrence's later prose style, but they are found with greater frequency, or at least with a peculiar intensity of effect, in *Women in Love*, as any reader who comes straight to this novel from, say, *The Rainbow*, will notice. The first is the persistent tendency of the prose to hanker for an idea or an attribute and its opposite at the same time – the antithesis being usually qualified by the rhetoric of 'and yet', 'but also' as well as 'odd', 'strange' or 'curious'. Extensive quotation would be tedious, but the reader will be able to collect several examples in five minutes of random reading from the book. Hermione 'like the fallen angels restored, yet still subtly demoniacal' (*Women in Love*, p. 24) and the mining village 'uncreated and ugly, and yet surcharged with this same potent atmosphere of intense, dark callousness' (p. 129) are instances of the sort of thing I have in mind. The passion for inclusiveness results in a language that is always hovering on the edge of paradox and sometimes thrusts beyond it into contradiction. A man and a wife can know each other 'heavenly and hellish, particularly hellish' (p. 327). Gudrun 'could not believe – she did not believe. Yet she believed' (p. 372). Gerald feels 'a mordant pity, a passion almost of cruelty' (p. 88).

Secondly there is a pervasive contrast between vehemence of tone and something which appears variously as either tentativeness or cloudiness of utterance. This occurs not only in situations where we may fairly assume that it is the character, not the author, who is in a state of uncertainty, as when Ursula feels Birkin's power: 'A strange feeling possessed her, as if something were taking place. But it was all intangible. And some sort of control was being put on her' (p. 145). It is also characteristic of such a celebrated and crucial moment as that in which Birkin tells Hermione what he 'gets' from copying the Chinese drawing:

> I know what centres they live from – what they perceive and feel – the hot, stinging centrality of a goose in the flux of cold water and mud – the curious bitter stinging heat of a goose's blood, entering their own blood like an inoculation of corruptive fire – fire of the cold-burning mud – the lotus of mystery.
>
> *Women in Love*, (p. 99)

The Romantic paradox – life and beauty rooted inescapably in corruption – is asserted with a convoluted violence, which seems to cast doubt on itself. The single opposition between Hermione's desire to 'know' (intellectually understand) and Birkin's 'knowing' (realising and responding to with one's whole being) is undercut by a sense that language is being used as a deliberate defence against communication, or at any rate with an overwhelming sense of its inadequacy, which seems to be the source of the vehemence.

Finally, there is hardly any other modern novel in which argument figures so prominently, and in which at the same time argument is so persistently devalued – summarised, parodied, dismissed, interrupted and trivialised. It would be only a slight exaggeration to say that discursive argument exists in *Women in Love* mainly in order to show its inadequacy as a mode of ordering experience, and to suggest that those most committed to it – Hermione, Sir Joshua, Gerald – are guilty of dangerous psychic self-deprivation. This would certainly account for the way in which what many would want to call Lawrence's message is at least twice parodied – in the *Telegraph* editorial and the Café Pompadour letter – as well as being echoed by, of all people, Hermione, in her diatribe against self-conscious knowledge (p. 44). It could be argued that Birkin's attack on her for bad faith points up precisely the defects of knowledge in the head. But this is to ignore the inescapable fact that Birkin, in his own way, argues more than anyone else in the novel, and that his 'arguments' appear to be an important element in his total impact; he does not convince only by his presence. It is true that in a neurotic civilisation people will tend to do too much talking about their ailments, yet it is not merely the quantity but the self-cancelling tendency of the argument that affects the reader. The way in which discursive argument seems to take on a serious importance ('It is because he had the genius of a great creative writer that he has been capable of this thinking,' Leavis tells us)[2] and then deflate itself is not unlike the way in which certain crucial scenes (notably the one where Birkin stones the moon in the water)[3] seem to cry out for 'symbolic' translation and then mock it, as the attempt to 'symbolise' a daisy in socio-political terms mocks itself in the conversation between Ursula and Birkin (p. 146). 'I don't mean anything, why should I?' says Birkin at one point (p. 446). And it is not only Birkin whose authority as a commentator is undermined. 'I don't trust you when you drag in the stars', Mino tells him. But the 'starry' rhetoric is often used by the author in his own person.

If we glance briefly at the circumstances in which Lawrence produced *Women in Love*, as well as at the wider Romantic tradition to which it in part belongs, we may also find factors which account for the novel's janiformity. Though it grew out of the same rich fictional raw material as *The Rainbow*, most of the later novel was written when Lawrence was in the throes of his agonised experiences of the First World War. In his

139

preface to the American edition he wrote: 'It is a novel which took its final shape in the midst of the period of war, though it does not concern the war itself.' The sense of universal catastrophe is palpable enough as we read and it is not difficult to understand why Lawrence seriously considered calling the novel *The Latter Days* or *Dies Irae*. Often in the novel we have the sense that the perspectives opened up imply a reader who is something other than a human being, something more like an impersonal life force:

> '. . . But what if people *are* all flowers of dissolution – when they're flowers at all – what difference does it make?'
>
> 'No difference – and all the difference. Dissolution rolls on, just as production does,' he said. 'It is a progressive process – and it ends in universal nothing – the end of the world, if you like. But why isn't the end of the world as good as the beginning?'
>
> 'I suppose it isn't', said Ursula, rather angry.
>
> 'Oh yes, ultimately,' he said. 'It means a new cycle of creation after – but not for us. If it is the end, then we are of the end – *fleurs du mal*, if you like.'
>
> *(Women in Love, p. 193)*

Again: 'No, death doesn't really seem the point any more' says Birkin. 'It curiously doesn't concern me. It's like an ordinary tomorrow' (pp. 228–9), and even more explicitly:

> Birkin looked at the land, at the evening, and was thinking: 'Well, if mankind is destroyed, if our race is destroyed like Sodom, and there is this beautiful evening with the luminous land and trees, I am satisfied. That which informs it all is there, and can never be lost. After all, what is mankind but just one expression of the incomprehensible. And if mankind passes away, it will only mean that this particular expression is completed and done. That which is expressed, and that which is to be expressed, cannot be diminished. There it is, in the shining evening. Let mankind pass away – time it did. The creative utterances will not cease, they will only be there. Humanity doesn't embody the utterance of the incomprehensible any more. Humanity is a dead letter. There will be a new embodiment, in a new way. Let humanity disappear as quick as possible.'
>
> (p. 65)

I am aware that this is a passge from fairly early on in the book and that the focus of Birkin's anti-humanity narrows to something like mere anti-Englishness. But one is a development from the other only in the case of Birkin, not in the novel as a whole, where the larger anti-humanity seems to me as persistent as the more human concern for dying so that one may be truly reborn. Birkin's occasional indifference to humanity and its fate seems to be endorsed by his creator: 'I cannot touch humanity, even in thought, it is abhorrent to me. But a work of art is an act of faith, as Michael Angelo says, and one goes on writing, to the unseen witnesses.'[4]

On the other hand the novel was finally called *Women in Love*, which suggests a more affirmative note as well as a less anti-human perspective. Further, although the positives of pure singleness of being and fulfilment within the chosen community are both part of the Romantic tradition,[5] there is a gap between the importance attached in that tradition to *yielding* to experience ('a wise passiveness' or a passionate abandon) and the prophet's assertiveness. *Women in Love* demands at least two incompatible things of Birkin. Put in their simplest terms, these are that he should both dramatise and assert the virtue of an abandonment to the depths of experience so that he may be renewed by the contact. In so far as the novel shows him doing this (by dying out of the world and returning to it in 'the freedom together' of his relationship with Ursula), we are wholly convinced. As a vehement and even violent spokesman for passivity he also evidently has the best of most of the novel's arguments, even when he turns them to mockery. But the second stance is incompatible with the first, and the incompatibility is surely more than a matter of the man who shouts about the value of silence being suddenly embarrassed by the sound of his own voice. That Lawrence himself was aware of the problem is shown by his description of Birkin in the abandoned prologue to the novel:

> In his most passionate moment of spiritual enlightenment, when like a saviour of mankind he would pour out his soul for the world, there was in him a capacity to jeer at his own righteousness and spirituality, justly and sincerely to make a mock of it all. And the mockery was so true, it bit to the very core of his righteousness, and showed it rotten, shining with phosphorescence. But at the same time, whilst quivering in the climax-thrill of sexual pangs, some cold voice could say in him: 'You are not really moved; you could rise up and go away from this pleasure quite coldly and calmly; it is not radical, your enjoyment.'[6]

Finally there is the problem of finding a language in which to communicate the incommunicable. Throughout *Women in Love* we come into contact with a perfectly conventional 'novel of character and circumstance' as identifiable in dialogue, description and event as the evidences of dissatisfaction with it. This dissatisfaction shows itself when, for instance, Birkin is described in terms which suggest the conventional novelist:

> He affected to be quite ordinary, perfectly and marvellously
> commonplace. And he did it so well, taking the tone of his
> surroundings, adjusting himself quickly to his interlocutor and his
> circumstance, that he achieved a verisimilitude of ordinary
> commonplaceness that usually propitiated his onlookers for the
> moment, disarmed them from attacking his singleness.
>
> (p. 22)

Or when the effort of ordering one's life is contrasted with the
'formlessness' of the picaresque novel (p. 340), or in Birkin's weariness
with the life at Breadalby because of its tedious familiarity: '. . . how
known it all was, like a game with the figures set out . . . the same
figures moving round in one of the innumerable permutations that make
up the game. But the game is known, its going on is like a madness, it is
so exhausted' (p. 110). The 'conventional novel' intermittently coming up
against all that which is resistant to it admirably mimes one theme of
Women in Love, which is new life urgent and struggling to grow out of old
forms. A novel in which character is vividly related to environment and
in which a central theme – say, the implications of modern marriage and
its relation to the possibility and necessity of companionship between
men – is included within a larger whole which appears to cast doubts on
the entire enterprise. 'A fate dictated from outside, from theory or from
circumstance, is a false fate', wrote Lawrence in his foreword to the
American edition of the novel.[7] But in the nature of the case, this 'false
fate' manifests itself as the 'conventional novel', while the 'promptings of
desire and aspiration' which the 'creative, spontaneous soul sends forth',
and which are 'our true fate, which it is our business to fulfil', not only
follow a different pattern, but are presented with an awareness that the
very presentation is a kind of falsification.

It is not enough, though it is certainly true to say that Lawrence's
novel deals with the theme that: 'Love is a thing to be learned, through
centuries of patient effort. It is a difficult, complex maintenance of
individual integrity throughout the incalculable process of interhuman
polarity.'[8] It is not enough, though it is certainly true to say, with Colin
Clarke, that the reductive process of corruption is a necessary part of the
regenerative and redemptive process. Corruption and regeneration,
orgiastic abandonmemnt and liberating freedom, insane will and
necessary self-discipline, proud singleness and egotistic separateness,
perverse anal intercourse and the healthy purging of sexual shame,
homosexual abomination and satisfying love between man and man –
almost any pair of apparent contrasts will do – are constantly losing their
distinctiveness, under the pressure of an urgent necessity to cry out the
truth, and an equally resolute determination not to preach expressing
itself in janiformity of idiom and structure. 'Art speech is the only

speech', but at the same time it is 'indirect and ultimate' and the times seemed to demand directness and the fictional world specificity. Characters are described in ways which seem to make their inner lives interchangeable and their external selves vivid but unimportant; events seem both to affirm and to deny any symbolic or representative meaning; and a whole range of key terms – 'obscene', 'mindless', 'mystic', 'dreadful', 'will', 'single', 'corrupt', 'unspeakable' are a few of them – point in opposite directions. The reader is constantly challenged to make a range of discriminations of the kind which I have catalogued earlier but which cannot be made consistently from *within the novel itself*. If we go outside the novel, of course, to the Romantic tradition in European and English literature or to Lawrence's discursive writings, we can make a convincing case for either reading of *Women in Love*, depending on whether we want mainly to use (with Leavis) *Psychoanalysis and the Unconscious* or (with Clarke) *The Reality of Peace* and *The Crown*. But this brings us to the question of the relation between the novel and discursive prose which, I have implicitly argued, is in this case a peculiarly baffling one.

No one who has read *Women in Love* is likely to feel that he has wasted his time or 'got nothing' out of it. But he will be more than usually at a loss to say what it is he has got, not because of the meagreness of the experience but because of its abundance. Working through the novel leaves one reader at least with the sense that its 'message' or 'messages' are snares and delusions: the final effect is the typically 'modern' one of having the experience and missing the meaning. One remembers Lawrence's own words: 'If you try to nail anything down in the novel, either it kills the novel, or the novel gets up and walks away with the nail.'

There is a perfectly ordinary sense in which this observation could be true of the relationship between any creative work and any 'message'; the significance of the one could not be derived from that of the other. There is a more complicated, even paradoxical, sense in which Lawrence's remark is relevant to janiform novels, for we could say that the tension between the 'messages' vivifies the novel instead of killing it. In the end one has to say that *Women in Love* is not janiform merely because its 'messages' point in opposite directions; one could, at least in theory, reconcile the two with some such formula as: 'Spontaneous–creative fullness of being includes corruption and degradation as phases rather than as opposites', though the synthesis leaves something out of each. Lawrence's novel does not merely deploy a series of paradoxes and contradictions in the service of a larger unity. It is centrally paradoxical because it is shot through with the continuous and continuously felt tension between the necessity of articulating a vision and its impossibility, and sometimes its undesirability. The defensiveness with which Lawrence writes of *Women in Love* in the American preface is to me both revealing and touching:

> Any man of real individuality tries to know and to understand what is happening, even in himself, as he goes along. This struggle for verbal consciousness should not be left out in art. It is a very great part of life. It is not superimposition of a theory. It is the passionate struggle into conscious being.[9]

Revealing because it points to the novelist's inescapable function (and intermittently that of some of his central characters) and touching because at one level (as when it is localised in Hermione, for example) it is the great modern sin. But it is not so modern, after all. Set against the passage just quoted these words from Lawrence's review of Trigant Burrow's *The Social Basis of Consciousness*:

> At a certain point in his evolution, man became cognitively conscious: he bit the apple: he began to know. Up till that time, his consciousness flowed unaware, as in the animals. Suddenly his consciousness split.
> . . . The true self is not aware that it is a self. A bird as it sings, sings itself. But not according to a picture. It has no idea of itself.[10]

Women in Love attempts to articulate a vision of paradisal singleness-of-being-in-relatedness both negatively and positively. The measure of its success is also the measure of its failure. The reader's fascination and his frustration have the same source.

Notes

All references to *Women in Love* are to the Penguin edition (1974).
1. CEDRIC WATTS, 'Janiform Novels', *English*, **24** (July 1975): 40–1.
2. F.R. LEAVIS, *D.H. Lawrence, Novelist* (London: Chatto and Windus 1955), p. 156.
3. Critical dissension over the interpretation of this celebrated scene is instructive and relevant. Most commentators, noting Birkin's reference to Cybele, 'the accursed Syria Dea' who emasculated her acolytes, interpret it as the male's attempt to annihilate the insatiable female. Mark Kinkead-Weekes and Colin Clarke see the scene, more plausibly in my view, as dramatising how 'the individuality of the ego gives way to a true individuality, though a precarious one' (Clarke, *River of Dissolution*, London: Routledge, 1969). The first group of critics, maintain that the moon's image finally re-forms, and that Birkin is defeated. For the last two critics, Lawrence's art shuts from our minds the idea of the moon's final re-formation, so that we are indeed left with a sense of 'precarious' individuality.

But the text gives us: '. . . until a ragged rose, a distorted, frayed moon was shaking upon the waters again, reasserted, renewed, trying to recover from its convulsion, to get over the disfigurement and agitation, to be whole and composed, at peace' (p. 280), where the rhythm and language of the earlier part of the sentence suggest the activity and agitation and the final cadence suggests rest and wholeness.

4. Lawrence, *Collected Letters*, ed. Harry T. Moore (London: Heinemann, 1962), vol. 1, p. 449.

5. CLARKE, op. cit., pp. 88ff. My debt to this book, even where I disagree with it, is overwhelming.

6. Lawrence, *Phoenix II*, ed. Warren Roberts and Harry T. Moore (London: Heinemann, 1968), p. 103.

7. Ibid.: 275.

8. Lawrence, *Psychoanalysis and the Unconscious* (London 1923), quoted in Leavis, op. cit., p. 149.

9. Lawrence, *Phoenix II*, p. 276.

10. Lawrence, *Phoenix*, (London: Heinemann, 1961), p. 377.

11 The Power of Nothing in *Women In Love**

Daniel O'Hara

Daniel O'Hara is Professor of English at Temple University, and Review Editor of *Boundary 2: an International Journal of Literature and Culture* (Duke University Press). The essay included here is an early version of the aesthetic, ethical and political issues which inform *Performing Foucault: Critical Theory as Cultural Politics* (Columbia University Press), a book O'Hara is currently completing which explores the social practices of self-fashioning in modern literature and postmodern criticism. The present essay at once deploys and challenges strategies invoked by Paul de Man and Michel Foucault, and in relation to *Women in Love* sees the novel, in its 'repetitive self-cancellation', as more radically deconstructive than even the rhetorical postures of the deconstructionist critics themselves. But O'Hara also claims that this power is 'harnessed' by Lawrence, rather than merely 'set loose' as a reflex of the discourse of human sexuality. (For further comment on this essay, see Introduction, pp. 20–1.)

In addition to the work in progress mentioned above, Daniel O'Hara has edited two collections of essays on critical theory, including *Why Nietzsche Now?* (Indiana University Press, 1985), and has written three further books on the subject, among them *Lionel Trilling: the Work of Liberation* (University Wisconsin Press, 1988).

> It's the old story – action and reaction, and nothing between.
>
> D.H. Lawrence

The question most insistently raised by recent literary criticism is the status and authority of the critic's own voice. Declaring that the idea of

---

* Reprinted from *Bucknell Review: A Scholarly Journal of Letters, Arts and Science*. Special Issue (ed. Harry R. Garvin), 'Rhetoric, Literature and Interpretation' (1983), **28**, 2: 151–64.

the self is a demonstrable fiction puts radically into question the critic who asserts this position. Of course, one strategy for avoiding this dilemma is the claim that the very rigor of the discourse that deconstructs the self recuperates the idea of the self on the metacritical level. Paul de Man has expressed this view most succinctly:

> Within the epistemological labyrinth of figural structures [in a critic's text], the recuperation of selfhood would be accomplished by the rigor with which the discourse deconstructs the very notion of the self. The originator of this discourse is then no longer the dupe of his own wishes; he is as far beyond pleasure and pain as he is beyond good and evil or, for that matter, beyond strength and weakness. His consciousness is neither happy nor unhappy, nor does he possess any power. He remains however a center of authority to the extent that the very destructiveness of his ascetic reading testifies to the validity of his interpretation.[1]

De Man, naturally, does not subscribe to this point of view. He asserts that no critic can master his discourse and no critic's discourse can achieve the kind of invulnerability to the ceaseless ironic reversals of language assumed by this position, not even the discourse that repeatedly enunciates this very principle:

> The discourse by which the figural structure of the self is asserted fails to escape from the categories it claims to deconstruct, and this remains true, of course, of any discourse which pretends to reinscribe in its turn the figure of this aporia. There can be no escape from the dialectical movement of the text.[2]

The critic who would expose the dreaded hand of the onto-theological tradition under every privileged figure in another's text should look first to the figures of his own text. And the metacritic who makes this assertion can never escape either the tradition he would subvert or the destructive discourse he has put into play. The dialectical movement of the text that de Man refers to here is, needless to say, a continuously arrested dialectic generated by the interplay of its grammatical structures, rhetorical figures, and logical maneuvers. There can be no final synthetic resolution: 'nothing, whether deed, word, thought or text, ever happens in relation, positive or negative, to anything that precedes, follows or exists elsewhere, but only as a random event whose power, like the power of death, is due to the randomness of its occurrency'.[3] The power of this nothing is what I wish to explore in Lawrence's *Women in Love*.

But first I want to raise another question: of what use is a critical position that reduces the writing of a text to the blind attempt of the critic to kiss a shattered mirror whole? For one thing, it helps to account for some of the stranger spectacles in recent criticism. A critic as sophisticated as Paul de Man, who knows the truth of deconstruction, would build into his own discourse the elements of a parodic reduction of his position. Such a critic would thereby enact the ironic, arrested dialectic of textual production that at every moment threatens to explode the critical project into convulsions of mockery. How else account for Harold Bloom's embrace of the Gnostic Sophia he previously scorned, or Edward W. Said's apparent obsession with Flaubert's Egyptian concubine, or Jacques Derrida's fascination with Nietzsche's misplaced umbrella?[4] To secure temporarily their critical authority from the threat of the aporia described by de Man these critics practice a radical form of modernist irony that places in the hands of the reader preliminary sketches for a parodic interpretation of the critic even as such irony protects the articulation of the critic's overall position. Like the great modernist masters of irony, Joyce, Mann, Valéry, or Lawrence, contemporary critics create in their texts ironic portraits of the authors of these texts. The principle is to do unto oneself before the text itself does one in.

This brings us to a second use of de Man's position, as well as to an example of de Man's own complex irony at work on himself. In his reading of an incident from Rousseau's *Confessions*, de Man, in a playful spirit, takes seriously Rousseau's attempt to excuse himself for accusing a servant girl, Marion, of the theft of a ribbon, which he himself had committed. De Man argues that when Rousseau asserts that he is innocent of blame, that he is not responsible because he had merely excused himself 'upon the first thing that offered itself', he is speaking correctly. For the linguistic machine has operated impersonally to produce from the play of signifiers the proper sonorous designation at hand, 'Marion'.[5] And in a scene from the *Fourth Rêverie* this machine has replicated its own figure and has dramatised the precarious position of the writer in relation to the seductive processes of textual production: 'I looked at the metal rolls, my eyes were attracted by their polish. I was tempted to touch them with my fingers and I moved them with pleasure over the polished surface of the cylinder.'[6] What staging of the critic's desire could be clearer than this scene?

De Man is arguing for the fundamental impersonality, anonymity, and arbitrariness of discursive practices. A kind of Kantian unconscious, a spontaneous play of linguistic and grammatical structures, or rhetorical tropes and metaphorical conceptions, interrupts and subverts the action of human intentionality. De Man announces this position, however, not with lamentation but with a kind of bewildering joy, a delightful freedom from any responsibility for one's utterances, an irresponsibility that explains the attractiveness of deconstruction and, as well, functions as the basis for any future critiques of the deconstructive enterprise. De Man names this curious freedom in which one self-consciously identifies with the agency of one's own enslavement and so anticipates all possible criticism: 'irony'. 'Irony is no longer a trope but the undoing of the deconstructive allegory of all tropological cognitions, the systematic undoing, in other words, of understanding. As such, far from closing off the tropological system, irony enforces the repetition of its aberration.'[7] The critic, no matter how aware, is condemned to this kind of freedom – the freedom of irony.

Different critics give different names to this systematic undoing of understanding. Bloom calls it 'influence', Lacan calls it 'the discourse of the Other', or the 'Unconscious', and Derrida calls it by various nondenominational names, but most consistently 'différance'. Each of these 'terms' functions for these critics as irony does for de Man here – a term I think is perhaps the most comprehensive. These master 'nonterms' allow the critic to perform any operation upon a text and it is all acceptable because his arguments have built into them the assumption of their own ultimate meaninglessness. Whereas critics and thinkers in the literary and philosophical traditions propounded concepts they asserted were univocal, stable, and pristine, contemporary theoreticians of deconstruction articulate sets of terms that are just the opposite: polyvalent, corrosive, and messy. Reading contemporary criticism is often like watching someone pirouette between the horns of a stuffed bull: all the simulation of meaning, but none of the actual risk.

Even as apparently 'relevant' a thinker as Michel Foucault is not immune from the seductions of his own irony. For example, in his introductory volume of *The History of Sexuality* Foucault places Lawrence as a representative of that modern effort to get sex to talk that is the peculiar form of the modern will to knowledge.

According to Foucault we delight now in the pleasure that arises from our power to make the supposedly unspeakable tell all:

> The medical examination, the psychiatric investigation, the pedagogical report, and family controls . . . function as mechanisms with a double impetus: pleasure and power. The pleasure that comes of exercising a power that questions, monitors, watches, spies, searches out, palpates, brings to light; and on the other hand, the pleasure that kindles at having to evade this power, flee from it, fool it, or travesty it. The power that lets itself be invaded by the pleasure it is pursuing. And opposite it, power asserting itself in the pleasure of showing off, scandalizing or resisting. Capture and seduction, confrontation and mutual reinforcement: parents and children, adults and adolescents, educators and students, doctors and patients, the psychiatrist with his hysteric and his perverts, all have played this

game continually since the nineteenth century. These attractions, these evasions, these circular incitements have traced around bodies and sexes, not boundaries not to be crossed, but *perpetual spirals of power and pleasure.*[8]

And Lawrence, according to Foucault, participates in this complex round of pleasure–knowledge–power that makes up the history of sexuality in the West from the end of the eighteenth century to the present.

Foucault, at the conclusion of his little book, quotes two statements from Lawrence – one from *The Plumed Serpent* and the other from *Psychoanalysis and the Unconscious* to show how Lawrence, as a major literary inventor of the discourse of human sexuality, seeks both to evade that discourse by making sex sacred and unnameable and to propose the fullest articulation yet of the thought of sex:

> 'It is sex', said Kate in *The Plumed Serpent*. 'How wonderful sex can be, when men keep it powerful and sacred, and it fills the world! like sunshine through and through one!'

> 'There has been so much action in the past', said D.H. Lawrence, 'especially sexual action, a wearying repetition over and over, without a corresponding thought, a corresponding realization. Now our business is to realize sex. Today the full conscious realization of sex is even more important than the act itself.'[9]

In other words, Lawrence is just an instance, a convenient illustration, of Foucault's hypothesis.

Foucault is able to assimilate Lawrence (among others) to his critical project because he, too, possesses a master 'non-term', *discourse*, which allows Foucault to proceed even as it implicates him to some extent in the critique he mounts against the Western 'will-to-knowledge'. Lawrence's work in his time, like Foucault's in our own, is the manifestation of a particular complex set of rules for the formation of texts on the subject of human sexuality. That is, Lawrence is a locus for the complex network of discursive practices dealing with the topic:

> . . . one is dealing with mobile and transitory points of resistance, producing cleavages in a society that shift about, fracturing unities and effecting regroupings, furrowing across individuals themselves, cutting them up and remolding them, marking off irreducible regions in them, in their bodies and minds. Just as the network of power relations ends by forming a dense web that passes through apparatuses and institutions, without being exactly localized in them, so too the swarm

of points of resistance traverses social stratifications and individual unities.[10]

How can one effectively respond to Foucault's unstringing of Lawrence's rainbow? After all, we, too, are implicated in a discourse that exceeds and subverts our understanding. This, above all else, we understand from reading Foucault.

Perhaps the only thing that one can do in this context is repose the Lawrence question by tracing our genealogy back to Lawrence and his most important work, *Women in Love*. In that way the text, I think, can be seen as anticipating and so subsuming Foucault's position on human sexuality. What this implies about the nature of contemporary criticism must be left for future discussion.

Lawrence presents a problem primarily because he appears to be both a modern continuator of the Romantic project of revising traditional religious ideas in terms of secular values and the finest representative of that modern tradition of writers, artists, and thinkers who would destroy the old so as to liberate the radically new. M.H. Abrams in *Natural Supernaturalism* argues the former position as follows:

> Much of what distinguishes writers I call 'Romantic' derives from the fact that they undertook, whatever their religious creed or lack of creed, to save traditional concepts, schemes, and values which had been based on the relation of the Creator to his creatures and creation, but to reformulate them within the prevailing two-term system of subject and object, ego and non-ego, the human mind or consciousness and its transactions with nature. Despite their displacement from a supernatural to a natural frame of reference, however, the ancient problems, terminology, and ways of thinking about human nature and history survived, as the implicit distinctions and categories through which even radically secular writers saw themselves and their world, and as the presuppositions and forms of their thinking about the condition, the milieu, the essential values and aspirations, and the history and destiny of the individual and of mankind . . . What Lawrence has done, in his unique and haunting [works] is to revise the Scriptural account of the fall and apocalypse . . .[11]

And Philip Rieff argues the latter position on Lawrence in his introduction to *Psychoanalysis and the Unconscious* and *Fantasia of the Unconscious*:

Lawrence shows himself as the most genuine of modern heresiarchs, chief and father – although only long after his death – over all the little heresiarchs: father-killers, ambivalent mother-lovers, culture-breakers, all those professional youngsters who swarm the literary horizon looking for an older generation with some left-over self-images that might be good for smashing. Lawrence senses how thoroughly even his elders had constructed their own morals to meet the new criterion of obsolescence. In his rage at the tyrannous permissiveness and publicity of modern life he is truly the revolutionary of the private life.[12]

Obviously, both Abrams and Rieff are seeing similar things. The terms in which they couch their arguments suggest as much. Where they differ is in their interpretation and evaluation of the essential Lawrence. Is he essentially one of the last Romantics, as Abrams defines the term, or is he the premier revolutionary of the private life, as Rieff claims? Or is he only an uneasy amalgam of both tendencies, like one of his own characters who he asserted were as changeable as the allotropic states of a primal element like carbon?[13] Perhaps Foucault is right and Lawrence is just another example of the modern discourse on human sexuality at work, which combines all the salient features of the religious rite of confession with the new *scientia sexualis* of Freud and Havelock Ellis?

What I want to propose in oppositon to these views of Lawrence is that in his finest work, in *Women in Love*, Lawrence is an apocalyptic ironist who says, in effect, a plague on all your houses. In his portrayal of Birkin and his prophetic anality, and in his presentation of Ursula's complex response to him, Lawrence undermines the claims upon his textual projects of both his religious heritage and the increasingly secularized modern world. For Birkin is a latter-day version of Edward Carpenter, the Edwardian prophet of human sexual freedom who is given Lawrence's own features in *Women in Love*. Lawrence shows us that Birkin's authority is radically suspect. Not only is he vulnerable to Ursula's penetrating remarks – 'She hated the *Salvator Mundi* touch'[14] – but he is the familiar compound ghost of displaced religiosity and self-conscious will-to-knowledge (as Foucault would put it) that haunts us all.

Edward Carpenter was an enormously influential late Victorian and Edwardian prophet of human sexual freedom, whose influence on Lawrence and his youthful circle of friends in the Midlands was particularly considerable.[15] Carpenter compounded Christian symbolism, Nietzschean speculations on the *übermensch*, esoteric lore, and the latest developments in the physiology of sex into a heady potion. He prophesied that the future of the earth would belong to an androgynous race of supermen who would reorganise society into freely loving democratic groups. It was as if all men might become in part Walt

Whitman, all women Sappho. The two most important of Carpenter's works are *Love's Coming of Age* and *The Art of Creation*, for in them Carpenter repeatedly described the future brand of relations between the sexes in the following terms:

> A marriage so free, so spontaneous, that it would allow of wide excursions of the pair from each other, in common or even in separate objects of work and interest, and yet would hold them all the time in the bond of absolute sympathy, would by its very freedom be all the more poignantly attractive and by its very scope and breadth all the richer and more vital – would be in a sense indestructible, like the relation of two suns which, revolving in fluent and rebounding curves, only recede from each other in order to return again with renewed swiftness into close proximity – and which together blend their rays into the glory of one double star.[16]

Carpenter saw in the increasingly uncertain natures and minds of sensitive and sickly young men signs of the coming times. These men were for Carpenter forerunners or prototypes of the master type that would renew the earth.

Birkin is an extremely close replica of Carpenter's prototype, which itself was created largely in the latter's own image. Birkin possesses an extremely fluid and unstable personality:

> He affected to be quite ordinary, perfectly and marvellously commonplace. And he did it so well, taking the tone of his surroundings, adjusting himself quickly to his interlocutor and his circumstance, that he achieved a verisimilitude of ordinary commonplaceness that usually propitiated his onlookers for the moment, disarmed them from attacking his singleness . . . he played with situations like a man on a tightrope: but always on a tightrope, pretending nothing but ease.
>
> (*Women in Love*, p. 14)

Birkin is capable of such radical changes from moment to moment, from one extreme position to another, from solemn preachiness to mock solemnity and self-disgusting silence, that he is said to be not a man at all by the Italian Contessa who visits Breadalby to attend Hermione's party, but 'a chameleon, a creature of change' (p. 85). Birkin is so much a creature of change that he is a connoisseur of decadence and dissolution: sick himself, he appreciates the various forms of sickness in all those around him: 'That dark river of dissolution. You see it rolls in us . . . the black river of corruption. And our flowers are of this – our sea-born Aphrodite, all our white phosphorescent flowers of sensuous perfection, all our reality, nowadays' (p. 164). And finally, Birkin even speaks of his salvation, the only kind he can now imagine, in terms of a reimagined marital relation that is clearly drawn from Carpenter's idea of a mystic conjunction:

> 'What I want is a strange conjunction with you' [he tells Ursula] – 'not meeting and mingling; you are quite right: – but an equilibrium, a pure balance of two single beings – as the stars balance each other.'
>
> (p. 139)

> 'I meant two single equal stars balanced in conjunction – . . . It is the law of creation. One is committed. One must commit oneself to a conjunction with the other – for ever. But it is not selfless – it is a maintaining of the self in mystic balance and integrity – like a star balanced with another star.'
>
> (pp. 142, 144)

Ursula naturally wonders after hearing this, as we do, whether Birkin means for her to be no more than a white dwarf companion of that blue giant who wants an intimate relationship with the god of the mines, Gerald Crich.

I do not want to leave the impression that Birkin is merely the enthusiastic Carpenter updated for more pessimistic times, given a futuristic glitter.[17] Rather, I want to suggest that Birkin represents that compound of religious and scientific ideas, given a Laurentian twist, which threatens to subsume Lawrence's creative life. Lawrence must exorcise this demon by means of this kind of ironic exposure – and he will continue to do so in ever more virulent forms in such later works as *Aaron's Rod*, *Kangaroo*, and *The Plumed Serpent* until he emerges free of this incubus in the beautiful final works, *The Man Who Died* and the death poems. Lawrence must repeatedly shatter the image of that would-be idol, Birkin/Carpenter, much as Birkin must stone the image of the moon ceaselessly re-forming on the surface of the surging waters in the 'Moony' chapter of *Women in Love*.

One of the most effective and most neglected examples of how Lawrence accomplishes this creative feat of self-destruction occurs – at least in part – in the chapter from *Women in Love* called 'Sunday Evening'. Earlier that day Ursula has returned from the disastrous Water Party on the Crich estate, where Gerald's sister, Diana, and Doctor Brindell have drowned in a senseless boating accident that reveals the fate facing the entire Crich family and the class to which it belongs. Birkin and Ursula have recognised their love for each other, and she longs passionately for his presence at the Brangwen home.

But by the end of the day on Sunday she has drifted into a mood of total resignation, a complete letting go, an acquiescence to the universal flux, and a new appreciation of 'the illimitable space of death' as the one last great mystery left unspoiled by modern man and his will to master the earth by translating God's relation to his creation into purely human terms, and in so doing botching and soiling everything with his science, technology and commercialism:

> But what a joy! What a gladness to think that whatever humanity did, it could not seize hold of the kingdom of death, to nullify that. The sea they turned into a murderous alley and a soiled road of commerce, disputed like the dirty land of a city every inch of it. The air they claimed too, shared it up, parcelled it out to certain owners, they trespassed in the air to fight for it. Everything was gone, walled in, with spikes on top of the walls, and one must ignominiously creep between the spiky walls through a labyrinth of life.
>
> (p. 185)

Only death presents Ursula with a 'window' onto a prospect of ultimate purification and renewal – of the earth purged of human kind. Even the mind and the body's most secret and sacred mysteries have been invaded, interrogated, and colonised in the name of human knowledge, mastery, and profit.

> Whatever life might be, it could not take away death, the inhuman transcendent death. Oh, let us ask no question of it, what it is or is not. To know is human, and in death we do not know, we are not human. And the joy of this compensates for all the bitterness of knowledge and the sordidness of our humanity. In death we shall not be human, and we shall not know. The promise of this is our heritage, we look forward like heirs to their majority.
>
> (p. 186)

The fatal beauty of *Women in Love* occurs when Ursula, rather than Birkin, speaks like this; we are tempted to agree with her that both the Romantic projects of natural supernaturalism and the modern will-to-knowledge have even destroyed the private life: nothing is left but the kingdom of death.

What happens next is that Birkin arrives at the Brangwen home just as Ursula's younger brother and sister, Billy and Dora, are going to bed. Birkin is wonderful to the children, so much so that Billy becomes 'angelic like a cherub boy, or like an acolyte' under the ministerings of

Birkin (one of Carpenter's signs of the prototype). But Dora becomes 'like a tiny Dryad that will not be touched' (p. 187). The children thereby clearly objectify in the scene the moods of Birkin and Ursula. For Ursula now hates Birkin with a passionate intensity that transports and transfigures her. Ursula sees in Birkin the idolisation of death that she herself has just given in to. She even transforms him into an image to occupy the center of 'the illimitable space of death': 'She saw him, how he was motionless and ageless, like some crouching idol, some image of a deathly religion. He looked round at her, and his face, very pale and unreal, seemed to gleam with a whiteness almost phosphorescent' (p. 188). Birkin becomes for her now a crystalline beam from the underworld in opposition to her 'pure dart of hate, her white flame of essential hate' (p. 190). She has been reborn in his presence as an avenging Persephone that would destroy his would-be phosphorescent Pluto. These are star-crossed lovers with a vengeance.

What has happened here in this chapter of *Women in Love*? A simple answer would be to say that Birkin, because he threatens Ursula's self-indulgent love of death (the only way she can conceive of her freedom), must be seen as deathly. He threatens to kill her death, and replace it with a relation with life. But such an argument would overlook the fact that Ursula is not just projecting onto Birkin her own recent obsession so that she might shed another of her sicknesses. Birkin is consistently associated in the novel with images of death, as indicated earlier. A better answer would be to say that Lawrence has shown Ursula in transition from an idolisation of the ultimate vacancy of death to the radical critique of such idolisation when it is embodied for her in the person of Birkin. This critique leaves her 'quite lost and dazed, really dead to her own life', and yet transformed by her 'hate . . . so pure and gem-like' (p. 190) – a demonic parody of Pater's aestheticism, his privileged moment of purely disinterested vision. Where does this leave the reader and Lawrence? Lawrence has established 'the illimitable space of death' as the last refuge of the transcendent religious ideal and, at the same time, he has undermined this refuge by exposing Birkin – made in the image of Carpenter's prototype of the androgynous *übermensch* – as the would-be prince of this kingdom – in Ursula's and our eyes. What is this peculiarly self-cancelling rhetorical gesture that subverts what it would set up by identifying it with what is thought to be its antithesis?

This textual phenomenon is like de Man's irony. But I would contend that it is not an exclusively linguistic thing, and that it is characteristic of modernist literature in general. It is harnessed by Lawrence, however, rather than being, as Foucault would have it, set loose within the discourse of human sexuality as the will-to-knowledge ceaselessly transforming the constellation of discursive practices of the West in an eternal recurrence of the Same. Lawrence dramatises in his novel the various forms of revisionary decadence from Gerald Crich's translation of the 'mystic word harmony into the practical word organisation' (p. 220) to Loerke's aesthetics of the machine (pp. 421–2), and passes a last judgment upon them all, especially upon that most prevalent form that delights in the expression of an apocalyptic resentment. Lawrence is thus left with nothing at all, with only the imaginary focal point that stands at the center of all these condemnations, like 'the illimitable space of death'.

Unlike his critical heirs, however, Lawrence refuses finally to name the resultant void, for even death is undone as a name in 'Sunday Evening', as we have seen. He does not call it 'irony', or 'discourse' or 'différance', or 'angst'. And his 'dark sun' is a designation that would explode the very idea of exploiting the abysses of paradox, ambiguity, and rhetoric, however conceived. The reader is left, as is Birkin, and presumably Lawrence himself, feeling like a modern version of Milton's Satan:

> To him, the wonder of this transit [to the Continent] was overwhelming. He was falling through a gulf of infinite darkness, like a meteorite plunging across the chasm between the worlds. The world was torn in two, and he was plunging like an unlit star through the ineffable rift. What was beyond was not yet for him. He was overcome by the trajectory.
>
> (p. 379)

As Joyce Carol Oates has argued, *Women in Love* is Lawrence's *Götterdämmerung*.[18] Through the wondrous power of the negative, Lawrence smashes 'the old idols of ourselves' (p. 47) to make room for the coming of new life – in whatever non-human form it might take: 'Well, if mankind is destroyed, if our race is destroyed like Sodom, and there is this beautiful evening with the luminous land and trees, I am satisfied. That which informs it all is there, and can never be lost. After all, what is mankind but just one expression of the incomprehensible' (p. 52). But, of course, this very attitude is called into question repeatedly, especially when Loerke and Gudrun delight in imagining the future of the earth as a cosmic catastrophe, blown apart into two equal halves by some ultimate explosive (p. 444).

Another way of putting this repetitive self-cancelation that defines the structure of the novel is to say that Lawrence sets up an opposition here between the fatal action of Western man that has transformed the earth and himself into a standing reserve of material for his designs and the pathetic reaction of those who attempt to critique, or to transcend, or to escape this fate in their various ways. For such reaction always ends up only repeating the crime in a more systematic fashion in yet another area of human existence. What Lawrence leaves the reader, then, is not de Man's linguistic machine, or Foucault's discursive network, but simply 'nothing' at all:

> 'Of course', he [Birkin] said, 'Julius [the Bertrand Russell figure] is somewhat insane. On one hand he's had religious mania, and on the other, he is fascinated by obscenity. Either he is a pure servant, washing the feet of Christ, or else he is making obscene drawings of Jesus – action and reaction – and between the two, nothing. He is really insane . . . It's the old story – action and reaction, and nothing between.'

(p. 88)

Mrs Lawrence's son never put the nature of his love any better: 'just one expression of the incomprehensible'.

Notes

1. PAUL DE MAN, *Allegories of Reading: Figural Language in Rousseau, Nietzsche, Rilke, and Proust* (New Haven, Conn.: Yale University Press, 1979), pp. 173–4.
2. Ibid., p. 187.
3. PAUL DE MAN, 'Shelley Disfigured'. *Deconstruction and Criticism* (New York: Seabury Press, 1979), p. 69.
4. See Harold Bloom, *The Flight to Lucifer: A Gnostic Fantasy* (New York: Farrat, Straus & Giroux, 1979); Edward W. Said, *Orientalism* (New York: Pantheon, 1978); and Jacques Derrida, *Spurs: Nietzsche's Styles*, trans. Barbara Harlow (Chicago: University of Chicago Press, 1979). See as well two of my review articles: 'The Romance of Interpretation: A "Postmodern" Critical Style'. *Boundary* 2, **8**, no. 2 (1980): 259–83, and 'The Freedom of the Master?', *Contemporary Literature*, **2**, no. 4 (1980): 649–61.
5. DE MAN, *Allegories of Reading*, p. 288.
6. Cited in ibid., p. 298.
7. Ibid., p. 301.
8. MICHEL FOUCAULT, *The History of Sexuality: An Introduction*, trans. Robert Hurley (New York: Pantheon, 1978), p. 45.
9. Ibid., p. 157.
10. Ibid., p. 96.
11. M.H. ABRAMS, *Natural Supernaturalism* (New York: Norton, 1971), pp. 13 and 324.
12. PHILIP RIEFF, introduction to D.H. Lawrence's *Psychoanalysis and the Unconscious* and *Fantasia of the Unconscious* (New York: Viking, 1960), p. xiii.
13. See 'Extracts from Letters', *D.H. Lawrence: Selected Literary Criticism*, ed. Anthony Beal (New York: Viking, 1966), pp. 17–18. The reference is to the famous letter of 5 June 1914 to Edward Garnett. For commentary on this letter, see Frank Kermode, *D.H. Lawrence* (New York: Viking, 1973), pp. 27–9.
14. D.H. Lawrence, *Women in Love* (New York: Viking, 1960), p. 121. Hereafter all references to the novel will be given in the text.
15. See *Emile Delavenay, D.H. Lawrence and Edward Carpenter: A study in Edwardian*

Transition (New York: Taplinger, 1971). I am greatly indebted to this excellent study. However, Delavenay is concerned with the relation of Lawrence's ideas to Carpenter's. He draws no formal or literary conclusion from the relationship.
16. Ibid., p. 91.
17. See Lawrence's letter to Edward Garnett of 5 June 1914.
18. JOYCE CAROL OATES, 'Lawrence's *Götterdämmerung:* the Tragic Vision of *Women in Love*', *Critical Inquiry*, 4 (Spring 1978): 559–88.

12 Alternatives to Logocentrism in D.H. Lawrence*

DANIEL J. SCHNEIDER

Daniel Schneider is Distinguished Professor at the University of Tennessee. He has published two books on Lawrence: the first, *D.H. Lawrence: the Artist as Psychologist* (University Press of Kansas, 1984), was a comprehensive study of the assumptions of Lawrence's psychology and a systematic analysis of the ways in which he worked his psychological laws into his fiction; the second, *The Consciousness of D.H. Lawrence: An Intellectual Biography* (University Press of Kansas, 1986), sought to lay bare Lawrence's effort to develop a religious alternative to contemporary scepticism and outworn belief. The present essay (which has had a short passage dealing with Lawrence on Walt Whitman cut from it) exemplifies Schneider's approach of scrupulously setting Lawrence's imaginative work in the context of his ideas – in this case exploring the apparent consanguinity of his thinking with that of deconstruction. (For further discussion of Schneider's contemporary reproduction of Lawrence, see Introduction, p. 21.)

Daniel Schneider is currently studying Lawrence's use of anthropology in the evolution of his thought.

D.H. Lawrence has been accused of a great many crimes against Logic and Reason, but no one has associated him with that frontal assault on traditional views of knowledge and logic that is known today as deconstruction. Yet it is illuminating to consider Lawrence in relation to deconstructionist thought if criticism is to appreciate the cogency of Lawrence's thinking about language and reality as well as the intelligence of his efforts to evade the snares of language. I am not arguing that D.H. Lawrence was a deconstructionist. Far from it; he often clung to the traditional view that language can be subjugated to thought and logic;

---

* Reprinted from *South Atlantic Review* **51**, 2 (May 1986): 35–47.

the view that, using language with care, one can avoid the snares of metaphor and of rhetoric generally. Also he would probably have opposed Paul de Man's contention that there is no 'privileged observer'(de Man, p. 10) – no one who can arrive at a correct evaluation of truth and significance. Yet it was part of Lawrence's quickness that he saw clearly the implications of an idea central in Nietzschean thought: that language, as instrument of the ideal consciousness, is a network of arbitrary signs and conventions that conceal a host of unexamined assumptions and that have no inevitable connection with 'presence' or with the validating 'intention' of the speaker. Early in his intellectual life Lawrence realised not only that words and knowledge do not correspond to being but also that mental or ideal statements cannot be taken as honest versions of the speaker's intention. All language is metaphorical; words do not mean what they say or say what is meant. Moreover, human intention is masked more often than it is revealed by 'writing'. Lawrence saw too that it is folly to presume that human conduct can be authorised or justified by an appeal to propositional truth; the only authentic appeal is to the wordless impulse of 'the Holy Ghost', that balancing center of the whole psyche which Lawrence believed makes adjustments far finer than any contemplated in the crude counters of language. For language, considered as instrument of the ego or ideal self, is always the enemy of truth and sincerity. One can go wrong in the mind – in words; only in 'the blood' and in the intuitive wisdom of the Holy Ghost can one know what one really desires, as apart from what one thinks one desires because of one's bewitchment by social pressures and the social lies of words.

The extent of Lawrence's attack on idealism – and on 'logocentrism', as Derrida would say – is revealed in his bold employment and adaptation of ideas that he found in four philosophers – Schopenhauer, Nietzsche, William James and Henri Bergson. All four provided arguments that fully supported his attack on 'knowledge' – and on what Derrida calls 'the myth of presence'. And they forced him to seek two closely related alternatives to the falsifications and the prison-house of language – first, the alternative of silence, touch, and wordless sympathy; second, the alternative of a knowledge which occupies 'a true place in the living activity of man'.

Schopenhauer established to Lawrence's satisfaction that the world as Idea is an illusion, a human fiction that does not correspond to the *Ding an sich*. Language, purporting to represent the real world, represents only the world as human idea, not the world as Inhuman Will. And all the terms of science are abstractions that 'fit badly':

> These 'laws' which science has invented, like conservation of energy, indestructibility of matter, gravitation, the will-to-live, survival of the

fittest: and even these absolute facts, like – the earth goes round the sun, or the doubtful atoms, electrons, or ether – they are all prison-walls, unless we realize that we don't know what they mean. We don't know what we mean, ultimately, by *conservation*, or *indestructibility*. Our atoms, electrons, ether, are caps that fit exceedingly badly. And our will-to-live contains a germ of suicide, and our survival-of-the-fittest the germ of degeneracy. As for the earth going round the sun: it goes round as the blood goes round my body, absolutely mysteriously, with the rapidity and hesitation of life.

But the human ego, in its pettifogging arrogance, sets up these things for you as absolutes, and unless you kick hard and kick in time, they are your prison walls forever.

(Lawrence, *Phoenix II*, pp. 397–9)

Because he was so keenly aware of the gulf between language and being, Lawrence was often indifferent to vocabulary in his own 'philosophy'. He knew perfectly well that the pre-Socratic philosophers, or theosophists like Hélène Blavatsky or James Pryse could not be regarded as speaking sober 'truth'. Yet the ideas of Heraclitus or of occultists could easily be accepted as metaphors expressing fundamental insights that were also in Herbert Spencer or in Ernst Haeckel. After all, scientific explanations were also metaphorical. It did not seem to Lawrence that the Heraclitean exchanges of fire and water or the Empedoclean oscillations of Love and Strife were *essentially* different from Spencer's idea of action and reaction, or that the polarity of male and female was *essentially* different from that of positive and negative electrons. If anything, the pre-Socratic philosophers seemed more *factual* than modern physicists because the Greeks spoke of a world perceived by sense – air, earth, fire, and water instead of atoms, electrons, and electromagnetic forces!

Nietzsche's analysis of 'the basic presuppositions of the metaphysics of language' – or, in 'plain talk, the presuppositions of reason' – carried the Schopenhauerian (and Kantian) skepticism still further, calling into question the presuppositions in language of 'unity, permanence, substance, cause, thinghood, being' (p. 482). Lawrence's essential agreement with these conclusions can be found everywhere in his writings, notably in 'The Crown', where Lawrence draws heavily on one of Nietzsche's teachers, Heraclitus:

If I say that *I am*, this is false and evil. I am not . . . Our ready-made individuality, our identity is no more than an accidental cohesion in the flux of time. The cohesion will break down and utterly cease to be . . . (*Phoenix II*, p. 384).

Only perpetuation is a sin . . . (p. 412). In Time and Eternity all is in flux (p. 413).
Memory is not truth. Memory is persistence, perpetuation of a momentary cohesion in the flux . . . (p. 414).
Men may be utterly different from the things they now seem. And then they will behold, to their astonishment, that the sun is absolutely different from the thing they now see, or that they call 'sun' (p. 415).

In addition to the metaphysical absence, Nietzsche established that there is psychological absence. There is no self-presence as a guarantor of meaning. The 'I' is a convention, and real intentions are masked by 'ideal' intentions – the intentions stated in language. The true meaning of any statement becomes an undermeaning, disguised desire, or envy or *ressentiment*. The task of interpretation becomes that of seeing through the subterfuge – penetrating the surface and discovering the 'underconsciousness' which contradicts the ideal consciousness. *Studies in Classic American Literature* is relentless deconstruction of the language to expose the hypocritical, masquerading self with its 'diabolic' intentions. American writers seldom say what they mean or mean what they say: they cannot, having been mesmerised by a false idealism.

William James's idea of the stream of consciousness, coupled with Bergson's emphasis on duration and on the falsifying nature of the abstractive intellect, supported the deconstruction of the 'I'. James, it will be remembered, argued persuasively that the physiological states of the body precede the 'I' which is conscious. According to James's theory of the emotions, we do not cry because we are sorry or strike because we are angry; rather, says James, 'we feel sorry because we cry, angry because we strike, afraid because we tremble' (James, p. 333). Ideas are always *belated* – mental activity is the effect of physical activity; and the self becomes a changing 'Thought' that appropriates the thoughts of past selves, or Thoughts. Lawrence seized on this idea of the belatedness of thought and the flowing, changing self as a complete justification for his attack on Idealism, which, instead of accepting the flux of the psyche, freezes the self into an unchanging ego and freezes the fluent world into fixed, limited categories that substitute for reality. Like Bergson, Lawrence recognised that the verbal counters employed by the abstractive intellect ignore process and organic change and obliterate the infinitude of detail and of variety in experience, reducing the concrete interconnectedness and flow of events to the limited, fixed categories of a non-existent 'mental' world.

The idea of the belatedness – and hence the falsity – of 'knowledge' is stated boldly in *Women in Love*, where Birkin argues, 'You can only have knowledge, strictly . . . of things concluded, in the past. It's like bottling the liberty of last summer in the bottled gooseberries' (p. 79). In *Fantasia of the Unconscious,* Lawrence argues eloquently that 'an idea is just the final concrete or registered result of living dynamic interchange and reactions' (or sympathetic and voluntary feelings). No idea 'is ever perfectly expressed until its dynamic cause is finished; and . . . to continue to put into dynamic effect an already perfected idea means the nullification of all living activity, the substitution of mechanism, and the resultant horrors of ennui, ecstasy, neurasthenia, and a collapsing psyche' (p. 83). If ideas could arise 'ever fresh, ever displaced, like the leaves of a tree, from out of the quickness of the sap', they might correspond to being; and Lawrence clings to the belief that such ideas are possible; but implicitly Lawrence seems to be arguing that any employment of language – which gives us 'an already perfected idea' – does violence to the reality which is the body's sympathetic or antagonistic response to immediacy.

Moreover, uniqueness and individuality are always falsified by language. One can say, with Hermione Roddice, that 'in the spirit we are all one, all equal in the spirit, all brothers there', but such language, with its buried metaphors drawn from mathematics, obliterates the reality of individual uniqueness. As Rupert Birkin bitterly replies:

> 'It is just the opposite, just the contrary, Hermione. We are all different and unequal in spirit – it is only the *social* differences that are based on accidental material conditions. We are all abstractly or mathematically equal, if you like . . . But spiritually there is pure difference and neither equality nor inequality counts. It is upon these two bits of knowledge that you must found a state. Your democracy is an absolute lie – your brotherhood of man is a pure falsity, if you apply it further than the mathematical abstraction.'
>
> (*Women in Love,* p. 96)

In *Psychoanalysis and the Unconscious,* Lawrence argues that the 'reality of individuality' is 'unanalysable' and 'undefinable' (p. 214). 'Cause-and-effect' cannot explain 'even the individuality of a single dandelion' (p. 214). Individuality is, in truth, that which cannot be stated or analysed in language because language always reduces the individual to the universal – always emphasises characteristics which are shared, common to all members of the class.[1] From this it follows, as in Bergson, that intuition rather than mental 'knowing' is needed if one is to register the subtlety and uniqueness of another individual.

Even one's self cannot be known. For 'knowledge is to consciousness what the signpost is to the traveller: just an indication of the way which has been travelled before' (*Fantasia,* p. 76). In immediacy, the reality is 'a constant current of interflow, a constant vibrating interchange', and as William James pointed out that the bodily state precedes mental awareness, so Lawrence identified the only true knowledge with the blood-consciousness – intuitive and instinctive awareness that is non-verbal. In this connection, one might recall that Nietzsche had argued that animals *think* all the time, but that verbal consciousness is a late development of the species and a crude instrument for dealing with living realities. Lawrence obviously accepted that argument, and stated it in various ways from *Study of Thomas Hardy* (1914) to the end of his life.

In his search for a living truth and a living belief undefiled by the lies propounded by the herd – the lie of idealism, of equality, of brotherhood, of love of neighbor, of the general welfare, of self-sacrifice and selflessness – Lawrence sought in three different ways to overcome the falsifications of logocentrism.

The first was not an alternative to logocentrism as such, but an attempt to invent a new language and a new kind of narrative structure that would lay bare the realities which conventional language obscures or falsifies. He must find a way to dispel the conventional idea of the self as a conscious ego, the conventional idea of 'personality' or 'character'. The artist must reveal, beneath the superficial personality or ego, what a woman really is – in herself or as the expression of the great inhuman will. Narrative structure must reveal the *forma informans* of the divine will, the artist's imagination must open the doors of perception and see things as they really are: infinite. The Blakean mission was what Lawrence set out to accomplish in *The Rainbow*, where the pattern of attraction and repulsion, unity and division, sympathy and resistance, synthesis and destruction, constitutes the very form of scenic development. The pattern is the divine will in action, *natura naturans*, the Heraclitean to-and-fro in the lives of Tom Brangwen and Lydia Lensky, of Will Brangwen and Anna, and of Ursula and Anton Skrebensky. Character is dissolved in the universal pattern – the pattern of the macrocosm – and, as Aldous Huxley observes in *Eyeless in Gaza*, human beings become 'anonymous' in Lawrence: 'psychological atomism' is rationalised into 'a philosophical system'. Thus Lawrence hoped that *Maya* would be overcome in a fiction that preserves the timeless form even as it captures the dynamism of the flux.[2] In his new work on *The Sisters* (1913), he felt that he had got rid of 'the Laocoon writhing and shrieking' of his earlier fiction and had captured 'something of the eternal stillness that lies under all movement, under all life, like a source, incorruptible and inexhaustible' – 'the great impersonal which never changes and out of which all change comes' (Lawrence, *Letters*, 2, pp. 137–8).

The second way to avoid the falsification of logocentrism was to insist on wordless physical communication. Men and women must depart from society and enter into new relationships with one another. In the Utopia which Lawrence perhaps unconsciously modeled after Haggs farm, where he had begun 'a new life' with the Chambers family, there would be a holy ground, or a holy center, 'an abiding place' which is 'the meeting ground', as Lawrence wrote in *The Plumed Serpent*. 'There needs a centre of silence', he wrote to Rolf Gardner on 3 December 1926,

> and a heart of darkness . . . We'll have to establish some spot on earth, that will be the fissure into the underworld, like the oracle at Delphos, where one can always come to . . . And then one must set out and learn a deep discipline – and learn dances from all the world, and take whatsoever we can make into our own. And learn music the same; mass music and canons, and wordless music like the Indians have.
>
> (*Letters*, p. 951)

Two years later, in another letter to Gardner, Lawrence wrote, 'You ought to have a few, very few . . . who would add together their little flames of consciousness and make a permanent core. That would make a holy centre: whole, heal, hale.' He goes on to say that the English 'must have kindled again their religious sense of at-one-ness. And for that you must have a silent, central flame of *consciousness* and of warmth which radiates out bit by bit' (*Letters*, p. 1031). To the psychoanalyst Trigant Burrow he wrote: 'And I do think that the only way of true relationship between men is to meet in some common "belief" – if the belief is but physical and not merely mental' (3 August 1927, in Moore (ed.), p. 933).

The 'belief' which is 'but physical', or the 'silent, central flame . . . of *consciousness* and of warmth' is what he called elsewhere 'the phallic consciousness' – the pre-verbal sympathetic awareness or responsiveness which, being rooted in sex, is essentially unitive, a force binding men and women, and men and men, and men and the cosmos together. Dance and wordless songs and rituals might augment the sense of unison. The 'civilisation of touch', if it could be established, would discover ways to do away with, or to penetrate beyond, the falsifications of language. For the blood cannot lie. (As the French mime Marcel Marceau remarked in a television interview, 'for lies you really need words'. The body cannot lie, or lies only with difficulty; hence, said Marceau, 'It is very difficult for a mime to tell lies.')

In his essay, 'A Propos of *Lady Chatterley's Lover*', Lawrence writes with an eloquence unusual even for Lawrence:

> the greatest need of man is the renewal forever of the complete rhythm of life and death, the rhythm of the sun's year, the body's year of a lifetime, and the greater year of the stars, the soul's year of immortality. This is our need, our imperative need. It is a need of the mind and soul, body, spirit and sex: all. It is no use asking for a Word to fulfill such a need. No Word, no Logos, no Utterance will ever do it. The Word is uttered, most of it: we need only pay true attention. But

who will call us to the Deed, the great Deed of the Seasons and the
year, the Deed of the soul's cycle, the Deed of a woman's life at one
with a man's, the little Deed of the moon's wandering, the bigger Deed
of the sun's, and the biggest, of the great still stars? It is the *Deed* of life
we have now to learn: we are supposed to have learnt the Word, but,
alas, look at us. Word-perfect we may be, but Deed-demented.

(*Phoenix II*, p. 510)

He goes on to call for rituals of the day and of the seasons, of life and of
death – a 'return to ancient forms', though these will have to be 'created
again'. The universe is dead for us, 'the abstracted mind' inhabits a 'dry
sterile little world' (p. 511). 'Mental, rational, scientific' knowing, which
is 'knowing in terms of apartness', must be replaced by religious and
poetic knowing, 'in terms of togetherness' (p. 512).

The emphasis on the deed instead of the Word is significant. To
Aldous Huxley he wrote in November of 1927, 'I myself am in a state of
despair about the Word either written or spoken seriously' (*Letters*, 1020).
It is not surprising that in many of his last poems he invoked 'holy
Silence' and lamented that 'man has killed the silence of the earth' (*CP*,
pp. 698, 725). 'What has killed mankind . . . is lies' (*CP*, p. 654), he
wrote, and 'since I hate lying', he said, 'I keep to myself as much as
possible' (*Letters*, p. 967). Again and again he sought to escape 'the petrol
fumes of human conversation' and to satisfy the 'great desire to drink life
direct/from the source, not out of bottles and bottled personal vessels'
(*CP*, pp. 646, 481). How, he kept asking, can one live a *real* life instead of
the mechanical, false life in which talk is like that at Hermione Roddice's
Breadalby – 'a rattle of artillery'? All speech which expressed the will of
the petty human ego was a form of aggression: bullying. The 'spiritual
will' was the will armed with words and slogans which it employed
everywhere to 'force' life. If the deep impulses of life were ever to be
realised, it was necessary to 'keep still', to 'keep quiet, and wait' (*CP*,
p. 514).

The third way to avoid the falsifications of logocentrism was to make
sure that the 'knowledge' acquired by the conscious ego is 'put into its
true place in the living activity of men' (*Fantasia*, p. 76). That is, the
knowledge which we express in words must always be subordinated to
the deeper knowledge which is pre-verbal and to the impulses of desire
and resistance which arise in the depths of the soul – the *authentic* desires
and hatreds of the deepest self.

Lawrence had no doubt that a knowledge which is merely mental or
rational is incapable of grasping truth. In his little poem 'Thought' he
distinguishes between thought which is 'the jiggling and twisting of
already existent ideas' and thought which is 'the welling up of unknown
life into consciousness'. Ultimately true thought was 'a man in his

167

wholeness wholly attending.' Such a man would show the wisdom which he defines in *Fantasia of the Unconscious* as

> a state of soul. It is the state wherein we know our wholeness and the complicated, manifold nature of our being. It is the state wherein we know the great relations which exist between us and our near ones. And it is the state which accepts full responsibility, first for our own souls, and then for the living dynamic relations wherein we have our being. It is no use expecting the other person to know. Each must know for himself.
>
> (*Fantasia*, p. 53)

The inclusion of the idea of 'responsibility' is necessary, for it is responsibility which enables him to distinguish between thought which is false and inauthentic and thought which is true and authentic. False thought is purely mental or verbal – it has no basis in the deepest self, the whole man; it is the thought of a *persona*, of a non-self created by 'writing'.

True thought is authorised by the deep commitment to the whole self. It is not, however, primitive. Following the passage above, Lawrence goes on to say that it is 'sophistry' and 'criminal cowardice' to pretend 'that children and idiots alone know best' (*Fantasia*, p. 53). The Dostoevskyan embrace of The Idiot is a dodge of full 'life-responsibility'. Thus Lawrence acknowledged that 'true knowledge' may depend to some extent on conscious and verbal elements; it is not *merely* unconscious and pre-verbal. In truth, it must be both conscious and unconscious. That paradoxical conclusion is at the root of Lawrence's important declaration: 'the supreme lesson of human consciousness is to learn how *not to know*. That is, how not to *interfere*. That is, how to live dynamically, from the great Source, and not statically, like machines driven by ideas and principles from the head, or automatically, from one fixed desire. At last, knowledge must be put into its true place in the living activity of man' (*Fantasia*, p. 76). . . .

In short, Lawrence believes that one can escape the prisonhouse of language, provided one knows the true place of mind and knowledge in the living of life. Above all, like the deconstructionists, one must understand that language may bear no connection with a speaker's original intention and that the structures of convention which masquerade as sincere or authentic truth are mere structures, dead, static, final. No words, no ideas, can convey the breath of life. On the contrary, all knowledge is, strictly speaking, the death of life, the death of being.

Lawrence did not carry his skepticism as far as Derrideans are wont to do. He clung to the traditional view that language is, or can be, subjugated to 'thought', and style to the notion of a plenitude of meaning. But it is obvious that the Lawrence who has been scorned as an irrationalist and a romantic had gone far beyond the simple realism of those who hold that knowledge can be achieved which is undistorted by metaphysical assumptions or by rhetorical snares. Lawrence's solutions to the problem of discovering truth – the solution of inventing a new language, of silence and physical communion, and of locating knowledge in 'the living activity of men' – may seem naive to those realists. But the 'realists' are also naive, and when one reflects that they would base their most important life-decisions on ideal statements, one is forced to reassess Lawrence's call for silence, phallic consciousness, and 'true knowledge'. In fact, of course, Lawrence was never the primitive he has been imagined to be. At the root of his appeal to silence and to phallic consciousness lay the sophisticated Nietzschean deconstruction of language and the Nietzschean awareness of the priority of life to reason or mind.

Notes

1. Cf. *Kristeva's* obsrevation (p. x) that 'the overly constraining and reductive meaning of a language made up of universals causes us to suffer', yet 'the call of the unnameable . . . issuing from those borders where signification vanishes, hurls us into the void of a psychosis that appears henceforth as the solidary reverse of our universe, saturated with interpretation, faith, or truth'. Lawrence's resistance to 'our universe', the universe created in words, branded him as 'psychotic' to many who simply could not understand the depth and ferocity of his religious rejection of convention and conformity.
2. For an exceptionally lucid analysis of problems closely related to those confronted by Lawrence – and by some contemporary critics – see *Krieger*, who points out that such critics as Geoffrey Hartman (in *The Unmediated Vision*) and Ihab Hassan (in 'The Dismemberment of Orpheus' and *The Literature of Silence*) view language and form as the 'totalitarian force that everywhere subdues the wayward to its overwhelming autotelic purposiveness, thus delivering death to our subjective freedom' (pp. 589–90). The equations developed by such critics (Hassan chiefly) are as follows: 'language equals sublimation equals symbol equals mediation equals culture equals *objectivity* equals abstraction equals death. As point-by-point apocalyptic alternatives, silence (as the identity of nothingness and the indiscriminate, chaotic all) has as its equations (instead of sublimation) indulgence, (instead of symbolism) flesh, (instead of mediation) outrage, (instead of culture) anarchy, (instead of objectivity) subjectivity, (instead of abstraction) particularity, (instead of death) instinctual life' (p. 590).
   Krieger's own view of poetry – that it is mediation that holds 'the dynamism of flux in its coils' when the poet makes the language 'his own' – would probably have appealed to Lawrence, who, as I have pointed out, believed that the quick of life *can* be captured in words provided that the writer does

not attempt to impose conclusions that are rigged in advance and that thus violate the trembling to-and-fro of life.

References

PAUL DE MAN, *Blindness and Insight: Essays in the Rhetoric of Contemporary Criticism* (New York: Oxford University Press, 1971).

WILLIAM JAMES, *Psychology* (Greenwich, CT: Fawcett, 1963).

MURRAY KRIEGER, 'Meditation, Language, and Vision in the Reading of Literature', *Issues in Contemporary Literary Criticism*, ed. Gregory T. Polletta (Boston: Little Brown, 1973), pp. 585–613.

JULIA KRISTEVA, *Desire in Language: A Semiotic Approach to Literature and Art*, ed. Leon S. Roudiez (New York: Columbia University Press, 1980).

D.H. Lawrence, *The Collected Letters of D.H. Lawrence*, ed. and with an introduction by Harry T. Moore, 2 vols (London: Heinemann, 1962).

D.H. Lawrence, *The Complete Poems of D.H. Lawrence*, ed. Vivian de Sola Pinto and Warren Roberts (New York: Viking, 1971). Here cited as *CP*.

D.H. Lawrence, *Fantasia of the Unconscious and Psychoanalysis and the Unconscious* (Harmondsworth, Middlesex: Penguin, 1960).

D.H. Lawrence, *The Letters of D.H. Lawrence*, ed. James T. Boulton (Cambridge: Cambridge University Press, 1981).

D.H. Lawrence, *Phoenix II: Uncollected, Unpublished, and Other Prose Works*, ed. Warren Roberts and Harry T. Moore (Harmondsworth, Middlesex: Penguin, 1978).

D.H. Lawrence, *Studies in Classic American Literature* (Harmondsworth, Middlesex: Penguin, 1977).

D.H. Lawrence, *Women in Love* (Harmondsworth, Middlesex: Penguin, 1979).

Nietzsche, Friedrich, *The Portable Nietzsche*, ed. Walter Kaufmann (New York: Viking, 1972).

13 Contexts of Reading: the Reception of D.H. Lawrence's *The Rainbow* and *Women in Love**

ALISTAIR DAVIES

Alistair Davies is a Lecturer in English and American Studies at the University of Sussex. The present essay contains a substantial cut – an extended comparative reading of Lawrence's wartime novels with the French novelist Roman Rolland's ten-volume work, *Jean-Christophe* (1904–12), which Lawrence apparently read in 1913, and with which Davies finds *The Rainbow* and *Women in Love* have similarities. His general aim in this, as in the attempt to explain Leavis's particular construction of Lawrence in the excerpt reprinted here, is to deconstruct the insularly 'English' representation of Lawrence's work (sustained even by contemporary Marxist critics like Eagleton and Williams, see Introduction, pp. 13, 17). Within his period, Lawrence can then be read in a *European* literary context (Rolland), his wartime novels internationalist in spirit and opposed to the idea of the nation-state; and Leavis's need to emphasise his Englishness can be seen to be determined in part by contemporary attacks on Lawrence during and after the war for his seemingly anti-English sentiments. Although I have located Davies's essay in the post-structuralist section of this Reader, it is only 'deconstructive' in the sense that its promotion of contextual reading helps to dismantle those pervasive historical and ideological representations of Lawrence which limit our perception of his work.

Alistair Davies is principally interested in Anglo-American modernism, about which he has published a number of articles.

---

* Reprinted from Frank Glóversmith (ed.), *The Theory of Reading* (Brighton: Harvester Press, 1984), pp. 199–202, 214–22; references renumbered from the original.

The Cambridge critic F.R. Leavis has, for many, provided in his *D.H. Lawrence: Novelist* (1955) the definitive readings of Lawrence's *The Rainbow* and *Women in Love*.[1] According to Leavis, Lawrence presented in *The Rainbow* a broad but intimate social history of England at the crucial points of its transformation from an agricultural into an industrial society. He described this process from firsthand experience, and as he described, he also enumerated the losses, in community, in human relationships, in contact with Nature, which the change entailed. Indeed, for Leavis, it is as a recorder of the social and cultural traditions, of the modes of life, of a certain nonconformist civilisation in English history, at the moment when industrial England interpenetrated and destroyed the old, agricultural England, that Lawrence has most value. In the modern period, Lawrence was, Leavis argued, 'as a recorder of essential English history . . . a great successor to George Eliot' (Leavis, *D.H. Lawrence: Novelist*, p. 107). *The Rainbow* was in the tradition of *Middlemarch* and might have been written:

> to show what, in the concrete, a living tradition is, and what it is to be brought up in the environment of one. (As to whether the tradition qualifies as 'central' I will not argue; I am content with recording it to have been that in the environment of which George Eliot, too, was brought up.) We are made to see how, amid the pieties and continuities of life at the Marsh, the spiritual achievements of a mature civilization . . . are transmitted.
>
> (Leavis, p. 105)

Lawrence, however, did not simply memorialise the nonconformist tradition out of which he (and George Eliot) had come. He showed, through the history of three generations of the Brangwen family, that the tradition was not only a shaping and sustaining power, but that its pieties and sanctions remained, even in the contemporary world, a living presence. Ursula's quest for spiritual fulfilment was in no essential measure different from that of her predecessors. The new kind of civilisation which had obliterated the world of Marsh Farm had not obliterated its spiritual heritage, its particular sacredness of vision. It was this vision which Lawrence had preserved and transmitted through his 'marvellous invention of form' which rendered 'the continuity and rhythm of life' (Leavis, p. 144). If the final section of the novel dealing with Ursula often seemed tentative, if her final prophetic passages were 'wholly unprepared and unsupported' (p. 142), the achievement of Lawrence's novel as a whole was undiminished. He had described, and, more importantly, had enacted 'the transmission of the spiritual heritage in an actual society' (p. 145).

Women in Love, Leavis continued, was a more complex work, in terms of its fictional technique and of its social vision. There were 'new things to be done in fiction, conceived as a wholly serious art, and it was for his particular genius to do them' (p. 147). Lawrence created here a panoramic novel of Edwardian and Georgian England before the sickness which he diagnosed within it had precipitated the country into the destruction of the First World War. 'After reading *Women in Love*, we do feel', Leavis asserted, 'that we have "touched the whole pulse of social England"' (p. 173). Lawrence's powers as a novelist lay in exploring the essential, or the inner spiritual history of England, and he presented with brilliant insight the brutality and self-destructiveness of Gerald, the perversity of Gudrun, and the positive and creative drives of Ursula and of Birkin. Yet, if his diagnosis was first-rate, his solution to the problems diagnosed was less satisfactory. Ursula and Birkin may have discovered, as a couple, a realm of values and of being which allowed them to withdraw from the downward rush to destruction of the civilisation around them, but their personal quest for salvation, a quest which led them to abandon England, was, Leavis acknowledged, perplexing and contradictory in a novelist so committed to social renewal. Lawrence perhaps had been defeated by the difficulty of life.

Leavis intended his study to champion Lawrence's peculiarly English vision, his peculiarly English genius, and in this, he was brilliantly successful. With *D.H. Lawrence: Novelist*, he established Lawrence's reputation in English and American criticism as the foremost English novelist of the century. Moreover, he drew attention not only to Lawrence's merits as a novelist but also to his importance as a modern thinker. Lawrence, he argued, had analysed the problems and the dilemmas of our present phase of civilisation, when industrial society and industrial values were becoming paramount, with an insight which no other modern thinker possessed. Yet there was a paradox in Leavis's approach, for while he related Lawrence's work to a definite historical moment, he did not concern himself with the precise literary, social or political context in which the novels were written. He did not have, it is true, the advantage of the textual histories of *The Rainbow* and *Women in Love* which have been produced since his study was first published. We now know in detail, for example, not only how Lawrence reworked *The Rainbow* and *Women in Love* from an earlier work, 'The Wedding Ring', but also exactly how he redrafted *The Rainbow*, after the outbreak of the First World War, giving (among other substantial changes) much greater prominence to Ursula's quest for freedom and independence. Even so, Leavis's disregard for the way in which the outbreak of the First World War might have affected Lawrence's reworking of *The Rainbow* and *Women in Love* is strange in a critic otherwise so conscious of the historical and social pressures upon Lawrence's writing.

It is a disregard which, in due course, led to a curious imperceptiveness in Leavis's reading. When Ursula, for instance, recovers from her illness, at the end of *The Rainbow*, she insistently repeats: 'I have no father nor mother nor lover, I have no allocated place in the world of things, I do not belong to Beldover nor to Nottingham nor to England nor to this world, they none of them exist. I am trammelled and entangled in them, but they are all unreal'.[2] These are hardly the words of a Dorothea Brooke, for Ursula does not believe that she should submit, as does George Eliot's heroine in *Middlemarch*, to the forms and limits of local and of national life, but seeks rather to find her identity by rejecting and transcending them. The contrast, indeed, is instructive: the importance of Ursula's quest lies precisely in her refusal to accept such forms and limits. How are we, therefore, to understand her words – and the quest for freedom which, in the last and longest section of the novel, inspires them? They have profound implications for Ursula's private life; but they have no less profound implications for her (and for our) political life as well. It is impossible to ignore their subversive intent. We need, Lawrence suggests, if we are to become free, if we are to become truly ourselves, to reject all national values, all national perspectives and all those human ties which, under present conditions, uphold the nation-state. *The Rainbow* was not simply a novel rewritten during the First World War: it became, in the process, a novel about, and in opposition to, those forces which made war possible. . . .

I have suggested that, if we are to understand D.H. Lawrence's *The Rainbow* and *Women in Love* accurately, we need to place them in the context not only of English but of European literature, and specifically, of French literature; and in the context, not of the fiction of the nineteenth century but of the fiction of the early twentieth century. It is an assertion which almost inescapably involves the following questions. If this is the case, why has a quite contrary interpretation of Lawrence, dating from F.R. Leavis's *D.H. Lawrence: Novelist* (1955) been established and accepted within the English critical tradition, even by recent critics, such as Raymond Williams and Terry Eagleton, who rebut the form, if not the content, of Leavis's reading of Lawrence?[3] By what process of critical revision has the individualist and anti-nationalist perspective which I have described been transformed into the epic, quintessentially English one of F.R. Leavis's study?

Again, the contextual method, conscious that criticism, like literature, and reading, like writing, has to be placed in its cultural, social and political context, helps us to find an answer. For Leavis, as he makes his case for Lawrence, does so by rejecting the specific charges made against Lawrence in the most influential literary journalism of the 1920s and the 1930s. Against Wyndham Lewis, who had argued in *Paleface* (1929) that Lawrence advocated capitulation to mindless instinct, Leavis argued that Lawrence made plain that 'without proper use of intelligence there can

be no solution of the problems of mental, emotional and spiritual health'
(Leavis, *D.H. Lawrence: Novelist*, p. 310). Against John Middleton Murry,
who had suggested in *Son of Woman* (1931) that Lawrence's fiction was
the record of his sexual failure and of his deep hatred of women, Leavis
asserted its health and normality. In *The Rainbow*, the pieties of life at
Marsh Farm, Leavis suggested, were clearly feminine and matriarchal:
Lawrence celebrated throughout the novel the moral and creative vitality
of women. Against Murry's assertion that Lawrence used his fiction after
The Rainbow as a vehicle for his 'thought-adventures', Leavis defended
the artistry of *Women in Love*. Against T.S. Eliot, who had suggested in
After Strange Gods (1934) that Lawrence was an ignoramus who had come
from an intellectual and spiritual tradition in decay, Leavis argued that
Lawrence's nonconformist background was one of rich and sustaining
intellectual life. He alerted Eliot to the 'extraordinary active intellectual
life enjoyed by that group of young people of which Lawrence was the
centre' (Leavis, p. 306). It was just such a rich and central tradition which
Lawrence celebrated in *The Rainbow*, and as he did so, he celebrated an
essential strand of English history. For the Congregationalism of
Lawrence's youth had played an important part in English civilisation as
Eliot would see if he read Elie Halévy. The English nonconformist
tradition was one from which the major works of nineteenth-century
English fiction, from George Eliot to Thomas Hardy, had come. This
tradition, and the fiction which it inspired, was not, as Eliot suggested,
eccentric, but stood at the heart of English cultural, political and moral
life.

Yet, in asserting Lawrence's normality, his love for and rootedness
within English values and traditions, Leavis was engaged in defending
Lawrence against a persistent and unusually grave charge, which
underlies the criticism of Lewis, Murry and Eliot, that Lawrence had been
no less than a traitor to his country during the First World War, and had
continued to be so after the War with his support for Bolshevism. The
allegation was seriously stated, and its truth widely accepted. It is a
measure of Leavis's success in cultural rehabilitation that this central
aspect of the immediate critical reception of Lawrence had been forgotten.

In the first two years of the First World War, Lawrence's public
opposition to the War brought charges of treachery and of lack of
patriotism, and the publication of *The Rainbow* in 1915, with its criticism
of the nation-state, seemed to confirm them. Certainly, the banning of
The Rainbow on the grounds of obscenity was widely, and correctly,
thought to be a political act.[4] The morbid sexual content of *The Rainbow*,
J.C. Squire argued in the *New Statesman*, revealing the prevailing
association of Lawrence with the German cause, was suspiciously
Hunnish. The book 'broods gloomily over the physical reactions of sex in
a way so persistent that one wonders whether the author is under the

spell of German psychologists'.[5] It was, however, with *Women in Love* in 1921 that the full case against Lawrence was made explicit. His most influential accuser was John Middleton Murry. 'It is part of our creed', Murry wrote in the *Nation and Athenaeum*, 'that the writer must be responsible; but it is part of [Lawrence's] creed that he is not.'[6] His lofty and semi-official tone, passing considered judgement in the public interest, came from his recent, war-time role as censor at the War Office, but it came also from the new function which he, the most noted editor of the period, assumed for English criticism after the War. The English writer and critic should now, he believed, speak in the name of and in the defence of the special wisdom of the English race, which had been achieved through its Christian and its Protestant history. That should be his creed, for the English writer and critic was heir to a strain of heretical individualism, an instinct for freedom. This was English culture's unique contribution, politically and culturally, to world society. Even so, the impulse to freedom should never be anarchic; the individual should come freely to accept the loyalties and the allegiances which bound him, as an Englishman, to his people and to its unique heritage.

From this perspective, Lawrence, whose passionate individualism made him the 'most interesting figure' in English letters, had to be censured. 'We stand by the consciousness and the civilization of which the literature we know is the finest flower', Murry insisted, but Lawrence was in rebellion against both: 'If we try him before our court he contemptuously rejects the jurisdiction. The things we prize are the things he would destroy; what is triumph to him is catastrophe to us. He is the outlaw of modern English literature; and he is the most interesting figure in it. But he must be shown no mercy.'

Murry's forensic language was not accidental. Lawrence was being tried *in absentia*. He, 'the outlaw of modern English literature', had repudiated his ties with and his allegiances to England and to English culture. His rejection of the decencies of English life, his opposition to the Allied cause in the War – which alone could explain his relish in portraying the collapse of English society in *Women in Love* and his own abandonment of England for foreign lands – these formed the implicit basis of Murry's public indictment.

Lawrence, Murry insisted, wanted above all to destroy that level of consciousness upon which European civilisation was founded. Through Birkin, who had 'a negroid as well as an Egyptian avatar', Lawrence advocated, Murry wrote, quoting *Women in Love*, 'sensual mindless mysteries to be achieved through an awful African process'. This process was, for Murry, a literal degradation, a falling back to the 'sub-human and bestial, a thing that our forefathers had rejected when they began to rise from the slime'. Lawrence, quite simply, delighted in imagining the overthrow of England by the forces of darkness and of barbarism. The qualities of Lawrence's genius 'no longer delight us', Murry had announced at the beginning of his review: 'They have been pressed into the service of another power, they walk in bondage and in livery.' Murry's language is vague and shrill, but its import would be clear to a contemporary audience. Lawrence had rejoiced during the War to think of England defeated by the Prussians whom he served, just as he rejoiced after the War to think of his native country overthrown by his new masters, the Bolshevists.

When Murry returned to Lawrence in his major study of Lawrence's novels, *Son of Woman* (1931), he made use of the new languages of psychoanalysis and of sociology, but his charge of treachery against Lawrence remained the same. Lawrence was, Murry argued, a dangerous demagogue, for the novel had become a vehicle for his 'thought-adventures', his aim as a writer 'to discover authority, not to create art'.[7] He had gone to America as a second Moses, as a Law-giver who 'should bring its soul to consciousness'. If the Mahatma Gandhi could convulse and revivify a whole Empire, he suggested, 'there was no reason why Lawrence should not give laws to a people' (Murry, *Son of Woman*, pp. 169–70). Lawrence's intention in America had been to bring about, through the disintegration of traditional, white consciousness, the end of Western civilisation. By comparing Lawrence's teaching with that of Gandhi, by suggesting their common revolt against the West, Murry indicated the revolutionary threat Lawrence's teachings were thought to pose.

But why should Lawrence do this? Murry found a ready psychological and sociological explanation in Lawrence's upbringing. Although born into the working class, with its warmth of human contact, Lawrence had been dominated in childhood by his mother. Having aspirations to middle-class gentility, she caused Lawrence to repress his sexual vitality as gross and vulgar. Accordingly, he grew up a guilt-ridden sexual weakling, 'a sex-crucified man' (Murry, p. 21), and remained 'a child of the woman' (p. 73), with deep resentment at his inadequacy and limitations. In his dreams, he was 'a wild, untamed, dominant male' (p. 73), yet he wanted also to be a child, with the happiness and oblivion of childhood.

Sons and Lovers, Murry suggested, had been an assertive fantasy of social and sexual independence. *The Rainbow*, which concentrated throughout on unsatisfactory relationships, first of Anna and Will, then of Ursula and Anton, reflected the failure of his marriage to Frieda. It was 'radically, the history of Lawrence's final sexual failure' (Murry, p. 88). Thereafter, he took his revenge upon the social order itself, which the mother and wife enshrined, in fantasies of destruction and of extravagant sexual assertion. *Women in Love*, in which Birkin/Lawrence demanded of Ursula a kind of sexual or sensual homage, was the first of a series of aggressive fantasies in which the female, insatiably demanding satisfaction, was annihilated by the man who could not satisfy her (Murry, p. 118). The woman was humiliated, and the man formed, in the place of marriage, emotional alliances with other men. Love was turned into hate, loyalty into betrayal and the quest for life became the unconscious veneration of chaos and of death. In *Women in Love*, Lawrence envisaged a whole culture within a death-miasma in order to 'feed his sense of doom and death and corruption; to fulfil his own injunction that "we must disintegrate while we live"' (Murry, p. 330). In his American writings, Lawrence exulted in the destruction of England and of Europe, and hoped for his own, vengeful resurrection by absorbing the dark blood-consciousness of America's primitive races. Yet for Murry, these writings, with their fantasies of leadership, with their celebration of primitive communism, merely expressed Lawrence's power-fantasies and his craving for death (p. 333). It was clear that the Bolshevist Lawrence, embittered by his sexual perversity and by his proletarian origins, wished, in the spirit of revenge, to destroy the normal and wholesome world of culture, refinement and adult relationship, from which he had been excluded.

Murry was not the only critic to find in Lawrence's work the example of a resentful or treacherous Bolshevist temperament. Wyndham Lewis, whose writings of the 1920s and 1930s were concerned to identify those writers who, in his opinion, were working towards the overthrow of the West by what he termed 'Oriental Bolshevism', found Lawrence to be the most prominent and the most dangerous foe of the West: 'In contrast to the White Overlord of this world in which we live, Mr Lawrence shows us a more primitive type of "consciousness", which has been physically defeated by the White "consciousness"', and assures us that the defeated "consciousness" is the better of the two'.[8] Lawrence was, Lewis suggested, 'a natural communist' because he was unmanly, preferring the mindless and feminine merging of Oriental Bolshevism to the masculine separateness of the Greco-Christian West:

> With *Sons and Lovers* . . . he was at once hot-foot upon the fashionable
> trail of incest; the book is an eloquent wallowing mass of Mother-love
> and Sex-idolatry. His *Women in Love* is again the same thick,
> sentimental, luscious stew. The 'Homo'-motive, how could that be
> absent from such a compendium, as is the nature of Mr Lawrence, of
> all that has passed for 'revolutionary', reposing mainly for its popular
> effectiveness upon the meaty, succulent levers of sex and supersex, to
> bait those politically-innocent, romantic, anglo-saxon simpletons,
> dreaming their 'anglo-saxon dreams', whether in America or the native
> country of Mr Lawrence?
>
> (Wyndham Lewis, *Paleface*, pp. 180–1)

Lewis suggested that Lawrence advocated Communism and homosexuality in order to encourage young Anglo-Saxons to repudiate the masculine dreams of Empire which had inspired their fathers, in favour of the feminine and homosexual fantasy of subjugation beneath an Oriental Bolshevist despotism. Lawrence was the most sinister and the most subtle propagandist against the West.

T.S. Eliot, similarly, saw Lawrence's ideas and writing to be the principal challenge to traditional values and ideals in England and America. What made the task of maintaining these values and ideals in the modern period particularly difficult, Eliot stated in *After Strange Gods* (1934), was the undermining of intellectual and religious orthodoxy by protestant heresies. The chief clue to the immense influence of Lawrence's work was to be found in the decay of Protestantism in England and America, and in the rise of a semi-educated public unable to grasp the intellectual definitions by which orthodoxy in thought and in religion had been maintained. In Eliot's view, D.H. Lawrence was the foremost example of heresy in modern Anglo-Saxon literature. Influenced by the degenerate Protestantism of his infancy, with its 'vague, hymn-singing pieties',[9] educated on a fare of English literature notable, in Eliot's judgement, only for its eccentric and individualist morality, Lawrence lacked 'the critical faculties which education should give' (Eliot, *After Strange Gods*, p. 58). Lawrence started life 'wholly free from any restriction of tradition or institution'. He had 'no guidance except the Inner Light, the most untrustworthy and deceitful guide that ever offered itself to wandering humanity' (Eliot, p. 59). It is hardly surprising, therefore, that Lawrence should come to see himself as a second Messiah, or that he should win a large following among 'the sick and debile and confused', appealing not 'to what remains of health in them, but to their sickness' (Eliot, p. 61). It was, nevertheless, the influence of Lawrence's supposedly ill-educated and perverse ideas upon the young with which Eliot concerned himself, for, following Murry and Lewis, he saw Lawrence as the instrument of sinister and demonic forces, which threatened to destroy the Christian West. 'His acute sensibility, his violent prejudices and passions and lack of social and intellectual training', Eliot argued, made Lawrence 'admirably fitted to be an instrument for forces of good or of evil' (Eliot, p. 59). It seems, for a moment, that Eliot will withhold final judgement, but his censure is all the more effectively made by being delayed. Not trained, he continued, as had been the mind of James Joyce, Lawrence's mind was not 'always aware of the master it is serving' (Eliot, p. 59).

A review of Lawrence's early critical reception reveals how much Leavis's championship of Lawrence involved an essentially liberal recovery of his work from the often hysterical and inflexibly reactionary misreadings to which it had been subject. Yet the cost of such a rehabilitation, as we have seen, was considerable, for as Leavis tried to counter the effect of previous readings, to cancel what he considered to be a distortion of Lawrence, he not only removed Lawrence from the literary and historical context in which he had written, but also made his work acceptable by ignoring its original political intentions. If we wish to read and understand *The Rainbow* and *Women in Love* accurately, we have, I believe, to restore them to their original contexts. This essay is an attempt to sketch one way out of many in which this can be done, and to show how much the past criticism of Lawrence's *The Rainbow* and *Women in Love* has proceeded by falsifying or repressing those original contexts.

Notes

1. F.R. LEAVIS, *D.H. Lawrence: Novelist* (London: Chatto & Windus, 1955).
2. D.H. Lawrence, *The Rainbow* (London: Heinemann, 1963), p. 492.
3. See RAYMOND WILLIAMS, *The English Novel from Dickens to Lawrence* (London: Chatto & Windus, 1970), pp. 177–9; Terry Eagleton, *Exiles and Emigrés* (London: Chatto & Windus, 1970), pp. 202–4; Terry Eagleton, *Criticism and Ideology* (London: New Left Books, 1976), pp. 157–61.
4. See EMILE DEVALENAY, *D.H. Lawrence: The Man and His Work. The Formative Years, 1885–1919* (London: Heinemann, 1972), pp. 235–48.
5. See R.P. DRAPER, *D.H. Lawrence: The Critical Heritage* (London: Routledge & Kegan Paul, 1970), p. 106.
6. See COLIN CLARKE (ed.), *D.H. Lawrence*, op. cit., pp. 67–72.
7. JOHN MIDDLETON MURRY, *Son of Woman* (London: Cape, 1931), p. 173.
8. WYNDHAM LEWIS, *Paleface* (London: Chatto & Windus, 1929), p. 193.
9. T.S. ELIOT, *After Strange Gods: A Primer of Modern Heresy* (London: Faber & Faber, 1934), p. 39.

14 Northernness and Modernism (*The Rainbow, Women in Love*)*

Tony Pinkney

Tony Pinkney is a lecturer in English at the University of Lancaster, and editor of *News from Nowhere*, a journal of critical and cultural theory and erstwhile organ of 'Oxford English Limited', the radical student-led pressure group for the reform of the traditional English syllabus. The essay reprinted here is only part of a chapter from Pinkney's 'new reading' of Lawrence, which also deals – prior to the start of the present excerpt – with his early novel *The Trespasser*. A further long passage is omitted in which Pinkney proposes a relationship between Lawrence in *The Rainbow* and German expressionism (especially the architecture of Gropius and the Bauhaus); the re-emergence of these motifs in *Women in Love* (Lawrence's 'gothic modernism' opposed to an arid classicism); and a (dizzyingly innovative) relating of this theme to the sexual imagery of the novel, in which a dry, anal symbolism replaces the 'wet' vagina/womb symbols of *The Rainbow*. As I have indicated in the Introduction (see p. 17), the chapter – indeed the whole book – deploys many elements derived from modern critical theory in a close textual reading which offers a genuinely renewed Lawrence – one in a sense recuperated from both Leavisism and Marxism/feminism as a textual site ripe for redevelopment.

Tony Pinkney is also the author of *Women in the Poetry of T.S. Eliot: A Psychoanalytic Approach* (Macmillan, 1984); *Raymond Williams: Postmodern Novelist* (Seren Books, 1991); and a number of articles in *News from Nowhere* (and elsewhere).

---

* Reprinted from Tony Pinkney, *D.H. Lawrence* (Harvester New Readings, Hemel Hempstead: Harvester Wheatsheaf, 1990), pp. 60–75, 94–99, 170–2; references renumbered from the original.

As Ursula Brangwen looks out over Beldover at the end of *The Rainbow*, she sees the novel's eponymous symbol 'making great *architecture* of light and colour and the space of heaven' [my emphasis].[1] This new metaphor is swept momentarily away by that familiar imagery of shells and kernels – dead rinds or forms contrasted with sensitive, new living content – that is so pervasive in the last sections of this book. But it then returns, emerging in the novel's closing sentence as a powerful utopian vision: 'She saw in the rainbow the earth's new architecture, the old, brittle corruption of houses and factories swept away, the world built up in a living fabric of Truth, fitting to the over-arching heaven' (*The Rainbow*, p. 548). At the end of *Women in Love* the architectural metaphor metamorphoses into a character, the sculptor Loerke, who argues for the integration of the individual arts within the building: 'sculpture and architecture must go together. The day for irrelevant statues, as for wall pictures, is over. As a matter of fact sculpture is always part of an architectural conception.'[2] True, the detailed position he goes on to elaborate is deeply contested by the novel in which he appears; yet thus far, in his demand for the reintegration in the building of the hitherto autonomous particular arts and crafts, it can agree with him.

Once alerted to this architectural preoccupation in the novels, we can begin to see how it pervades their every detail – above all in *The Rainbow*. Metaphorically or literally, everyone is feverishly building in this text. Tom Brangwen may begin like 'a broken arch thrust sickeningly out from support', but when he and Lydia Lensky at last 'joined hands, the house was finished' (p. 134). Will Brangwen is a devoted student of church architecture, and when he settles next to Cossethay church determines 'to have the intimate sacred building utterly in his own hands': 'it was the church *building* he cared for . . . He laboured cleaning the stonework, repairing the woodwork, restoring the organ' (p. 251). His woodshed, that 'smelled of sweet wood and resounded to the noise of the plane or the hammer or the saw' (p. 259), casts the glamour of the act of building over his daughter Ursula, so that years later when the family moves into a new house in Beldover, she 'could use her father's ordinary tools, both for woodwork and metal-work, so she hammered and tinkered' (p. 478). Such literal mastery of the arts and crafts of building is metaphorically paralleled throughout; after getting a grip on school-teaching in Brinsley Street School, Ursula 'had put in her tiny brick to the fabric man was building, she had qualified herself as co-builder' (p. 475). Her father by now is Art and Handwork Instructor for the County of Nottingham, her uncle Tom is the friend of a famous engineer in London, her boyfriend Anton Skrebensky is in the Royal Engineers and, in case of war, would 'be making railways or bridges, working like a nigger' (p. 356). Even the most resolutely 'organic' of the novel's episodes transmutes itself into a mode of building: in the famous scene in the cornfields with Will, Ursula 'set down her sheaves making a part house with those others', and Anna Brangwen, lost in a hot fecund storm of pregnancies, has none the less 'settled in her builded house, a rich woman . . . She was a door and a threshold' (p. 238). This Brangwen passion for building then communicates itself to the environment at large. Ursula's hair is 'chiselled back by the wind', and simple objects do their uncanny best to metamorphose, in the Brangwen presence, into sculptures or mini-buildings; 'curiously monumental that box of sweets stood up'. Such is the architectural energy of the family that any building they enter at once seems to spring into active construction; when Ursula strolls into the church in Derby, 'the place re-echoed to the calling of secular voices and to blows of the hammer' (p. 341).

'In my father's house are many mansions', quotes Lydia Brangwen; but in Lawrence's novel there are many houses – or other buildings and constructions. Most anciently, there is the 'high place, an earthwork of the Stone Age men' on the Sussex Downs, where Ursula insists on sleeping out with Skrebensky. But these earthworks are oddly echoed, millennia later, by the 'raw bank of earth' thrown up when the canal linking the collieries of the Erewash valley is dug in the 1840s; subsequently this embankment bursts, destroying Tom Brangwen. Bridges prove to be a key motif in the novel. Will Brangwen has a strange sense of the presence of Angels as he passes under the Canal Bridge on his way to Marsh Farm. If Skrebensky builds bridges, Ursula and her father leap recklessly from them to the point where, once, she drops forward on to his head and nearly breaks his neck; and for all Ursula's later attacks on Skrebensky, verbal and sexual, she has to concede to him that India 'did need his roads and bridges'. There are the memorable buildings of the Marsh Farm itself – the barn into which Tom takes the child Anna during her mother's labour, or the hayloft in which he sees her silhouetted in embrace with Will years later. It is hard to say whether the Brangwen 'blood-intimacy' is a function of this domestic architecture, or vice versa; at any rate, 'there was in the house a sort of richness, a deep, inarticulate interchange which made other places seem thin and unsatisfying' (p. 142). Yet to Anna in rebellious mood the farm suggests a quite different kind of building, 'the torture cell of a certain Bishop of France, in which the victim could neither stand nor lie stretched out, never' (p. 143). Will and Anna's cottage next to the church at Cossethay, with its magical woodshed and later the refurbished parish room, belong evidently to the same Brangwen architectural culture. But as the novel enters 'The Widening Circle' of its later chapters, new types of architecture and settlement enter its consciousness: the new industrial town Wiggiston, with 'no meeting place, no centre, no artery, no organic formation', an anti-city if ever there was one; Brinsley Street School, 'intimating the church's architecture for the purpose of domineering'; the 'countryhouse near Oxford', to which Skrebensky takes Ursula, a forerunner of Breadalby Manor in *Women in Love*; or the Italian hotel in London in which, for a brief liberated moment, the lovers can feel as if 'this world of England has vanished away'.

When the teenage Ursula dreams passionately of Christ, she concludes: 'it was not houses and factories He would hold in His bosom' (p. 331). But then what kind of architecture would he embrace? As it progresses, *The Rainbow* begins to articulate its rejection of one culturally hegemonic answer to that question. When Ursula contemplates Jove's incarnation as a bull, she affirms: 'Very good, so he had in Greece. For herself, she was no Grecian woman' (p. 321). Later, it is an index of the spiritual disintegration of Winifred Inger that she appears 'dressed in a rust-red tunic like a Greek girl's . . . firm-bodied as Diana' (pp. 334–5). Even when, in more positive mood, Ursula 'tried hard to keep her old grasp of the Roman spirit . . . gradually the Latin became mere gossip-stuff and artificiality to her' (p. 48). This rejection of classicism is virtually a family heritage. Both Ursula's father and her uncle Fred are great readers of John Ruskin, and it is Ruskin's work – above all his great chapter on 'The Nature of Gothic' (1853), which William Morris aptly termed 'one of the very few necessary and inevitable utterances of the century'[3] – that we must invoke to grasp the rejections of both industrial mechanism and classicism in *The Rainbow*.

'He had always, all his life, had a secret dread of Absolute Beauty . . . So he had turned to the Gothic form, which always asserted the broken desire of mankind in its pointed arches, escaping the rolling, absolute beauty of the round arch' (p. 280). This is Will Brangwen rather than Ruskin, at the point when the former is just about to succumb to the 'absolute beauty' of some obscure and perverse renewed sensual relationship with his wife; but it expresses Ruskin's cultural position effectively none the less. Broken and irregular, the Gothic arch is a creaturely architecture; it refuses the abstract symmetries of both classical Greek architecture and modern industry, since these both, as Ruskin argued, inhumanly reduce craftsman or worker to a mechanism blindly carrying out a geometrical plan handed down from above. In contrast, the Gothic cathedral, 'savage', 'changeful' and 'redundant', gives scope to the creative capacities of its workmen, its communal grandeur coming about as a result of their joy in their own labour process. An architectural preference thus opens on to the most far-reaching social and political judgements: Ursula's father reads Ruskin and tinkers with the fabric of the local church; she, remaining in this truly his daughter, cries 'why don't they alter it?' as she contemplates the subjection of the colliers to 'the great machine' in Wiggiston.

All the modes of building and architectural styles I have surveyed in the novel have their ultimate social implications, but these are all in the

long run organised around the *Gothic*, which dominates the book.[4] In love
with 'medieval forms', Will and his young wife resolve that 'one by one,
they should visit all the cathedrals of England' (p. 242); one of the great
turning points in their relationship, which I shall discuss below, takes
place in Lincoln Cathedral, and Southwell Minster near Nottingham is a
favoured site for excursions throughout the novel. Nor is it just English
cathedrals that so fascinate Will: purchasing a German architectural text,
he exults, 'Did not Bamberg Cathedral make the world his own?' (p. 206).
This Gothic allegiance then holds good in the next generation, partly
redeeming even the horrors of Victorian Gothic. An undergraduate at
Nottingham College, Ursula finds that 'its rather pretty, plaything, Gothic
form was almost a style, in the dirty industrial town' (p. 480); at least
temporarily it evokes for her 'a reminiscence of the wondrous, cloistral
origins of education'. And in a scene little noted by critics of the novel,
Ursula and Skrebensky very directly replay their parents' crucial
encounter in a great Gothic cathedral – with the difference that it is now
the Goth rather than the classicist who emerges reinvigorated:

> for some reason, she must call in Rouen on the way back to London.
> He had an instinctive mistrust of her desire for the place . . . The old
> streets, the cathedral, the age and the monumental peace of the town
> took her away from him. She turned to it as to something she had
> forgotten, and wanted. This was now the reality; this great stone
> cathedral slumbering there in its mass.
>
> (*The Rainbow*, p. 507)

If Paul was 'Norman' and Miriam 'Gothic', so too, it seems, are
Skrebensky and Ursula. In the final analysis, even the rainbow itself is a
Gothic arch, since the earth's 'new architecture' (which will in fact be its
old architecture restored) can be seen in it.

Will Brangwen dreams of 'the establishment of a whole mystical
architectural conception which used the human figure as a unit' (p. 323) –
in contrast to the austere geometricism of ancient classicism or modern
manufacture. In one sense, as for Ruskin himself, this stress on the
'human figure as a unit' means that the workman is a creative contributor
to the overall construction, fertilely adding to a form capable of infinite
variation, rather than the alienated executor of a scheme delivered from
elsewhere; hence the emphasis throughout the novel on active
craftsmanship, almost in the spirit of William Morris himself. But
Lawrence also adds a powerful new dimension to this analysis – which is
indeed *The Rainbow*'s most distinctive contribution to the British 'Gothic'
tradition. The relation between the Gothic and the body is not simply
that of the craftsman's toiling muscles. For the Gothic cathedral itself is a
body, and more specifically a female body, a womb. It is at this point that

the Gothic is a mode of utopian architecture leading towards socialism in Ruskin and Morris, and the Gothic as a subversive female literary form uniquely intersect – as Anton Skrebensky seems obscurely to guess by buying Ursula a copy of *Wuthering Heights* early in their relationship.[5]

In a fine account of *The Rainbow* in her *Sexual Politics*, Kate Millett has stressed the prevalence of womb imagery in the novel, but she only hints at the further, crucial point that the womb is also a cathedral. 'So entirely does the womb dominate the book', Millett comments, 'that it becomes a symbol, in the arch of Lincoln cathedral, or in the moon, of the spiritual and the supernatural.'[6] But the novel is rather more explicit than this; 'I think it's right', announces Ursula, 'to make love in a cathedral' (p. 343), and when characters respond to the 'pregnant hush of churches' or their 'murky interiors, strangely luminous, pregnant', we are not simply in the presence of a dead metaphor. The churches and cathedrals of the novel certainly seem fecund enough: in Cossethay church at Christmas 'the arches put forth their buds', and the Lamb in the stained-glass window remains sufficiently in touch with the actual lambs born on Marsh Farm to bring the natural cycles and rhythms of generation into the very body of the church. The very first occurrence of the arch motif in the book (when Tom feels like a 'broken arch') features in the context of Lydia's pregnancy. Even craftsmanship is most itself when it is in contact with the womb of the female, as when Will carves his figure of Eve: 'he sent the chisel over her belly, her hard, unripe, small belly' (p. 158). And buildings themselves seem to have contractions of a kind, as when Will finds that 'the walls had thrust him out and given him a vast space to walk in'.

A cathedral is a rainbow, as at Lincoln: 'when he saw the cathedral in the distance . . . his heart leapt. It was the sign in heaven.' A cathedral is, moreover, female: "There she is," he said. The "she" irritated her. Why "she"?' Because, as Will realises and Anna as yet does not, the building is a giant womb: 'he was to pass within to the perfect womb', his soul 'quivered in the womb in the hush and gloom of fecundity, like seed of procreation in ecstasy', the cathedral contains 'the embryo of all light' and is 'spanned round with the rainbow' (p. 242–3). Since rainbows are cathedrals are wombs, rainbows too can 'give birth'; indeed, such are the extraordinary transformations of imagery effected in this novel that the rainbow (or Gothic arch) comes ultimately to represent the legs of a woman opening in childbirth, ejecting the new life into the world. Anna Lensky is born in precisely this metaphorical way, parturition by courtesy of the rainbow: 'her father and her mother now met to the span of the heavens, and she, the child, was free to play in the space beneath, between' (p. 134). When Anna dances naked during pregnancy – 'she stood on proud legs, with a lovely reckless balance of her full belly' (p. 191) – we must understand her to be, remarkably, both cathedral and rainbow at once, Gothic mass perched as it were upon one of its own arches. Or, in reverse, the womb is a cathedral from whose arches or rainbows one must be expelled in the act of labour, as the novel movingly articulates in its reflections on Anna: 'She was a door and a threshold, she herself. Through her another soul was coming, to stand upon her as upon the threshold, looking out, shading its eyes for the direction to take' (p. 238). Any 'new architecture' which does not somehow build into its very fabric these crucial female and human experiences will be doomed from the start, binding itself over in advance to the dead abstractions of Wiggiston.

For the centrality of the Gothic cathedral in the symbology of *The Rainbow* projects political messages which contradict those allowed at the level of overt rhetoric or character analysis. In *Culture and Society* Raymond Williams notes that in much of his social thinking 'Lawrence is very close to the socialism of a man like Morris': 'in his basic attitudes he is so much within the tradition we have been following, has indeed so much in common with a socialist like Morris, that it is at first difficult to understand why his influence should have appeared to lead in other directions'.[7] Williams does not evoke questions of aesthetics or architecture here, yet this point could have been powerfully reinforced by stressing the Ruskinian and Morrisian lineage of *The Rainbow*'s most commanding symbol. But we must expand, as well as reinforce, Williams's argument, by taking on board the 'feminisation' of the Gothic which this novel effects; the 'Gothic socialism' of Morris is now on the verge of becoming a socialist-feminism. This claim may seem excessive, given that the book's explicit treatment of women's emancipation, as incarnated in figures like Winifred Inger or Dorothy Russell, is at best uninterested, at worst actively hostile. The novel's commitment to an emergent feminism is a narrative, not a discursive, allegiance – in its slippage from male to female protagonist after the first generation. Certainly there is much residual resistance to this shift in the book, and indeed, the novel's anti-feminist rhetoric must in a sense be understood as its 'vengeance' upon its own inner narrative drive. But to compare Tom Brangwen with any of the later male figures – Skrebensky, Uncle Tom, Mr Harby – is to grasp at once that it is now the Brangwen women who embody the potential utopian energies of the culture.

Evoking Southwell Minster for Anna, Will remarks, 'I like the main body of the church – and that north porch' – (p. 151); and it is to the theme of Northernness that I now wish to return. In its stress on medieval architecture and handicrafts, *The Rainbow* might seem as culturally nostalgic as Ruskin or Morris at their worst, harking back to a happy Hobbitland that preceded some cataclysmic 'dissociation of sensibility'; F.R. Leavis, relating the book back to George Eliot's literary provincialism, leaves much the same impression in his emphasis on its 'essentially English' nature. Yet it is specifically the earth's *new* architecture that Ursula finds shadowed forth by her rainbow, and Leavis's exemplary 'English' novel in fact cannot even narratively get underway until a half-German, half-Polish *emigrée* bumps into Tom Brangwen in a country lane; two generations later the book will still be drawing powerfully upon its East European heritage, as Ursula dreams 'how she was truly a princess in Poland, how in England she was under a spell' (p. 312). The 'Northern' architectural tradition in which *The Rainbow* is grounded is, I shall argue, open from the very start to a distinctively 'modernist' consciousness. Though the novel engages in heated debate with anti-Northern or classicist versions of modernism, it does this not so much to discredit as to incorporate them, to concede their limited, merely relative validity within an over-arching Gothic modernism – at which point *The Rainbow* can be seen to rejoin the contemporary Northern modernism being developed in Germany during the very period of its own composition.

In its opening 'mythic' chapter, while the Brangwen men work in the fields in a 'drowse of blood-intimacy', their women look beyond to the world of cities, freedom, 'outwardness', 'range of motion', education – in short, to the forces of modernity. Such values become focused for the young Tom Brangwen in his encounter with the foreign gentleman with his 'monkey-like self-surety' at Matlock. If the values of formality and detachment can be partly found within the class-system of his own society, as with Alfred's mistress Mrs Forbes in her 'visionary polite world', they are considerably intensified in the recognisably modernist deracination that Lydia Lensky embodies, alternately suffering from and glorying in it. Lydia, like so many modernist writers, is an 'exile and *emigrée*' – a condition which is at least as much spiritual as geographical. She has entered a realm of irony and moral relativity, 'laughing when he [Tom] was shocked or astounded, condemning nothing' (p. 98), Lydia brings into the English Midlands the ambience of the great European capitals: Berlin, where her husband was educated, Vienna, where they spent their honeymoon, Warsaw, even London, whither they had first fled. Product of a restless, sophisticated cosmopolitanism, she is indeed 'an *emancipée*', 'very "European"', representative of 'the new movement just begun in Russia' – or, as Tom puts it in his blacker moments, '"a foreigner with a bad nature, caring really about nothing, having no proper feelings at the bottom of her"' (p. 100). Marrying the Midlands to modernism, the Erewash to Europe, Lydia kickstarts the whole narrative into motion.

Yet both she and Tom remain, for all this, deeply inarticulate figures, and the novel's attempt at integrating opposed modes of consciousness must begin all over again and at a much higher level of theoretical clarity in the second generation. Anna, like her mother, 'wanted her distance. She mistrusted intimacy'; she is 'of another order than he [Will], she had no defence against him . . . his real being lay in his dark, emotional experience of the Infinite' (p. 199). Their key clash, as I have noted, takes place in Lincoln Cathedral, after that visit to Baron Skrebensky, with his 'faculty for sharp, deliberate response . . . detached, so purely objective' (p. 240), which so intensifies Anna's own innate desire towards modernist unrootedness. As Will's spirit surges to ecstasy along the sweep of the Gothic arches, Anna

> caught at little things, which saved her from being swept forward headlong in the tide of passion that leaps on into the Infinite in a great mass . . . So she caught sight of the wicked, odd little faces carved in stone . . . These sly little faces peeped out of the grand tide of the cathedral like something that knew better. They knew quite well, these little imps that retorted on man's own illusion, that the cathedral was not absolute. They winked and leered, giving suggestion of the many things that had been left out of the great concept of the church . . . a note which the cathedrals did not include: something free and careless and joyous.
>
> (*The Rainbow*, pp. 245–46, 248)

The novel's local sympathies are heavily with Anna here; Will's ecstatic vision is defeated and, for him, permanently disenchanted. Yet his wife's case against the Gothic can be answered as, in terms of its own overall architecture, *The Rainbow* well knows. Will thinks of 'the ruins of the Grecian worship, and it seemed a temple was never perfectly a temple until it was ruined and mixed up with the winds and the sky and the herbs' (p. 248). This is indeed true of a Greek building, whose classicist perfection is exclusionary in exactly the sense Anna intends, its symmetrical elegance being premised upon the abolition of the disorder of Nature. But the Gothic cathedral as it were *contains* its own ruins, brokenness (or 'savageness', 'changefulness', 'grotesqueness' and 'redundance', in Ruskin's terms) is a constitutive part of its aesthetic – as the novel has already acknowledged in referring to the 'broken desire of mankind' expressed in its pointed (rather than round) arches. And if it comes to 'something free and careless and joyous', the cathedral contains that in the process of its own making, for it is, as Morris so many times stressed, the collective product of its craftsmen's pleasure in their labour. The Gothic deconstructs the rigid model of inside/outside that Anna erects here. Its outside is its inside; even the sly stone faces that denounce its incompletion are, after all, part of it. The Gothic contains its own 'negation', which thereafter ceases to be its negative pure and simple, and is rather granted local validity within a more generous total system which exceeds it. The Gothic cannot simply be counterposed to human sensuous fulfilment as Anna here intends since, as we have seen, it is above all 'a whole, mystical architectural conception which used the human figure as a unit'. Will and Anna may indeed be, as the novel ruefully admits, 'opposites, not complements'; but then Lincoln Cathedral contains them both, the 'close Brangwen life' and modernist dissociation. And that other Lawrentian arch, the rainbow, equally mediates between earth and sky.

At the Skrebensky's, Anna deplores Will's 'uncritical, unironical nature', and the two epithets announce that the Lincoln Cathedral episode is not just a turning point in this particular personal relationship but also a major intervention in the modernist aesthetic debates of the early years of this century. For in the classicist modernism into which Arnoldian Hellenism mutates in our own century, 'criticism', 'consciousness' and 'irony' are cardinal virtues. If Katherine Mansfield's *In a German Pension* was a practical literary assault on Wagnerian emotionalism, its theoretical equivalents are the prose writings of T.S. Eliot and T.E. Hulme. Irony, in Eliot's famous essay on Andrew Marvell, becomes 'wit', a pluralistic 'recognition, implicit in the expression of every experience, of other kinds of experience which are possible'.[8] It is a Latinate, gentlemanly value, to be defended against both the 'dream world' of English nineteenth-century poetry (which Eliot exemplifies, not accidentally, from the work of William Morris) and that 'confusion of thought, emotion, and vision' of the 'Northern' tradition instanced by *Also Sprach Zarathustra*.[9] Eliot's wit is Hulme's 'classical attitude', and the latter's aesthetic polemic in 'Romanticism and Classicism' takes us very close to the Lincoln Cathedral pages of *The Rainbow* – again not accidentally, since Hulme's target here is the writings of John Ruskin. Just as Anna in the cathedral caught at 'little things', so Hulme sets out to prove 'that beauty may be in small, dry things'; if she aims to avoid 'being swept forward headlong', so too for Hulme's classicist poet 'there is always a holding back, a reservation'; Anna resists the arches as they 'leap on into the Infinite in a great mass', and Hulme derides a Romantic aesthetics which 'always drags in the infinite' or a poetry with 'the word infinite in every other line'. In stark contrast,

> in the classical attitude you never seem to swing right along to the infinite nothing. If you say an extravagant thing which does exceed the limits inside which you know man to be fastened, yet there is always conveyed in some way at the end an impression of yourself standing outside it, and not quite believing it, or consciously putting it forward as a flourish. You never go blindly into an atmosphere more than the truth.[10]

This is Anna's position exactly. 'Classicist' it may term itself, but we can see in it recognisably modernist forms of mobility, provisionality, scepticism, a cold distance and detachment. Yet as we have seen, Lincoln Cathedral incorporates, not expels, such insights, its small, sly, leering faces articulating 'wit', 'ambiguity', 'paradox' (T.S. Eliot, William Empson, Cleanth Brooks respectively). If the Hulme and Eliot texts did indeed constitute a 'modernist counter-revolution against the Wagnerian revolution', as Stoddard Martin maintains, then *The Rainbow* forms a decisive second revolution against the classicist restoration – something in the order of an October 1917 to its February. What *The Trespasser*, with *In a German Pension* in its rifle sights, could only adumbrate, the Gothic modernism of *The Rainbow* marvellously substantiates. . . .

Women in Love is a much 'easier' or 'cooler' novel to read than *The Rainbow*: at the most banal level, the reader's heart rarely quails before page upon page of dense text without either paragraph break or dialogue, as it so often does in the earlier novel, and the much greater number of chapters lend themselves much more readily to coffee-breaks. Marginally longer than its predecessor, *Women in Love* has twice as many chapters, a difference which comes in the end to feel qualitative as well as just arithmetical. For the distinctive narrative prose of *The Rainbow* – cluttered with metaphor, heavily rhythmic and repetitive, hastening across dozens of pages with barely a pause for breath – has been purged away in its sequel. That prose in its surging, incantatory, 'tidal' rhythms is offered as *enacting* as well as thematically pondering deep continuity or generational transmission in a culture both settled and changing. Its characteristic narrative 'unit' is extended in chronological span: the months or years of Lydia Lensky's recovery in England, the decade of Anna or Ursula's girlhood, the lifetimes of the marriages of Tom and Lydia or Will and Anna. The 'event' as a narrative category is thoroughly decentred, submerged like the grinning gargoyles at Lincoln within more fundamental rhythms; only in the last chapters, as the world of modernity comes painfully into being, do events as such come into focus. The language of the novel is, so to speak, a 'prose of the womb', enacting the minute, remorseless but almost imperceptible organic accretions that take place within the fertilised female body; it is not a prose of orgasm, for all Lawrence's subsequent reputation, but a language of orgasm's consequences across months and then decades to come. Nor can we understand this prose by dubbing it 'stream of consciousness', though it has some affinities with the contemporary experiments of James Joyce and Virginia Woolf. For 'stream of consciousness' too is premised upon an inside/outside model that *The Rainbow* disallows: outside, the mendacities of official public rhetoric or the banal clichés of mass-culture; inside, the authentic, 'lived' language of the sub- or unconscious. But the language of Lawrence's novel is neither inside nor outside in these terms: charged though it is with the carnal opacity of the body's deepest desires, it is also – as its heavy complement of Biblical rhythms and images suggests – the language of a common culture. In this sense, indeed, it is the stylistic equivalent of the Gothic cathedral, uniting public labour with personal joy and creativity.

Women in Love, however, operates quite differently. Frank Kermode has described the book as a set of 'linked parables', a phrase which effectively captures the discrete, even disjointed nature of its key episodes.[11] Narratively, it is premised utterly upon the event. The characteristic time-span of a chapter is a single vivid instant: Birkin stoning the image of the moon in the pond, Gerald viciously restraining the Arab mare as the train rattles by, the rabbit Bismarck tearing Gudrun's flesh. The prose is 'cooler' than that of *The Rainbow*, functional and disenchanted, carefully delimiting rather than enthusiastically swamping its object. If the language of the former novel is 'hysterical' (in the strict sense, pertaining to the womb), the staple linguistic medium of *Women in Love* might speculatively be described as 'anal', enacting 'dry' moments of orgasmic fierceness with no consequences beyond their own intensity. More specifically, there is a return in *Woman in Love* to that sharply visualised mode of presentation that characterised *Sons and Lovers*; this book too is an Imagist novel. That it should be so represents, like so much of the Birkin/Ursula relationship at its centre, a capture of the novel by the very modernism it opposes. For so much of its overt rhetoric is determinedly anti-visual; even Halliday suspects that 'life is all wrong because it has become much too visual' (*Women in Love*, p. 132), and Birkin wants 'a woman I don't see'. But the famous scenes that comprise the book are all too visible in its own terms, 'objective correlatives' which memorably externalise what in *The Rainbow* remained on the whole the inarticulable feel and stuff of unconscious process. In the end, indeed, the individual chapters of *Women in Love* become instances of that modernist minimalism which the novel – searching for a scapegoat for its own proclivities – attacks so fiercely in Gudrun. However intense they are, they remain 'little carvings . . . small things that one can put between one's hands'.

If *Women in Love* begins as a 'Gothic' attack upon classicist modernisms, why, in terms of both style and thematic content, is it dragged so remorselessly backwards until it becomes an exemplary instance of precisely that which it set out to destroy? The answer seems to lie in a fundamental error of strategy upon Lawrence's part: what he assumes to be a neutral technical apparatus that he can turn to his own Northern purposes turns out to belong secretly to his enemies all the time. *Women in Love* is a synchronic rather than diachronic text: *The Rainbow* is about a place that passes through time, whereas its successor is about a time that passes through places – the Midlands of the Brangwens, the London of the Pompadour café, the Alpine landscapes of the later chapters. Such geographical range is both cause and effect of the 'cataloguing' impulse which so deeply governs this text – that desire to enumerate a whole host of modernist manifestations (minimalist carvings, Picasso reproductions, Futurist paintings, Loerke's industrial friezes, the Russian Ballet, the primitive art of Africa and the West Pacific) in order to reject them comprehensively. The book aims to leave no aesthetic stone unturned, to hunt down every last curio in the modernist cabinet. In doing so, however, its initial catalogue expands until it becomes, as it must, a virtual encyclopaedia of modernist art – at which point an apparently innocuous strategy delivers the disruptive sting in its tail. For the 'encyclopaedia' could never be a neutral totting up or diagnosis of modernism, for it is itself a – perhaps even the – distinctive modernist genre (or anti-genre), as Eliot's *The Waste Land*, Joyce's *Ulysses* and Pound's *Cantos* testify.[12] Moreover, the modernist 'encyclopaedia' is specifically a mutation of the classicist literary tradition, as Eliot's Arnoldian critical sympathies in *The Sacred Wood*, the role of Tiresias in *The Waste Land* itself, or the Homeric sub-structure of *Ulysses* all suggest; it is an attempt – desperate enough in all conscience – to salvage the classical heritage amidst the cultural, political and military crises of the early twentieth century. In the nineteenth century, the Arnoldian 'best self' disinterestedly aspired to know 'the best that has been thought and said', achieving Hellenic comprehensiveness rather than Hebraic intensity of focus. The same drive towards totality motivates its early twentieth-century successors; but the emergent phenomenon of an apparently classless 'mass culture' has eroded any secure boundary between 'high' and 'low' culture, Arnold's best and the mere rest. The twentieth-century classicist must then be comprehensive on a scale Matthew Arnold himself could never have dreamed of, scooping every last scrap and ort of contemporary culture, the whole range of its national, regional, class and professional languages, into the modernist text. If the social crisis cannot be mastered, if a secure meaning and structure, a 'best self', cannot be distilled from it, its elements can at least be collected, catalogued, 'encyclopaedised' – thereby affording at least the raw materials of a synthesis which someone somewhere, under more propitious cultural conditions, might one day make. On the basis of the Gothic modernism of *The Rainbow*, *Women in Love* heroically takes on the whole range of contemporary modernisms – classicist abstraction or minimalism and its sensationalist-primitivist counterparts – yet by virtue of this very gesture, it unknowingly becomes part of the very tradition it is assailing, an encyclopaedia worthy to rank with the masterpieces of Eliot, Joyce and Pound. What looks like a neutral strategy – the inventory of the enemy's positions – turns out to be in itself a genre – more specifically, the enemy's own genre; and this initial slippage in the project of *Women in Love* then reacts back upon both language and narrative structure, as well as the central sexual relationship of the novel, reprogramming them in its own classicist–modernist image. And the initial Gothic-modernist image is by then comprehensively defeated.

It is worth emphasising that this is a defeat. The relation between these two novels is not benign, as if they were Siamese twins developing from the author's ur-conception, *The Wedding Ring* or *The Sisters*; nor is it simply a matter of totting up, as so many critics have done, the pluses and minuses across both texts: the 'decline' of Ursula in the latter counterbalanced by its less fervid prose style, and so on. For these two novels stand in a relation of lethal antagonism. Each claims that it contains the other: *The Rainbow* incorporates the modernist consciousness of its successor in the form of the ironical gargoyles of Lincoln Cathedral; *Women in Love* turns its predecessor into the slide-show Ursula projects from her train window, downgrading historicity and settlement in the name of Futurist mobility. These are, ultimately, texts we must choose between, and our own deepest cultural commitments will be engaged in that choice. My own allegiances here are clear enough, premising themselves centrally on the claim that though *The Rainbow* can indeed fruitfully 'contain' *Women in Love*, *Women in Love* can only undialectically expunge *The Rainbow*, sloughing off both English-regional realism and Gothic modernism in the process. Seventy years on, the Lawrentian texts still involve us in this process of high-risk self-defining assessment; the notion of detached scientific analysis of them, rather than impassioned evaluation and taking of sides, seems still a long way off. But what we have learned in that intervening period is that the urgent cultural choice once offered to us by F.R. Leavis in the form, 'Lawrence or Joyce?', must now be more carefully reformulated as '*The Rainbow* or *Women in Love*?', Gothic modernism or the classicist–modernist Encyclopaedia.

Notes

1. D.H. Lawrence, *The Rainbow*, ed. John Worthern (Harmondsworth: Penguin, 1981), p. 548.
2. D.H. Lawrence, *Women in Love*, ed. Charles Ross (Harmondsworth: Penguin, 1982), p. 518.
3. Cited in John Ruskin, *Unto This Last and Other Writings*, ed. Clive Wilmer (Harmondsworth: Penguin, 1985), p. 75.
4. Judith Wilt also sees Lawrence as 'the "modernist" artist who is closest to the subtle, yet comparatively unprotected, unironic return to Gothic energies', but hers is a Gothic of ghouls and vampires rather than Ruskinian cathedrals. See her *Ghosts of the Gothic: Austen, Eliot and Lawrence* (Princeton: Princeton University Press, 1980), pp. 231–92.
5. I have attempted a general theory of modernism along these lines in 'The

woman's building: notes towards a Gothic modernism', *News from Nowhere*, **10**, forthcoming.

6. KATE MILLETT, *Sexual Politics* (London: Virago, 1977), p. 258.
7. RAYMOND WILLIAMS, *Culture and Society 1780–1950* (London: Faber, 1958), pp. 210–12.
8. T.S. ELIOT, *Selected Essays*, Third enlarged edn (London: Faber, 1951), p. 303.
9. T.S. ELIOT, *The Sacred Wood: Essays on poetry and criticism* (London: Faber, 1950), p. 158.
10. T.E. HULME, *Speculations: Essays on humanism and the philosophy of art*, ed. Herbert Read (London: Routledge, 1960), p. 120.
11. FRANK KERMODE, *Lawrence* (London: Fontana, 1973), p. 73.
12. For a lively early discussion of the genre, see Hugh Kenner, *The Stoic Comedians: Flaubert, Joyce and Beckett* (London: University of California Press, 1962).

Further Reading

What follows is a highly selective list of books and articles, drawn from the last twenty years' mass of Lawrence scholarship, which seem to me interesting in themselves and which might also have found a place in this Reader had there been space. James C. Cowan's *Annotated Bibliography*, vol. II (details in Note 6 of the Introduction) gives the fullest account of works about Lawrence, at least up to 1975, and his Introduction to that volume offers a useful digest.

I have not reincluded here the many additional works referred to in the course of my Introduction and its notes, or in the Headnotes – except in the case of collections of essays where reference has been made only to a single contribution within them.

The Further Reading has been roughly sectionalised at once to guide the reader and to approximate the general features of the body of the collection. I have offered a parenthetical comment on individual works where it seemed helpful to do so.

(1) General and formal

BURGESS, ANTHONY, *Flame into Being: the Life and Work of D.H. Lawrence*. London: Heinemann, 1985. (An account by another novelist of not dissimilar disposition.)

EGGERT, PAUL, 'D.H. Lawrence and his Audience: The Case of *Mr Noon*', *Southern Review: Literary and Interdisciplinary Essays*, **18**, 3 (November 1985): 298–307. (One of the few helpful essays as yet on Lawrence's 'newly published' novel.)

GORDON, DAVID J., 'Sex and Language in D.H. Lawrence', *Twentieth-Century Literature: A Scholarly and Critical Journal*, **27**, 4 (Winter 1981): 362–75.

KERMODE, FRANK, *Lawrence*. London: Fontana, 1973. (An excellent example of sophisticated textual reading.)

LAWRENCE, D.H., *Mr Noon*, ed. Lindeth Vasey. Cambridge: Cambridge University Press, 1984. (Latter-day addition to the Lawrence œuvre.)

LEAVIS, F.R., *Thought, Words and Creativity: Art and Thought in Lawrence*. London: Chatto & Windus, 1976. (Further later reflections by the creator of *D.H. Lawrence: Novelist*.)

SAGAR, KEITH, *D.H. Lawrence: Life into Art*. Athens: The University of Georgia Press, 1985. (A 'history-of-ideas' critical biography.)
WORTHEN, JOHN, *D.H. Lawrence and the Idea of the Novel*. London: Macmillan, 1979. (A formal/thematic reading.)

(2) Lawrence and society

ALDEN, PATRICIA, 'Lawrence: Climbing Up', Chapter 4 of *Social Mobility in the English* Bildungsroman: Gissing, Hardy, Bennett, and Lawrence. Ann Arbor: University of Michigan Research Press, 1986. (Explains Lawrence's class background as refracted in the novels.)
DELANY, PAUL, *D.H. Lawrence's Nightmare: The Writer and his Circle in the Years of the Great War*. Hassocks, Sussex: The Harvester Press, 1979. (A critical reading informed by socio-biography.)
SANDERS, SCOTT, *D.H. Lawrence: The World of the Major Novels*. London: Vision Press, 1973. (A highly regarded reading related to specific historical circumstances.)
SCHECKNER, PETER, *Class, Politics and the Individual: A Study of the Major Works of D.H. Lawrence*. Rutherford, N.J.: Fairleigh Dickinson University Press, 1985. (A descriptive account of how Lawrence's class and politics inform his writing.)
WRIGHT, ANNE, *Literature of Crisis, 1910–22:* Howards End, Heartbreak House, Women in Love *and* The Waste Land. London: Macmillan, 1984. (*Women in Love* contextualised by both historical period and contiguous contemporary texts.)

(3) Lawrence and women

DIX, CAROL, *D.H. Lawrence and Women*. London: Macmillan, 1980. (A personalised account in defence of Lawrence's treatment of female characters.)
HEATH, JANE, 'Helen Corke and D.H. Lawrence: Sexual Identity and Literary Relations', *Feminist Studies*, **11**, 2 (Summer 1985): 317–42.
LERNER, LAURENCE, 'Lawrence and the Feminists', in Mara Kalnins (ed.), *D.H. Lawrence: Centenary Essays*. Bristol: Bristol Classical Press, 1986. (A somewhat predictable, male critic's defence of Lawrence's sensitivity and complexity.)
NIXON, CORNELIA, *Lawrence's Leadership Politics and the Turn Against Women*. Berkeley: University of California Press, 1986. (Something of a companion piece to Judith Ruderman's book represented in this Reader.)

(4) Collections of essays

COOPER, ANDREW (ed.), *D.H. Lawrence 1885–1930: A Celebration*. Nottingham: D.H. Lawrence Society, 1985. (With Foreword by Glyn Hughes.)
GOMME, A.H. (ed.), *D.H. Lawrence: A Critical Study of the Major Novels and Other Writings*. Hassocks, Sussex: The Harvester Press, 1978.

D.H. Lawrence

HEYWOOD, CHRISTOPHER (ed.), *D.H. Lawrence: New Studies*. London: Macmillan, 1987.

KALNINS, MARA (ed.), *D.H. Lawrence: Centenary Essays*. Bristol: Bristol Classical Press, 1986.

MEYERS, JEFFREY (ed.), *D.H. Lawrence and Tradition*. London: The Athlone Press, 1985.

MEYERS, JEFFREY (ed.), *The Legacy of D.H. Lawrence: New Essays*. London: Macmillan, 1987.

SALGĀDO, GĀMINI and DAS, G.K. (eds), *The Spirit of D.H. Lawrence: Centenary Studies*. London: Macmillan, 1988.

SMITH, ANNE (ed.), *Lawrence and Women*. London: Vision Press, 1978.

SQUIRES, MICHAEL and JACKSON, DENNIS (eds), *D.H. Lawrence's 'Lady': A New Look at Lady Chatterley's Lover*. Athens, Georgia: University of Georgia Press, 1985.

Index